Toolkits

A practical guide to planning, monitoring, evaluation and impact assessment

Louisa Gosling with Mike Edwards

the Children

Save the Children UK is a member of the International Save the
Children Alliance the world's leading independent children's rights
organisation, with members in 29 countries and operational programmes
in more than 100.

Save the Children works with children and their communities to provide
practical assistance and, by influencing policy and public opinion, bring
about positive change for children.

Published by
Save the Children
17 Grove Lane
London SE5 8RD
UK

First edition published 1995
Revised and updated second edition published 2003

ISBN 1 84187 064 1

Typeset by Avon DataSet Ltd, Bidford on Avon, Warwickshire B50 4JH

Edited by Annabel Warburg

CONTENTS

Acknowledgements

This edition of *Toolkits* has been based on contributions, comments and advice from a large number of people from Save the Children UK programmes throughout the world, and from outside the organisation. All of these contributions have been invaluable in guiding both the content and style of the book. Members of the Learning and Impact Assessment Network of Save the Children UK have played a crucial role in identifying new issues to be incorporated, contributing to the content and commenting on the new chapters. Individuals throughout the organisation – too numerous to name – have contributed ideas, experience and individual case studies. Many people from different sections of the London office have also put a great deal of time and effort into reading and commenting on various drafts of the different tools and chapters of the book. The whole process has been diligently guided and managed by Marta Foresti with support from Simon Starling, Carrie Stebbings, and John Wilkinson from the Learning and Impact Assessment team in London. Any mistakes, inaccuracies or tracts of poor writing are entirely the responsibility of the author.

Preface to the new edition

After consultation with people who use *Toolkits*, it was decided that a new edition should incorporate the following changes:

- **Greater recognition of the role of planning, monitoring, review and evaluation for learning**, both in the short and long term, and for ensuring good practice, and improving both policy and practice.
- **More emphasis on assessing the wider impact of work** and considering the short-term and long-term implications of interventions; also more emphasis on attribution (if there has been a change, how do you know what caused it?) (See the new Chapter 9 on impact assessment.)
- **More emphasis on advocacy** and on how it can be monitored and evaluated (See Chapter 11 and Tool 13.)
- **A shift from 'needs-based' towards 'rights-based' approaches to development.** Save the Children is a children's rights organisation, and therefore adopts a rights-based approach to programming. This new edition aims to show how the key principles of children's rights can be applied to existing approaches to planning, monitoring, review and evaluation. (See Chapter 1 for further discussion of rights-based programming.)
- **More experience of using participatory approaches**, and in particular promoting the participation of children. Experience shows that children's views, insights and ownership are of great value for all development activities, not only for child-focused agencies. There are new case studies throughout the book to illustrate how children can participate. (See also Chapters 2 and 3 and Tool 1.)
- **More emphasis on work with partners.** This means adopting a more inclusive approach to planning, monitoring, review and evaluation. New case studies have been included to illustrate this.
- **The development of SPHERE minimum standards for humanitarian emergency programmes.** Chapter 10 has been redrafted to show how these can be used in planning, monitoring, reviewing and evaluating emergencies.

How to use *Toolkits*

Toolkits should be used as you would a real 'toolkit', by selecting the particular tools (in this case, approaches or techniques) that you need to deal with a specific problem.

Development work rarely conforms in practice to the ideal models found in the textbooks. The same is true for the techniques and approaches described here. When applied in practice, they always have to be adapted to local circumstances. The case studies illustrate some ways in which this has been done.

Monitoring and evaluation tools are not new and many of them are simply ways of using common sense systematically. They are designed to assist in the whole strategic planning process by providing some of the means to make decisions in changing circumstances in a systematic way.

Structure of *Toolkits*

This book has three Parts:

Part 1 should be read first when undertaking any planning, monitoring, review, evaluation or impact assessment. It looks at general issues that are relevant to all these exercises.

- **Why planning, monitoring, review, evaluation and impact assessment are essential to development work** and how they link to planning and decision-making (Chapter 1).

The remaining chapters in this Part examine the basic considerations that need to be applied throughout assessment, monitoring, review and evaluation if the findings are to be useful and relevant. These underlying principles are:

- **Involve the relevant people** (Chapter 2).
  - Who should participate in planning, monitoring, review, evaluation and impact assessment? Who uses the results?
  - Feedback of the findings to those involved in the work.
  - Confidentiality.
  - Working with partners: NGOs, governments and other agencies.
  - Who should carry out the exercise: programme staff or outsiders?
  - Different approaches: participatory, non-participatory and joint.
- **Recognise and deal with differences and discrimination** (Chapter 3).
  - Recognising differences within and between groups and avoiding discrimination against the least powerful.
  - How can the differences be analysed?
  - Avoiding discrimination in assessment, monitoring, review and evaluation.
  - Overcoming barriers and making sure different groups can participate: making sure children, women, people with disabilities, and different ethnic groups are involved.
  - Principles for good practice.
- **Be systematic about the analysis and collection of information** (Chapter 4).
  - The principles of being systematic: trying to be objective and avoiding bias.

– Quantitative and qualitative methods for collecting and analysing information.
– When to use different methods: what kind of information is required, what is the purpose of the exercise, and what resources are available?

Part 2 looks in more detail at the processes of planning, monitoring, review, evaluation and impact assessment.

- Chapter 5 looks at a sequence of questions that must be addressed when **planning all assessment, monitoring, review, evaluation and impact assessment exercises.** These questions form the basis of the terms of reference required for the exercise, so Chapter 5 should be read together with the relevant chapter from Chapters 6–9, which look at specific points connected with carrying out each process:
- **assessment and programme planning** (Chapter 6)
- **monitoring** (Chapter 7)
- **review and evaluation** (Chapter 8)
- **impact assessment** (Chapter 9)
- Chapter 10 looks at questions that are specifically relevant in **emergency situations**
- Chapter 11 considers how **advocacy work** can be monitored and evaluated.

Part 3 describes in detail the different tools and techniques that are referred to in the previous sections. The strengths and weaknesses of each technique are listed and references for further reading are given. This section should be read in conjunction with Parts 1 and 2, referring to the tools that are relevant to your own situation.

This new edition was written by Louisa Gosling.

Part I
Underlying principles

Chapter 1
The importance of planning, monitoring, review, evaluation and impact assessment

The role of planning, monitoring, review, evaluation and impact assessment for good programme management...

When *Toolkits* was first published in 1995 many people saw planning, monitoring review and evaluation as something imposed on them from outside, mostly by donors. There is still enormous pressure from donors, who increasingly impose stringent proposal and reporting requirements when funding programmes. But the importance of proper planning, monitoring and evaluation as an essential ingredient of good programme management practice is now much more widely accepted by development practitioners.

. . . and for learning

It is also recognised as the means whereby all the different people involved in the different stages of a project or programme can learn from it:

- Immediate lessons can be learnt: what are the issues? how should they be addressed? is the work going well or badly? is the work appropriate to the situation? how is the situation changing and why? how should the work be adjusted?
- There is also more focus on longer-term lessons: what sort of interventions are most effective? what impact – positive and negative – do they have on different groups in the short and long term? how should future policy and practice be changed in the light of these lessons?

The first section of this chapter gives a brief explanation of the terms planning, monitoring, review, evaluation and impact assessment, as they are used in *Toolkits*, together with an overview of how they fit into good management practice in development programmes. The second section of this chapter discusses how a rights-based approach to development affects programme design, implementation and evaluation.

Section 1: Programme cycle

Assessment and planning

(See Chapter 6.)

Assessment and planning are the processes of identifying and understanding a problem and planning a series of actions to deal with it. There are usually a number of different stages in this process, but the end result is always to have a clear and realistic plan of activities designed to achieve a set of clear aims and objectives. At the planning stage of a project or programme, information about the main issues and about the context is vital for a good understanding on which to base the work. Information is needed about: the people in the area affected by the work; government policies and programmes; social, economic and political systems; cultural beliefs and attitudes; roles of men, women and children; vested interests; and what other organisations are doing.

Aims are needed to give an overall focus to the work and to give direction to programme planning and design. They relate the work to the principles, values and mission statement of the agency, to its overall strategy, and to the broader issues of local plans and national development strategies.

Objectives clearly express the change you are trying to bring about – and therefore what the work is trying to achieve – so that activities can be designed to meet them. If objectives are clear, everyone has the same idea of why they are engaged in specific activities, and progress related to achieving objectives can be measured. As things change and develop, it may be necessary to alter the objectives on the basis of what is learned or what changes during implementation.

Monitoring

(See Chapter 7.)

Monitoring is the systematic and continuous collecting and analysing of information about the progress of a project or programme over time. It is useful for identifying strengths and weaknesses in a project or programme and for providing the people responsible for the work with sufficient information to make the right decisions at the right time to improve its quality.

Information about the work, about the impact it is having and about the external environment needs to be collected and analysed on a continuous basis. The results can then be fed directly back into the planning process and any necessary changes can be made. Monitoring ensures that the work stays on course by checking that activities are implemented, measuring progress towards objectives, identifying problems as they come up, identifying strengths that can be built on, and adapting to changing circumstances.

Monitoring is the key to good planning. If monitoring systems work well, evaluation is necessary less often; and when it is needed, it is much easier to carry out.

Review and evaluation

(See Chapter 8.)
Review is the assessment at one point in time of the progress of a project or programme. The basic purpose of a review is to take a closer look than is possible through the process of monitoring. Reviews can be carried out to look at different aspects of a project or programme and can use a range of criteria to measure progress. Appropriate decisions can then be taken about the direction the work should take.

The difference between an evaluation and a review is not always clear-cut, but an evaluation is usually more formal than a review, often carried out by external researchers in order to ensure independence. It is an assessment at one point in time that can have different purposes, including verifying whether objectives have been achieved, what impact it had on different stakeholders and how it can improve in the future.

The process of reviewing or evaluating work is also vital if people are to learn from experience and if they want to use their experience to influence others. Recognising and understanding failures and successes is equally important.

Impact assessment

(See Chapter 9.)
"Impact assessment is the systematic analysis of the lasting or significant changes – positive or negative, intended or not – in people's lives brought about by a given action or series of actions." (Chris Roche, p 21, *Learning to Value Change: Impact assessment for development NGOs*, Oxfam, 1999)

Impact assessment therefore considers more than the immediate, predicted outputs of an intervention (project or programme) and is much more concerned with the implications in the medium and long term. This crucially should include examples of expected, unintended, positive and negative impacts.

In order to measure lasting change meaningfully at the end of a programme, it is vital that change processes are tracked throughout its life cycle. Understanding and measuring change should therefore be a focus of on-going monitoring and other key stages of the programme cycle.

The programme spiral

Figure 1.1, the 'programme cycle' (see page 6), shows how assessment, monitoring, review and evaluation feed back into the planning of work as parts of a continuous process. Moreover, this process depends on the elements of the cycle being seen as a combination, rather than separate exercises. Together, they represent a mechanism to ensure that development workers:
• think about what they are trying to achieve before they start

- develop the most effective plan of action to achieve their objectives
- ensure that they monitor how effective they are being
- take action to address any problems that arise along the way
- take every opportunity to learn from the experience, and feed the learning back into future policy and practice.

Figure 1.1. Programme cycle

In other words, make sure you think systematically about something before you take any action, and after you have acted, reflect on what you have done before doing anything else.

However, development work is never straightforward and in reality does not always follow the ideal 'programme cycle'. Since all development work involves learning and change at every stage, it is useful to think in terms of a spiral rather than a cycle (Figure 1.2).

In this way, it is possible to see how experience gained through different

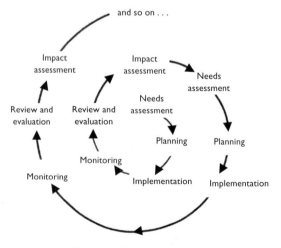

Figure 1.2. Programme spiral

activities can be incorporated into future ones. Planning, monitoring, review, evaluation and impact assessment are the essential components of a strong and effective programme spiral.

Section 2: Rights-based development

The shift from 'needs-based' towards 'rights-based' approaches to development

Rights-based programming has recently gained increasing popularity among development NGOs, UN organisations, and donors. This is particularly true for Save the Children, which, as a children's rights organisation is increasingly applying a rights-based approach to its programmes. Rights-based programming combines human rights and human development as Figure 1.3 shows.

Figure 1.3. Complementary systems and approaches: development and human rights

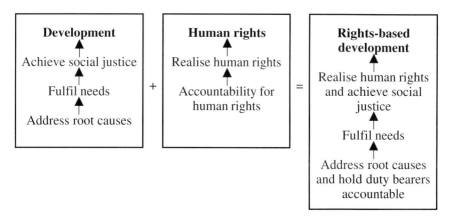

As a Save the Children publication, this book will concentrate on children's rights[1], which are set out in the UN Convention on the Rights of the Child.

How does this affect planning, monitoring, review, evaluation and impact assessment?

Rights-based programming means taking a different approach to programme design, implementation and evaluation. Attention shifts from the needs of people to the duties and responsibilities of those around them to respect, protect and fulfil their rights. Responsibility for this is distributed between

---

[1] See *An Introduction to Child Rights Programming: Concept and application*, Save the Children policy guidelines.

family, community, civil society organisations, national and local governments, international institutions, business and the media. All those with responsibility to respect, protect and fulfil children's rights are defined as duty-bearers. Development workers need to find out what is preventing people's rights from being realised in any particular situation, who is responsible for these rights, and on this basis decide what can be done about it by different agencies.

Table 1.1 Key features of a needs-based approach and a rights-based approach in relation to children

Needs-based approach	Rights-based approach
Children deserve help	Children are entitled to help
Governments ought to do something but no one has definite obligations	Governments have binding legal and moral obligations
Children can participate in order to improve service delivery	Children are active participants by right
Given scarce resources, some children may have to be left out	All children have the same right to fulfil their potential
Each piece of work has its own goal but there is no unifying overall purpose	There is an overarching goal to which all work contributes
Certain groups have the technical expertise to meet children's needs	All adults can play a role in achieving children's rights
Looks at specific, immediate situation	Analyses root causes

All the chapters of this book refer to implications of child rights programming. The key implications are:

- *Accountability to rights-holders*: All those who have responsibility for children's rights, ie, duty-bearers, are accountable to the rights-holders. This affects the emphasis and purpose of planning, monitoring, review and evaluation and means interventions are aimed at holding duty-bearers accountable.
- *Broader analysis*: Instead of focusing on the particular needs of a particular target group and the immediate causes, a rights-based analysis looks much more widely at all levels of responsibility around the child. It also looks at the broader context of the issue and its causes at different levels, and at the links between different organisations. This affects how a situation analysis should be carried out, setting aims and objectives, and approaches to monitoring and evaluation. (See Chapters 5, 6, 7 and 8.)
- *Broader impact*: The root causes of rights violations should be addressed as well as the immediate problems caused by such violations, so that programmes should all have an advocacy aspect. Impact assessment is needed to understand and learn about the broader impact of

development activities. (See Chapter 9 and Chapter 11.)

- *Participation:* The participation of children in decisions that affect them is a right and therefore children are entitled to it. (See cases studies and examples throughout; also Chapter 2.)
- *Non-discrimination and equality*: All children have the same right to fulfill their potential. Make sure that the rights of all children, even those who are least visible, are respected in the analysis, planning, monitoring, evaluation and impact assessment. (See Chapters 2 and 3.)
- *Best interest of the children* should come first. This is a useful test to apply to setting programme objectives and priorities. (See Chapter 6.)

Summary

Programme cycle

- Planning, monitoring, review, evaluation and impact assessment are essential for good programme management, for learning, and for accountability.
- They involve analysing the situation, setting clear programme aims and objectives, and identifying methods and indicators that will provide information about the process and impact of the work.
- The 'programme spiral' brings these processes together to make sure development workers think systematically about what they are doing before they start, while a programme is being implemented, and when it has finished in order to inform future practice.

Rights-based development

- Rights-based programming means that the attention shifts from the *needs* of people to the *duties* of those around them to respect, protect and fulfill their rights.
- This affects the *focus* and the *approach* to programming and therefore to planning, monitoring, review, evaluation and impact assessment, because:
    - all duty bearers are accountable to rights-holders
    - a broader situation analysis is required, focusing on people's rights and responsibilities
    - programmes should aim to have an impact on the root causes of rights violations, as well as immediate problems
    - people have a right to participate in decisions that affect them
    - all people have rights and this emphasises the importance of non-discrimination and equality
    - the best interests of the children should come first.

Chapter 2
Involving the relevant people

Who should be involved? This is one of the most important questions to be answered when undertaking any sort of planning, monitoring, review or evaluation.

This chapter begins by considering the importance and advantages of encouraging participation by a wide range of people, but also points to some of the potential pitfalls that need to be avoided. There is a list of questions that can be posed in order to help determine who should be involved. In particular, it is important to know who will use the results. A stakeholder analysis may help to decide when and how people should be involved, and examples are given of how this can be used. Examples are also given of the ways in which people may take part at particular stages of an exercise. As in all development work, there are many ethical issues to consider – the first part of the chapter ends with a list of the key issues.

Decisions about who should be involved in planning, monitoring, evaluation or impact assessment become more difficult if a project works in partnership with others. Some general principles of work are discussed in the second part of the chapter, including Christian Aid's useful definition of 'a good partnership'.

Finally, we consider the relative advantages and disadvantages of using people from outside the agency to carry out the exercise.

1. Why is participation good practice?

The success of planning, monitoring, review and evaluation depends on involving the right people at the right time. It is important to think systematically about who should be involved, to avoid unintentional bias. The least powerful, visible and assertive people (women and children, for example) should have as much opportunity to be involved as those with more confidence and status. Extra effort is needed to enable them to become equal parties in the exercise. (See Chapter 3 for more detail on avoiding discrimination.) Moreover, a rights-based approach to development requires the active, free and meaningful participation of those affected by the work. In the case of children, they are considered as active holders of human rights which they can exercise in accordance with their maturity and experience. This includes the right to express their views on decisions that affect them.

Encouraging a range of people to participate helps to strengthen the following:

Access to the work: Participation means talking to different groups and considering their points of view. It helps to ensure that different groups are aware of the work, that activities are not unintentionally biased according to gender, disability, caste or age, and that all groups in the target population have access to the programme and its outputs.

Relevance and effectiveness of the work: Drawing on the experience, priorities and views of different people helps illuminate key issues and concerns. The true nature of problems and the viability of alternative solutions becomes clearer. It is vital to understand local attitudes which can affect the relevance of a programme.

Ownership of the work: People's interest in and commitment to the work will be proportional to their sense of ownership (the extent to which they can influence decisions and feel that their real needs are being addressed).

Joint enterprise: Realisation by all or most of the stakeholders of how much their effectiveness depends on their working together in a coordinated way.

Sustainability: If the work is to be carried on by local agencies or government it can only be sustained if they have been closely involved in decision-making from the beginning.

Capacity-building: Participation can help develop analytical, planning, monitoring and evaluation skills essential for good programme management, and for developing relationships with other donors.

Empowerment: People can be empowered by knowing that their views, opinions and experiences are taken properly into account, by having more control over development activities that affect them, and through developing new skills.

Note of caution

While it is generally accepted that participation is essential for planning, monitoring and evaluation, experience shows that there are common dangers and pitfalls which need to be avoided:

- What participatory decision-making systems already exist? There is a danger that new systems for participation are created unnecessarily instead of building on existing procedures.
- Power relations: participatory approaches can reinforce the interests of those who are already powerful.
- Resources: participatory approaches are neither quick nor easy.
- Cultural appropriateness of participation: What is the most appropriate way of involving different groups?
- Does participation extract local knowledge or the knowledge local people think the researchers want to hear?
- Participatory approaches can mask the power dynamics and conceal the 'backstage' operations.
- Participation may raise unrealistic expectations.

- What are the current priorities, food (for example) or research? Sometimes it is more important to act quickly.
- There are a number of ethical issues to be considered (see below).

2. Who should participate?

The decision about who should participate depends on the following questions:
- Whose rights are affected by the programme? For a rights-based approach to programming, *rights-holders* should participate actively in claiming their rights. This includes children.
- Who takes decisions about the programme?
- What do you need to know? Whose views, priorities and experience would be relevant?
- Who has an interest in analysing problems and working out appropriate solutions? This should include those whose interests are less obvious or outspoken.
- Who will be expected to act on the decisions?
- Whose active support is essential for the success of the programme?
- Who is likely to feel threatened by the possibility of changes to the programme?

The answers to these questions will determine which *stakeholders* should be involved. A stakeholder is any person, group of people or institution who or which has an interest in a particular project or set of activities.

(See Chapter 3 for particular issues around the involvement of children and young people, disabled people, and gender issues.)

3. Who uses the results?

This is another question that must be answered when undertaking any planning, monitoring, review or evaluation. The results will be of interest to different stakeholders who will put them to different uses.

Stakeholder analysis is a tool which can help answer this question. The first stage is to analyse who are the different stakeholders (for example, see the list in Table 2.1), what are their interests in the work, and what is their interest in being involved in assessment, monitoring, review, evaluation or impact assessment. Try to imagine and verify who will be overlooked or excluded and how to encourage their visibility and direct involvement (see Tool 12). Table 2.2 (page 14) shows how the project and different stakeholders may benefit from the findings, and from participating in the process.

Usually the results of planning, monitoring, review and evaluation will be used in a number of different ways by a combination of stakeholders. The key

Table 2.1 Potential stakeholders

Community members	• Rights-holders and *duty bearers* relevant to the work (in rights-based programmes it is essential that they should participate)
	• key informants (for example, midwives and teachers)
	• established community representatives (for example, elders and village committees)
	• special interest groups within the community (for example, the different ethnic groups or clans, single parents, disabled people and their families, women's groups)
	• men and women who are affected by the work, or who are targets of advocacy
	• children and young people, including the very vulnerable
	• non-beneficiaries
Government and partners	• government officials at national or local level, as duty bearers for child rights, and as partners
	• staff and managers from partner organisations
Programme and project	• programme or project managers
	• programme or project staff
Others	• policy-makers within or outside the agency
	• people involved in advocacy
	• those who are opposed to the work
	• donors
	• other agencies involved in similar work

point is to ensure that you know who the exercise is principally for and the main types of information they need. This will determine the approach to be used and who should be involved.

4. When and how should people be involved?

The degree and timing of participation can vary. In some cases, all the people who are taking part in the exercise may take decisions together. In other cases, a range of people may be invited to discuss and comment on various options but the decisions will be made by a smaller group. In some cases a wide range of people will be involved in the whole process. In others they may be involved at the planning stage and in drawing conclusions at the end. The appropriate degree and timing of participation will depend on the needs of the particular programme, costs involved and on the constraints imposed by power relations and the decision-making structures of the agencies involved (see pages below). The second stage of *stakeholder analysis* is to decide what sort of involvement the different groups should have and at what stage. The levels of participation range from 'being informed' about something, to being in control of the process. There are various models of this. It is good to be clear and honest about the

Table 2.2 Potential benefits to different stakeholders

Stakeholder	Potential benefit
Beneficiary/ community	• Sense of ownership through participation • Empowerment for change through self-reflection • Empowerment by developing new skills • Empowerment by having more control over development activities that affect them
Partners: CBO/NGO, government counterpart	• Information for planning and strategic choices • Development of good practice • Improved reporting to funding agency • Improved information for fund-raising • Capacity building in project planning and monitoring and evaluation techniques • Improved information for advocacy • Sustainability of project improved
Project officer	• Development of good practice • Assessment of project impact/cost-efficiency • Capacity building in project planning and monitoring and evaluation techniques • Improved reporting to programme officer • Improved information for advocacy
Programme Director	• Information for programme strategic choices • Development of good practice • Recognition of project impact/cost efficiency • Improved accountability to government and donors • Improved information for fund-raising • Improved information for advocacy
Globally (for agency)	• Examples of good practice • Improved accountability to stakeholders • Demonstration of project effectiveness to other stakeholders
Donors, international agencies	• Sharing of experience as to supervising the monitoring of project effectiveness • Recognition and implementation of good practice • Reporting to governments/parliaments

degree of participation at different stages. Also consider what is realistic given the resources, existing contacts and time available (see Tool 12). Participatory methods are discussed in Tool 1.

Stakeholders can participate in different stages of planning, monitoring, review and evaluation, as shown in the example that follows.

Formulating objectives and key questions for the exercise

A typical process of group work to select objectives and key questions:
- Produce a statement about the purpose of the planning, monitoring, review or evaluation exercise with which everyone can agree.
- Consider the needs of different people involved in the work. Which people are at the forefront and which are less visible? What are the visible and invisible needs? It is important to emphasise the less visible or they will be left out. What are their primary concerns? Which issues would they like the exercise to concentrate on? In what way do the issues raised concern different people?
- Review the programme objectives and how different people view them.
- Select objectives for the exercise. Prioritise these if necessary.
- Formulate questions that will answer or clarify the main objectives.
- Identify indicators for measuring progress and impact. These need to be:
  - consistent with the social and cultural context in which the programme is operating
  - locally relevant
  - relevant to all the different groups involved.

Formulating objectives and indicators for the programme

Stakeholder involvement in this is often vital. One useful way of looking at the problems a programme aims to address and formulating objectives and indicators is to use a *problem tree* (see Tool 6).

For example: A focus group was conducted with young people and teachers at the Children First Project in Spanish Town, Jamaica. The focus group drew a problem tree around the issue of 'risky sex'. They identified its causes and its results. From this tree the project was able to work out its impact indicators, based on the causes and the unwelcome results, and on what behaviour the project was trying to encourage and prevent.

Designing tools for gathering and analysing information

Different participants can be involved in:
- designing, testing and using questionnaires
- drawing up and field-testing relevant practical checklists for observation
- selecting questions for semi-structured interviews
- designing other tools such as maps, transects, and other PLA techniques.

> **For example: Evaluation of female-headed households project, Tajikistan**
> One of the aims of this evaluation, which used 15 children aged 12–16 as
> evaluators, was to help the participants identify changes that had taken place
> in their lives as a result of the project. Before the interview process began the
> child evaluators drew three pictures: the first depicting the scene in a village
> before the project; the second the inputs that Save the Children had given to
> the various categories of female-headed household; and third the impact the
> project hoped to produce on the village. The pictures were used as a way of
> attracting the interviewees' attention, and as prompts for semi-structured
> focus group questioning. It took the children some time to use the pictures
> they had drawn in the interviews they carried out, but when they did so they
> reported that they had been very successful. Those being interviewed clustered
> round to see the pictures so they became the natural focus for the interview
> process.

As researchers: Gathering and analysing information

Participants can be involved in gathering information using the methods selected.
It is important to train participants to reach a common understanding about
concepts (like community, disability, inclusion, etc) and to standardise ways of
collecting and recording the information so that analysis is easier afterwards.

Any ethical issues also need to be carefully considered, for example, how
sensitive issues will be dealt with, and what follow-up is available. Where children
are involved as researchers it is important to make sure they are respected in their
own right and protected from abuse (see 'Ethics' on page 17).

The relationship between researchers and the groups they are interviewing is
important.

> **For example:** When children (12–16 years) acted as evaluators in Tajikistan,
> they carried out interviews with other children to explore the effects of the
> Save the Children UK programme. Early on it was found that they were not
> empathising with the interviewees, instead they were interrogating them and
> as a result upsetting them. The evaluation team carried out intensive role
> play with the children, which resulted in them taking a more caring and
> sensitive approach.

Analysis

Group analysis of group activities (see Tool 1) can be a good way for people to
reflect on their own experience, to discuss strengths and weaknesses, and to see
how different people they work with view the problems. Alternatively, the
findings can be analysed by a few individuals and then discussed with a larger

group. When analysing the findings it is important to look for problems and solutions without apportioning blame to individuals. (See also Tools 1, 3, 5, 6, and 7 for tools for participatory analysis.)

Reporting findings

The final written report is usually produced by one person, but it should be made available to all those involved in the exercise, written in an accessible style, and translated as necessary. Those involved should have the opportunity to amend the final report and contribute their views. Results can also be presented verbally at meetings and workshops using photographs, diagrams, drama, video, and so on. (See Tool 10 on visual presentation methods.)

Feedback of the findings to those involved in the work

It is important to present feedback about the results of planning, monitoring, review and evaluation to all those who have been involved in the exercise. For example, if the communities affected by a community health programme are expected to contribute actively to the work, then they must be informed about how this work is progressing, the effect it is having, and future plans. If a member of the community is on the review/evaluation team s/he may well be the best person to communicate outcomes with communities. Meetings and/or audiovisual presentations may be a good way of doing this. (See Tool 10.)

It is equally important that lessons learnt from experience are fed back into the agency systematically so that they can be used in future programme planning, policy development and advocacy.

5. Ethics

Ethical decisions occur at all levels of planning, monitoring, review and evaluation, and in encouraging people to participate. It is important that the following general issues are considered before the exercise and are regularly reviewed as it progresses.

- **Participation and protection**: ensure that work with vulnerable groups, such as children and young people, is in their best interest and does them no harm. Consider the power imbalances and assess any possible dangers at an early stage. Ensure that you follow your organisation's child protection policy. If children are the main evaluators they must be given the respect and power to help design and change the methods used.
- **Raising sensitive issues**: Ensure there is follow-up to deal with sensitive issues which may be raised as a result of the exercise.
- **Conflicting agendas**: Adults, children, and organisations come to the exercise

with their own agendas. It is important to be honest about these and negotiate differences.

- **Informed consent**: Ensure that the researcher, especially if he or she is a child, knows what they are being asked to do and that they have a right to say no to anything. Also that the necessary consent is obtained to interview young people.
- **Purposes of research**: Participants should know the purpose of what they are undertaking and what the activity they undertake contributes towards.
- **Confidentiality and trust**: Be honest with the researchers and respondents, so that they know if confidentiality will ever be broken and what the parameters are. Make sure that no confidential information is made available to those who might misuse it. If necessary make the personal information unrecognisable (change names, places, and so on).
- **Clarity**: Be clear about how much time the process is likely to take up, and what the likely outcomes will be.
- **Payment**: Consider how much to pay researchers, and whether also to pay respondents, compensating them for the time they give up.

6. Working with partners: NGOs, governments and other agencies

When an agency works with partners, the issue of who should be involved in planning, monitoring, review, evaluation and impact assessment becomes more complicated. The requirements and opinions of all partners need to be voiced clearly at all stages. They can then be discussed and negotiated. It is important to be as open, honest and explicit as possible. Although different partners may have the same long-term aims, they may have different requirements when it comes to planning, monitoring, review, evaluation and impact assessment.

Planning

In planning, for example, the objectives of a funding agency and those of an implementing agency may differ. An additional objective for the donor may be the institutional strengthening of the partner agency, or the dissemination of a particular experience in order to influence policy. For the implementing agency an additional objective may be to test the viability of a positive relationship with their funder. The objectives of both partners need to be made explicit so that there is no confusion about who is trying to do what. This will make monitoring, review and evaluation easier and less open to misunderstanding. This could be more difficult when working with large organisations or government departments where different groups within the agency may have different objectives.

Monitoring

Monitoring of performance is often more sensitive than the monitoring of expenditure, although both are essential for the purpose of accountability. The processes of defining objectives, developing activities and assessing progress can help to develop a stronger relationship between partner agencies. It can also clarify roles and identify areas where the relationship needs to be strengthened. Regular monitoring in which all partners participate actively will make it easier to identify and face problems together as they arise. It also provides an opportunity for partners to offer information and resources to each other.

For example: The Programme for Abused and Exploited Children (PAEC) in the Philippines is implemented by Save the Children in collaboration with several local organisations working with exploited children. Save the Children programme staff monitor the work with individual partners, and with partners as a group. Monitoring with individual partners enables them to help clarify the concepts used by Save the Children and the partner; it helps identify gaps in the programme of the partner based on an agreed framework of intervention and on agreed theoretical handles (view of the child and childhood, child rights, resilience); monitoring visits provide an opportunity to discuss issues around programme implementation.

Monitoring with partners as a group enables them to: discuss the progress of the overall programme, identify significant achievements, issues to be addressed, and facilitate learning from each others' experience; enhance collaboration among themselves, and links with government and other institutions; facilitate partners' understanding of their role within Save the Children programmes, and enable them to locate their work within the overall PAEC programme.

Review and evaluation

In review and evaluation, similar principles apply. An approach that ensures the participation of all stakeholders is vital if the results are to be accepted and used by the different partners. The process should also help partners develop the skills for future monitoring and evaluation. The design of the evaluation or review should be determined by the different viewpoints and expectations of the groups involved. A participatory review or evaluation can also help create a partnership for future joint planning.

All reviews and evaluations contain a large element of judgement (about progress against objectives, management and organisational competence, approaches to work, etc). It is often difficult to get people to see this in positive terms, especially if these judgements come from outside the project, programme, office or agency concerned. Participation of all partners at the planning stage of the review or evaluation can help minimise the sense of threat. Sometimes an external judgement is needed if things are going badly wrong, financially or otherwise. In this case it is important to be honest, and to make it clear that the purpose of the review or evaluation is to enable decisions to be made on the future of the work or the donor's relationship to it. One ingredient for a review/ evaluation to be successful with a specific implementing partner is that both the implementer and funder are 'learning organisations'. If it is suspected that this is not the case the issue must be brought into the open at the earliest opportunity.

Most important of all, make sure you have a clear idea of who and what the exercise is for so that it can be designed accordingly. An evaluation that aims to help those involved to strengthen their work may look very different from one that attempts to influence policy or enable a decision on future funding to be made.

The following principles of good partnership show how joint systems for monitoring and evaluation can promote good partnership.

Principles of Good Partnership
Christian Aid works exclusively through partner organisations in different countries. They have defined the principles of good partnership as follows:

> A partner is someone we want to co-operate with in order to achieve a common goal.

A good partnership is one that adheres to the following principles:

1. Compatibility and clarity of mission and methodology: a goal-oriented relationship requiring the specification of each partner's objectives, approaches and methods and the extent to which these are shared.

2. Clarity of expectations and commitment: a clear notion of what each partner will contribute to and expect from the partnership and how this will be of benefit to them (and their constituencies) in the long term. This requires an understanding of the distinctive competencies of all parties and should aim to maximise and develop the strengths of both. The time frame of commitment agreed should provide room for manoeuvre and adequate time to build a relationship. This may mean being willing to provide funds over a long time period and to cover at least some of the core costs of the partner.

3. Commitment to the pursuit of equity: both parties should seek to make the relationship as equitable and horizontal as possible, recognising, and actively working to minimise inherent power imbalances.

4. Mutuality, respect and trust:
- respecting and valuing the contribution of both parties (beyond the financial)
- transparency – a nurtured openness concerning policy, strategies, priorities, decision-making, negotiations with third parties, finances, sources of funding and reporting requirements – ie, no hidden agendas
- openness to dialogue, criticism and change, particularly when conflicts of interest or disagreements arise, and a willingness and ability by both parties to be constructively critical of each other within an overall framework of support and solidarity.

5. Joint agreement on ways of working:
- developing a common understanding of problems and the most appropriate ways to solve them
- agreeing goals and strategies and mechanisms for learning from joint experience
- reciprocal accountability – agreeing ways in which success and failure will be measured both for joint work and the partnership as a whole, and recognising and accommodating the need for accountability of both parties to their own constituencies, donors, trustees and supporters
- sharing information and actively working to deepen understanding of each other's organisations
- agreeing conditions under which partnership will end.

7. Who should carry out the exercise: insiders or outsiders?

Programme staff and management must be involved in all planning, monitoring, review and evaluation activities. The main purpose of all these exercises is for them to analyse what the programme is for, how it can be developed and improved, and take action accordingly. Their learning can also be fed back into policy development and used for advocacy. If programme staff are not actively involved, they will gain nothing from the exercise and any resulting decisions will be more difficult to put into effect. They may even be antagonised by the experience and this will have a negative effect on the programme.

Programme staff are familiar with the programme and know the constraints and why things are done the way they are. On the other hand, it may be difficult for them to find time to stand back and reflect, especially when running an emergency programme; to look critically at what they have been doing when they have been working in a certain way for a long time; and to speak openly and/or consider different viewpoints when a hierarchy is well established.

For these reasons, it is sometimes useful for someone from outside the programme to be involved, either as the person responsible for carrying out the activity or as a facilitator. In these situations, it is vital to find the right person for the job, with relevant experience and skills. They might come from another part of the same agency which is not directly involved in the work, from outside the agency, or both. They must have clear terms of reference drawn up and agreed by the programme staff. Extensive discussion with programme staff at the planning stage of an external evaluation or review is essential and will help minimise any anxieties about being 'judged' by an outsider. Table 2.3 gives a summary of the relative advantages and disadvantages of *'insiders'* and *'outsiders'* taking part in planning, monitoring, review or evaluation.

Different combinations of insiders and outsiders will be most appropriate in different situations. One of the most commonly used approaches is to combine the advantages of an objective and experienced input from outside specialists, with the benefits of involving staff and people affected by the work.

A joint assessment, monitoring, review or evaluation can be:

- a process carried out by a team which includes outsiders and insiders
- a process carried out by outside specialists but which includes the active participation of insiders in all or some of the process.

This approach is useful where the organisation wants to take a critical view of its work, but make sure that inside perspectives are properly represented, and maximise learning from the exercise. The involvement of insiders is also likely to make the organisation more committed to the findings.

Some words of caution

- When outside specialists are involved, there is a danger that they will dominate the process and have a greater influence on the conclusions and recommendations than insiders, due to their perceived expertise, and the fact that they may have a higher status, be paid more and have limited time available for the exercise. The nature and extent of participation by different groups should be made clear during the exercise and in the final report.
- There is a danger that the outsider may be the person who learns the most from the process, and the programme itself will not benefit from the learning.
- The time available for the exercise may be limited by the availability of outside specialists, allowing less time for effective participation.

To make sure it works:

- Ensure enough time is given to preparing the exercise, and for consultation between insiders and outsiders before it begins.
- Ensure that the relationship between insiders and outsiders is clarified in the

Table 2.3 Advantages and disadvantages of 'insiders' and 'outsiders' in planning, monitoring, review or evaluation.

	Insiders	Outsiders
Who	• Staff, managers and partners • Individuals and groups (eg, children) affected by the work. • Non-beneficiaries	• Staff from same agency but another programme • External consultants with specialist expertise in technique field, or specialist understanding of country or region
Advantages	• Know the organisation • Know the programme • Understand organisational • behaviour and attitudes • Known to staff • Less threatening • Greater chance of adopting recommendations • Less expensive • Build internal planning, monitoring, evaluation capability • Contribute to programme capacity • Familiarity with programme • Familiarity with context • Know constraints	• Objective • No organisational bias • Fresh perspectives • Broader experience • More easily hired for longer periods of time • Can serve as an outside expert • Not part of the power structure • Can bring in additional resources • Trained in evaluation • Experienced in other evaluations
Disadvantages	• Objectivity may be questioned • Organisational structure may constrain participation • Personal gain may be questioned • Accept the assumptions of the organisation • Not trained in evaluation methods • No special technical expertise • Acceptability by outsiders (credibility?) • May have difficulty avoiding bias	• May not know organisations • May not know of constraint affecting recommendations • May be perceived as an adversary • Expensive • Contract negotiations may take time • Follow up on recommendations not always there • Unfamiliar environment • Learning from process leaves the programme • May miss out on important insights
Role of leader	• Facilitator, with skills in participatory techniques, particular skills needed to increase participation of children • Need good communication and listening skills	• Consult with others, but ultimately responsible for drawing conclusions and making recommendations
When is it useful?	• Any rights-based programme where rights holders have right to participate • Social development projects • Where an aim is to enable groups to develop organisational capacity • Where active participation of different groups is essential for success of the work • Where there is an opportunity to do so	• When a particular type of expertise is needed • To take a more objective view, from someone who does not have vested interest in the programme or organisation • To gain a wider view of a project or programme • When a donor needs specific information about the programme

terms of reference. For example, the outsider should act as facilitator to maximise learning by insiders.

- When the insiders are children this will affect the approach of any outsider involved.
- Ensure the terms of reference clearly state the planning, monitoring, review or evaluation objectives, and specify where these may differ for the insiders and outsiders.
- Ensure enough time is left for proper consultation between insiders and outsiders in analysing the findings and drawing conclusions. Time often runs out towards the end of the process.

(See Tool 8, Using consultants, for more on this.)

Summary

- Stakeholder participation is recognised as good practice in development programmes because it can strengthen the effectiveness and impact of the work.
- People have a right to participate in decisions that affect them, through involvement in planning, monitoring and evaluation.
- There are many common pitfalls and dangers in adopting participatory approaches, which need to be carefully considered so they can be avoided.
- Stakeholder analysis can be used to help decide who should participate, and how they could benefit from participating.
- There are different levels of participation, which range from being informed about a process, to being in control of it.
- Participatory approaches can be used at different stages and for different tasks in planning, monitoring, review, evaluation and impact assessment.
- Ethical issues concerning participation must be considered, particularly where children are involved.
- Working with partner organisations requires particular sensitivity, transparency, and clarity in planning, monitoring, evaluation and impact assessment. The requirements and opinions of different partners must be respected.
- Insiders and outsiders can be involved in planning, monitoring, review, evaluation and impact assessment. Each has advantages and disadvantages. A combination is often the best solution, with careful planning to make sure the insider/outsider relationships work well.

Chapter 3
Recognising and dealing with differences and discrimination

The aim of the first part of this chapter is to help you analyse the community in which your work is based, in order to identify the many groups it contains, relationships between and within these groups, and their needs, interests and priorities. If the differences between groups are not properly recognised and understood, unintentional bias and discrimination can creep in.

The second part of the chapter looks at practical ways of avoiding bias and discrimination in planning, monitoring, review and evaluation. Examples are given of involving children, women, disabled people and people from minority ethnic groups. These apply not only to specific exercises, but to development work as a whole. They are summed up in a list of principles of good practice.

Recognising differences, avoiding discrimination

All societies, communities and families are made up of different groups and interests. It is vital to understand the differences and relationships that exist between these groups, and to avoid discriminating against those who are less visible, less powerful and less assertive. All people have rights that should be respected without discrimination. Most development work aims to benefit all ethnic groups, women, children and people with disabilities. Yet they are often prevented from participating in development activities because of physical, institutional or cultural barriers, and the personal prejudices of individuals.

As a result of discrimination:

- the rights and needs of these groups may be ignored, and their perception of problems and priorities, benefits and costs may be overlooked;
- they may have little or no influence over development activities that affect them, and therefore not feel part of them. They may not even know about the activities, the potential benefits and how these are expected to affect their lives;
- the impact of a project or programme on their lives (positive and/or negative) may never be measured or even recognised.

For development agencies, this is unacceptable. A principle of most development work is a belief in the inherent dignity and equality of all people. The United Nations Convention on the Rights of the Child states:

> 1. States parties shall respect and ensure the rights set forth in the present Convention to each child within their jurisdiction without discrimination of any kind, irrespective of the child's or his or her parents' or legal guardians' race, colour, sex, language, religion, political or other opinion, national, ethnic or social origin, property, disability, birth or other status.

The barriers that result in discrimination must be recognised and understood before they can be overcome, since they can only be tackled in a way that is relevant to the culture, programmes and individuals concerned.

Discrimination can happen knowingly or unknowingly. The more powerful and assertive members of a community are often unaware of the needs and skills of the less powerful. For example, men may not know about the concerns of women, and the work done by women is often valued less highly than the work of men. Adults may not know how children feel; community members in general may not recognise the capacities and experiences of disabled people and their families; and people from majority ethnic groups may not recognise the different viewpoints of minority groups.

It is therefore vital to understand the differences and inter-relationships that exist between groups. It is also important to recognise the differences and inter-relationships that exist within and across groups, for example, between older married women and younger unmarried women, children from different ethnic and religious groups, disabled people from poor and from wealthy families, and children of different age groups. Some differences reinforce each other: for example, female children often suffer more discrimination than male children.

Analysing differences

In planning and managing development work, it is important to analyse differences within communities and households to avoid discriminating unintentionally against particular groups. It is also important to monitor how the work affects these differences. The analysis can be done in various ways. One method is to examine: people's activities and responsibilities; the resources to which they have access and the benefits they receive from them; their needs, interests and priorities.

Activities and responsibilities
These include all the daily tasks and activities (including leisure) involved in maintaining a home, making a living, and fulfilling social obligations.

- Who does what? How are activities and responsibilities shared out and organised in communities and households? What roles and activities are carried out by different ethnic groups, women, girls, men, boys, and disabled people?

- How might this affect the way in which the objectives of the project or programme can be achieved?
- What effect will the project or programme have on the distribution of tasks in communities and households?

For example, training or income generation projects for women may result in them keeping their daughters away from school to look after younger siblings.

Resources and benefits

All development work requires the use of resources, and undertaking development work usually generates benefits for individuals, households and communities. It is important that the resources and benefits are for as many people as possible and do not discriminate against any group or individual.

- What resources do different groups have access to? What resources do they have control over? What implications do these patterns have for programme/ project activities? How can a project contribute to increasing access to and control over resources for the least powerful groups?
- What benefits do different groups each receive from the different activities undertaken, and from the use of resources? What benefits do they have control over? What are the implications for programme or project management? How can access to and control over benefits be increased for the least powerful groups?

Resources include: productive resources (such as land, equipment, tools, cash, credit, income earning skills and opportunities); political resources (such as representative organisations, leadership, education, information, public sphere experience and self confidence); and time. Benefits can include food, clothing, shelter, cash, income, assets, education, training, political power, prestige, status, and opportunities to pursue new interests.

> **For example:** An Action Aid study in Nepal showed that men always make decisions regarding money. The only possessions over which women have control are their pewa. This is a gift given to girls, which can be taken with them to their husband's house. Girls and women also supplement their pewa and save for pewa by carrying out income earning activities. It was suggested that this should be addressed in any discussion about the use of credit and savings schemes targeted at women.

Needs, interests and priorities

All individuals have immediate practical needs as well as long-term 'strategic' interests. Both must be met to improve the quality of their lives, but the priorities of different people will vary according to their particular circumstances.

- **What are the immediate practical needs of different groups?**

For example, the practical needs of parents are usually related to food and water, the health and education of their children, and increased income. Children need all of these and they need to play. Disabled people have the same practical needs as everyone else, and may also sometimes need specific types of help.

Projects that aim to meet practical needs and improve living conditions may preserve and reinforce traditional relations between the groups by working through existing structures dominated by the more powerful.

- **What are the long-term interests of different groups?**

For example, empowering women to have more opportunities, greater access to resources and more equal participation with men in decision-making is in their long-term or 'strategic' interest, and should also have a positive impact on the lives of the majority of the world's children (and men). It is in the long-term interest of children to ensure that their rights are respected and protected. Strategic interests for disabled people include changing the attitudes that

---

For example: Indicators to measure improvements in girls' and women's status

Distinction between practical needs and strategic needs is useful in this example:

Indicators that measure how well women's and girls' **practical needs** are met:	• Provision of: food and water, fuel, housing, reproductive and general healthcare • Increased access to: formal education, sex education
Indicators that measure how well women's and girls' **strategic** **needs** are met:	• Increased access to training in: negotiating skills, leadership skills, self-esteem • Increased awareness among girls and boys of: girls' needs and issues, discrimination against girls. (For instance, are boys speaking up about girls' rights to education?) • Increased participation in the project (eg, numbers of girls speaking at user group meetings) • Changes in traditional gender division of labour, ie, the amount of time girls and boys spend on activities that are usually done by the other gender (eg, In a community-based project for refugee children, how much time do boys spend on care work such as cooking?) • Decrease in gender-based violence (eg, decrease in numbers of reported cases of rape and domestic violence)

discriminate against them. Strategic interests for people from ethnic minority groups include changing attitudes that discriminate according to race, colour or religion.

- **What are the priorities of different groups?** What practical needs are most pressing, and what long-term interests are most important to them?

Attitudes, socialisation, discrimination practices

Discrimination against different groups is common in all societies. In order to understand how this affects the involvement of different groups in development, consider the following questions:

- What are the general attitudes towards different groups? – eg, children are often considered to be ignorant, irresponsible, immature, incapable, a nuisance, and to be made use of
- What is their role in society?
- What are the practices that reinforce discrimination?

Avoiding discrimination

It is important that planning, monitoring, reviews and evaluations are designed to take account of the differences and inter-relationships between and within groups that have been analysed. This can be done in the following ways:

- The **design** of the assessment, monitoring, review or evaluation should take account of differences and inter-relationships at all stages: when drawing up the terms of reference, defining aim and objectives, collecting and analysing information and drawing conclusions. For example, a situation analysis should look at how different groups may be discriminated against in terms of their rights being violated or protected, and by analysing differences as shown above.
- The exercise should use **methods** that make it easier for different groups to participate.
  - Which tools are most suitable for use with each group?
  - When should they be used, what time of day, what season is most convenient for different groups?
  - How can the tools best be used to make the groups more comfortable with them, so they can express their views as freely as possible?
  - Where should they be used: at home, in public meetings, in schools, while carrying out daily chores?
  - Who should use them: how does the gender, age, disability, language and ethnic origin of the programme staff affect the ability of different groups to participate?

- What attitudes, skills and experience are needed to use the techniques effectively?
- **Awareness**: ensure that the people carrying out the assessment, monitoring, review or evaluation are aware of the issues involved.
- **Disaggregate** all the data according to the different ways in which the information has been grouped (for example, by age and gender, age and ethnic group, ethnic group and gender). The groups that are relevant in different situations will vary.
- **Indicators** must be selected to make sure it is possible to measure programme progress and impact in relation to the relevant groups.
- **Lessons learned** from assessment, monitoring, review or evaluation should be made available to all the relevant groups.

Avoiding discrimination in organisational structures and policy

An anti-discriminatory approach should also be applied to the organisations concerned in any development programme and incorporated into all planning and decision-making. An anti-discriminatory approach can be strengthened by the following:

- **Participation of minority groups in the planning cycle from the start.**
- **Developing appropriate local equal opportunities policy and practice**. This means removing the organisational barriers that operate against particular groups of people. Equal opportunities in employment practice should cover: recruitment (advertising, application forms, job descriptions, person specification, shortlisting and interviewing); terms and conditions of employment (maternity and paternity leave, working arrangements); promotion and career development.
- **Training** staff, managers and volunteers to be aware of gender, disability, racism and the needs of children. Everyone has to understand the equal opportunities policy, and all training should take account of it. All training must be related to the circumstances, programmes and individuals concerned.
- **Recruiting** staff who are already aware of and behaving in line with equality issues.

Examples of ways to involve different groups

Children and young people

Most development organisations hope to benefit boys and girls of different ages through their work. The reasons for ensuring children's participation include:

- **Values and principles**: Many agencies are concerned with the lives, welfare and rights of children. This should include the right of young people to have

their opinions on matters that affect them taken into account in accordance
with their maturity.

- **Relevance**: Children's participation in planning, monitoring, review and
  evaluation gives insights into their best interests, their priorities and
  perspectives, and shows how policies and programmes affect them. It is
  essential to make sure the objectives and activities of projects and programmes
  are relevant to them, their lives and their needs.
- **Effective action**: If programmes are based on real insights into children's
  priorities, views and lives, rather than assumptions, they will be more likely
  to meet their objectives. Where children and young people have been centrally
  involved in planning, monitoring and evaluation they can be more centrally
  involved in decision-making and follow-up action.
- **Measure impact on children**: Bringing about meaningful change in children's
  and young people's lives involves asking them about the impact we are
  having. This means getting them involved in the process of deciding how to
  monitor, what information to collect, and how to interpret it.
- **Empowering children and young people**: Children and young people can
  gain skills and a sense of empowerment when their opinions are taken into
  account in planning, monitoring and evaluation.

Children may be prevented from participating because adults, including
programme staff, do not believe that they can add much to a programme; think
they are too young, too inexperienced or too passive; or think that they are too
disoriented by their experiences, especially in an emergency, to contribute useful
information and opinions.

These obstacles can be addressed by the careful selection and training of
staff, to make sure they elicit and consider children's views and have appropriate
expectations of what and how children can contribute. For example, children
may be too young to be asked what the programme objectives should be, but
they may have clear ideas about their problems, priorities and expectations.

Children can be involved, according to age and sex, in the following ways:
- As researchers or evaluators.

For example: In Bangladesh, Save the Children was working with street children
who had spent time in jail. The young people acted as researchers and
interviewed their peers about their experiences of incarceration to generate
debate among policy makers and NGOs in view of the common abuse suffered
by these children. Involving children brought fresh perceptions to the research,
the data gathered was of high quality, the young interviewees enjoyed being
interviewed by peers, they could raise issues and ask questions in a way adults
could not; the conclusions are more powerful when those affected carry out
research. Problems encountered included difficulty in contacting the young

people, getting the right incentives for them to take part, discussing some sensitive issues, and harassment by adults while carrying out research.

- Children can be asked their views directly.

For example: In one needs assessment children were asked what they did and did not like doing. They replied that they did not like getting up early, in the dark, to walk for over three hours to collect water, which often made them late for school. This was the origin of a water programme.

- Children can be encouraged to raise and discuss issues in groups.

For example: Theatre for Development (see Tool 10) is a good tool for enabling children to raise difficult issues. It was used in Pakistan to enable school children to discuss issues around sexual health and the effectiveness of the health education programme in school.

- Children can also give information by indirect means.

For example: In one routine walk around a refugee camp a small girl was approached and asked why she was sitting apart from other children. She replied that she was sad because camp officials had separated her from her brother. This led to a policy change in the camp: to keep brothers and sisters together, rather than dividing children up by age.

- Observation of children's needs and behaviour.

For example: Young children in pre-schools cannot be asked to participate in assessing the quality of care, but guidelines for observation can be prepared based on the principles of early childhood development and ways of providing care which are culturally appropriate. Indicators of good practice have been developed in this way for monitoring education work in Sri Lanka.

Communicating effectively with children may also require a different approach from communicating with adults. For example meetings may need to be shorter with more frequent breaks. Certain skills and techniques can be employed to make children feel at ease and talk about their lives. They may feel most at ease at home, in school, in groups or alone. Different techniques will be needed to communicate with children of different age groups. If you wish to involve children in assessment, monitoring, review and evaluation, it is essential to understand these techniques and ensure that they are used effectively.

For example: Some research was carried out with child domestic workers. Child domestic workers are often very isolated inside their employers' homes, and interviewing them may make them fearful of the consequences of upsetting their employers. Interviews should therefore be conducted in a neutral setting, where the child feels comfortable. It is also necessary to build up the child's confidence by interviewing over a period of time, and not asking difficult questions straight away. Interviewing can be very stressful for a child and interviewers should be aware that a child might become upset or depressed about a particular subject. Researchers should therefore only conduct interviews if they are prepared to provide follow-up help to the child.

These skills and techniques are described in the *Communicating with Children* by Naomi Richman and *Street and Working Children: A guide to planning* by Judith Ennew (see 'References and further reading'). Further **ethical issues** to consider when working with children and young people are discussed in Chapter 2.

Women

The full participation of women is a fundamental principle for any development programme. However, this principle is often difficult to put into practice because of inequalities between genders in many cultures and societies. The participation of women needs to be facilitated, for example, by ensuring settings in which women feel comfortable, and by helping women to define and express their own needs.

Barriers to women's participation include:

- lack of time due to heavy workloads and family responsibility
- lack of experience and confidence
- lack of education, training and access to information
- lack of mobility
- difficulty in talking to outsiders
- lack of familiarity with procedures
- deference to men
- fear of retribution (eg, physical violence)
- specific cultural constraints.

For example: In a long-term community development project in India, supported by the Aga Khan Rural Development Programme, the women in the village were asked what interventions would be of greatest assistance to them. They carried out a task analysis, showing how long they spent on each of their daily activities. This demonstrated that they worked 18 hours every day, and their most time-consuming tasks were collecting fuel and grinding corn. As a result they requested pressure cookers and a village corn mill.

The men of the village, however, were against this. They felt that food cooked in pressure cookers and grain that is not milled by hand is less nutritious and does not taste so good. They felt that the women were not as short of time as they claimed, but spent too much time chatting. The rural development team then asked the men to carry out a task analysis for their wives. When the men added up the time needed for each activity and found how many hours the women spent working each day, they were amazed. They then visited other villages where people used pressure cookers and mills and found that the food was, after all, acceptable.

Ways of helping to overcome barriers to participation include:

- **the careful choice of appropriate staff:**
  All staff should be aware that there is a gender dimension to every issue and action. In recruiting new staff, women and men should be given equal opportunities, and both should be assessed for their awareness of gender issues.

- **staff training in gender awareness:**
  Training should be related to local circumstances and the programmes concerned. It is important to use local expertise as far as possible, which may include local staff, gender specialists or representatives from women's organisations.

- **careful choice of time and place of meetings**, to ensure that women can attend and can speak freely about their concerns:
  Time and resources may need to be allocated to developing appropriate situations. It may be possible to meet women where they gather in the course of their daily activities, for example, while collecting water. It is often best to meet women without men, and to have separate meetings for older women and younger women. Issues to consider include:
  - childcare provision to allow women to attend meetings
  - taking time to explain concepts
  - training in confidence-building with women
  - working with men to increase their understanding of the need for women's involvement.

Disabled people

People with impairments form part of any community. They are 'disabled' by the physical, social and institutional barriers that exclude them, and because of the beliefs and attitudes of others. All projects can aim to eliminate these barriers and meet the ordinary needs of disabled children and their families, while disability projects may focus on special needs such as rehabilitation, correction of impairment, and special education. Everybody should be seen as having some common needs and some individual needs. This must be taken into account in any planning, monitoring, review or evaluation exercise.

The best way to ensure that there is a disability perspective in all development work is to involve disabled people and their families in decision-making.

Barriers to the participation of disabled people include:

- being invisible and overlooked in the community
- being forgotten in activities that do not specifically focus on disability
- lack of information for disabled people and lack of information about disability
- isolation due to cultural beliefs and attitudes (for example, thinking epilepsy is contagious, or the family is cursed)
- lack of self-esteem to speak out, interact and advocate joint interests
- lack of knowledge about how to involve disabled people
- physical access to buildings
- transport problems.

These barriers can be overcome, for example, in the following ways:

- Identify the different local, national and regional disabled people's organisations, and find out how best to work with them. For example, they may be involved in discussions about planning, monitoring and evaluation, in helping to recruit disabled people as staff or in designing training courses.
- Ensure that offices, latrines, health centres and other parts of the community infrastructure are designed to take into account the needs of people with impairments. This includes those who have wheelchairs, who have problems climbing stairs, who cannot squat easily or who have visual impairments.
- Consider the types of transport that are available, and recognise that carers of disabled children are often homebound. Try to identify families with disabled children and find ways for them to take part in community activities, or at least to be consulted in planning, monitoring and evaluation.
- Ensure that different kinds of disabled children and adults are considered and represented in training materials, both in pictures and text. Include disability in all the training courses, welcome disabled children and adults to take part.
- Develop or strengthen a referral system in the country for disability issues through links with NGOs, DPOs (disabled people's organisations) and other resource organisations.
- Promote disability awareness amongst staff, partners and communities, for example through training, campaigns, and awakening materials.

Minority ethnic groups

All ethnic groups should be involved in, and benefit from, development work on an equal basis.

Barriers to the participation of less powerful ethnic groups include the following:

- Personal prejudice about the abilities of individuals from these groups. For example, people from one ethnic group may believe that everyone from another is stupid, dishonest, or lazy.
- The language used by ethnic minorities is often different from the official national language.
- People from ethnic minority groups are often considered to be second class citizens, who are less important and whose opinions are not valued.

Ways of overcoming these barriers include the following:

- Find out about ethnic languages, communication channels and levels of literacy to make it possible to communicate effectively with different groups.
- Include the groups' own organisations and leaders in activities.
- Organise language and literacy training in the official national language with people from different communities.
- Ensure that training materials, health education materials and other literature include pictures of people from different ethnic groups.
- Take into account the different traditional practices and values in all activities.
- Provide awareness training for programme staff to foster mutual respect and understanding between different groups.
- Ensure that members of different ethnic groups are included on any team carrying out the planning, monitoring, review or evaluation exercise.

Summary

Principles of good practice

It is important to address the particular constraints that can prevent different individuals and groups from becoming involved in activities that affect them. There are also certain common features in all types of discrimination. As a general rule, discrimination against different groups can be addressed in planning, monitoring, review and evaluation by:

- analysing the differences within communities and households
- ensuring that all the relevant views and interests have a voice
- providing awareness training in equality issues for those carrying out the exercise
- using the right tools in the right way at the right time

- disaggregating data and selecting indicators according to relevant groups
- making sure the findings are made easily available to all the different groups.

These principles should always be applied in planning, monitoring, review and evaluation to avoid discriminating against children, women, disabled people, ethnic minorities, and any other groups that may be excluded in some way from the development process.

Chapter 4
The systematic collection and analysis of information

The principles of being systematic

Planning, monitoring, review, evaluation and impact assessment all depend on the systematic collection and analysis of different kinds of information. The purpose of being systematic is to understand a situation or problem fully and not from a single, personal viewpoint. The systematic collection of information is simply a way of searching for a balanced view. The degree of academic rigour required will depend on the purpose of the particular planning, monitoring, review or evaluation exercise. In some cases informal and ad hoc information collection will be more appropriate than a carefully planned study. In any case it is important to recognise the influence of bias, and how to overcome it.

This chapter gives a brief outline of the general tools that can be used to collect information in a systematic way. It begins by discussing how to recognise ways in which bias can be introduced into an exercise and how to minimise it. The chapter then goes on to describe qualitative and quantitative methods of collecting information and how to decide which method is most suitable for a particular situation.

Objectivity and bias

No research can be completely objective, however scientific the methods used. The researcher's questions are based on his or her experience, perceptions and assumptions. These will influence the design and hence the results of the research. It is important to recognise this when presenting information, and to acknowledge the assumptions that have been made. However, bias can be reduced by using quantitative and qualitative research techniques in a systematic way.

Bias means that a situation is represented from a particular angle. This can happen if one side of an argument is supported more than another, if some types of information are given more importance than others, or if the results are influenced too much in one direction by the way data is collected. Research can still be valid if bias is recognised and acknowledged. But if it is not acknowledged, then the results will be misleading.

Bias can be introduced when a study is designed

For example:

- The selection of samples, or who will be questioned in a community, may not represent the population it claims to represent. Who is asked, where they live, and when the survey is carried out will influence results. For example: men will have a different view of the community from women; a village near a road will have different problems from a more remote settlement; many people will not be available at certain times of the day or year. (See summary of types of sampling, below.)
- The way questions on a questionnaire are worded may lead people to answer in a particular way.

Summary of types of sampling:
(From *Impact Assessment for Development Agencies*, Chris Roche)

Random sampling:
Simple random sampling: A group of people are selected at random from a complete list of a given population.
Stratified or systematic random sampling: This ensures that sub-groups within a given population are included in the sample, by randomly sampling within each of these sub-groups.
Cluster sampling: By selecting geographic clusters of villages or households within a given population, time and money is saved; this technique thus allows more people or groups to be contacted in the time available.
Staged sampling: For large populations, one may need to sample within samples. For example, an NGO's Rural Development Programme works with 63,846 village organisations through 372 area offices. Each of these villages contains a number of households. Therefore, to assess its impact, the NGO selected a sample of areas within which a random sample of households was interviewed.
Random walk: Instructions are given to the interviewer to follow a random route and interview individuals (take first road right, interview at second house on your left, continue down the road, interview tenth household on your right, and so on).

Non-random sampling:
Quota sampling: Based on information about a population, quotas of certain types of people or organisations are selected for interview; common criteria for quotas are age, gender, occupation, and whether people live in project or non-project areas.
Genealogy-based sample: Select entire families and their relatives rather than households.

Chain sampling or snowballing: Select a first contact and then ask them whom you should talk to next. This method is useful for identifying minority groups or occupations within communities.

Matched samples: Similar pairs of villages, projects, or groups of people are selected in order to compare them (project groups and non-project groups are an example).

Repeat sample methods:

Panel or cohort surveys: A set of people or organisation is contacted several times over a relatively long period.

Repeat survey: The entire survey process is repeated, including sampling.

Rotating survey: This is a combination of the panel and repeat survey methods: one fraction of the sample is changed each time the survey is repeated, another fraction remains the same.

For more details see P Nichols, *Social Survey Methods* (see 'References and further reading' section).

Bias can be introduced when data is collected

For example:

- Measuring equipment may not be properly calibrated. For example, if a set of weighing scales is not set to zero properly, the objects it is weighing may seem heavier or lighter than they really are.
- The same equipment may be used in different ways from one measurement to another.
- The way people ask questions (if they are in a hurry, by the tone of their voice, by their body language) may encourage people to answer in a particular way.
- The attitudes of researchers towards particular groups may affect the way they ask questions and record answers.
- The researchers themselves (their gender, social and educational background, particular interests, etc) may influence the way people respond to them.
- The way questions and answers are translated into different languages may affect their meaning.
- If the variables used are not clearly defined, different people may interpret them differently.

Bias can be introduced in data analysis

For example:

- Different statistical tests carried out on the same data can give slightly different conclusions.
- Variables may be classified in different ways.

- If data is not disaggregated to show the differences between certain groups (by gender, age, ethnic groups, etc), the final results will not reflect the true variations within the sample.

In qualitative research it is especially difficult to avoid bias when analysing the data. It is important to recognise your own bias and the bias of the researchers.

Ways of minimising bias
Bias is inherent in most methods of collecting data, whether it is quantitative or qualitative. But there are ways of minimising it by careful training and supervision, and by cross-checking information.

Cross-checking, or triangulation is always essential in collecting information. This can be done through:
- different people collecting the information, each with different skills, experience and viewpoints
- using different tools and techniques to collect and analyse information about the same issue. For example, questions about the wealth of a household can be cross-checked by observation of the way a house is built, the possession of certain objects, etc
- using different sources of information: in other words collecting information from different people, in different places, and at different events. For example, the type of sampling method used is very important (see summary on page 39)
- checking for internal consistency. For example, in interviews about household food income, it is possible for the interviewer to add up the total amount of food income reported and compare it with the household's consumption needs.[1]

(Qualitative techniques for cross-checking are discussed in more detail in Tool 1, under PLA techniques.)

For example: The Health Action for Schools project in Pakistan underwent its final evaluation by an external evaluator from the Child-to-Child Trust. The quantitative data had been derived from classroom observations, field visits and so on. Qualitative data for the evaluation was assessed from focus group discussions with teachers, head teachers, health co-ordinators, and children. Other tools used included mapping exercises, role-plays, individual interviews and visual exercises. Children's participation was a major feature in the above activities, as their input was correlated with the responses of teachers, parents and head teachers to verify both how the health lessons were taught (the methodology and sequential process) as well as to examine the health content knowledge of children.

---

1 *The Household Economy Approach: A resource manual for practitioners*, Save the Children Development Manual 6, 2000

Training and supervision can be used. For example:

- Weighing babies: make sure people use the same equipment, look at the scales from the same angle, and set the scales to zero each time.
- Using a questionnaire: make sure that the wording of questions and the way they are asked (tone of voice, body language, general attitude) do not unduly influence the answers.
- Interviewers should be trained and given clear guidelines.
- Researchers should take care to avoid discriminating against certain groups (see Chapter 3).
- All variables should be clearly defined.
- All data should be classified consistently and in a way that will help produce relevant information. For example, if the findings are to be used to show how the work has affected the well-being of children, data should be collected and analysed in appropriate age groups. Data should also be disaggregated by gender, disability, and ethnic groups where relevant.
- Questions and answers must be translated carefully.

Precision and accuracy

"It is better to be approximately right than precisely wrong." (attributed to Keynes)

It is possible to measure something very precisely, using good techniques or well designed surveys. However, the measurement will only be accurate if it is both precise and unbiased. It is important to recognise that some measurements can be precise but inaccurate, and others can be imprecise, but more or less accurate. For example, data may appear to be precise if it is based on numbers, such as specific population figures, but if these population figures are out of date (particularly in areas where migration has taken place), the calculations will be wrong and entirely misleading. For the purposes of planning, monitoring, review and evaluation, being approximately right is usually all that is required.

Beware of assumptions

Assumptions underlie many decisions in development work. It is important to recognise what assumptions are being made. (See Tool 3: Logical framework analysis). It is equally important to recognise false assumptions when carrying out research.

For example: Pratt and Loizos (1992) identify some more pitfalls, which can cause problems in development-related research:

- Avoid false certainty about people's class.
- Do not assume solidarity – 'to share a characteristic is no guarantee of a sense of having "something in common".'

- Do not assume community – 'living near to each other [does not] automatically lead to something called "community spirit".'
- Do not read rural patterns into urban contexts (or vice versa).
- Avoid over-reliance on particular informants.

Quantitative and qualitative methods

Before collecting information from the field, it is essential to examine existing information, including relevant books, reports and surveys. This will help formulate questions and avoid duplicating previous studies. Information can be collected from the field and then analysed using quantitative and/or qualitative methods.

Quantitative methods

Quantitative research methods are used to collect data that can be analysed in a numerical form. They pose the questions:
who, what, when, where, how much, how many, how often?

Things are either measured or counted, or questions are asked according to a defined questionnaire so that the answers can be coded and analysed numerically. For example:
How many people said that when sick they would:
1   go to a traditional healer?
2   go to the local health centre?
3   go to the pharmacist?
4   go to family member?
5   other?

Statistical analysis can be used on quantitative data to give a precise description of the findings in terms of averages, ratios, ranges, etc. (see Tool 2).
Quantitative techniques are useful when you need to:
- provide accurate, precise data
- have a broad view of a whole population
- identify major differences in the characteristics of a population, and find out which sectors of the population are worst affected
- test whether there is a statistical relationship between a problem and an apparent cause
- produce evidence, or hard data, to prove that certain problems exist, or to justify a particular strategy to donors, government, and other decision-makers
- establish clear baseline information that can be used for evaluating the impact of a project or programme later on.

For example: The Household Economy Approach, developed at Save the Children, uses a range of methods to find out how households belonging to different wealth groups are likely to be affected by 'shocks' to the economic system, such as crop failure, or war. One method is a quantitative assessment of how much food, in calories, the household requires to survive, and how it obtains these calories using different sources of food income in a normal year. This provides a baseline to show how severely households will be affected if their access to any of the food sources is restricted. This approach has been used effectively to obtain food aid from donors.

Surveys

The most common quantitative research tool is the survey. Surveys are often used in development work to:

- look at the **size and distribution** of a specific problem (for example, a nutrition survey)
- investigate **characteristics of a population** that will be relevant to a project
- look at the **relationship between different variables** to see if there is a pattern
- collect **baseline data** on selected indicators early in a programme which can be compared with data collected later on, to see whether the programme has had any impact
- identify the **project beneficiaries**: household surveys can be used to identify the people who fit pre-defined criteria to receive assistance
- collect **epidemiological data** on diseases: to identify the population at risk, look at patterns of disease transmission, etc.

(See Tool 2, for a brief description of survey methodology with its strengths and weaknesses.)

Qualitative methods

Qualitative research methods are designed to help build up an in-depth picture among a relatively small sample of how the population functions, what the key relationships are, and how different aspects of life are linked together. They also reveal how people understand their own situation and problems, and what *their* priorities are. A range of techniques are used: interviews, focus groups, and other forms of enquiry such as video diaries, drawing, drama, and so on.

The essence of qualitative research is that it is flexible. Questions are asked in an open-ended way and the findings are analysed as data is collected. This means the design of the study can be continuously modified to follow up significant findings as they arise. The research poses the questions *how* and *why*. Qualitative methods (discussion, observation, etc) are used informally all the time, but the results can be subjective and impressionistic. When qualitative research is done systematically, the findings are as reliable and objective as those produced by quantitative methods.

Qualitative, in-depth analysis is useful when:

- planning a programme, to understand implications of social change
- a thorough understanding of a topic in a particular context is needed
- information is needed about what people think about their situation or a problem and what their priorities are
- selecting appropriate indicators for qualitative change (for example, to show whether a situation is getting better or worse)
- there is a shortage of time and money (it is often cheaper and quicker than a quantitative survey).

For example: The Household Economy Approach uses qualitative techniques to define: what social unit most closely matches the definition of a household, (ie, a group of people who work together as a production and consumption unit); what are the criteria that differentiate poor and rich households; how are households grouped within the economy; and what proportion of the population falls into each group.

Participatory methods

Participatory methods are designed to provide an opportunity for people to analyse their own situation and reach their own conclusions about possible solutions. Participatory approaches are based on qualitative research techniques, but are fundamentally different from conventional 'research' because the information is not extracted for analysis by outsiders. The whole process of designing the research, and collecting and analysing information is done by insiders, who then have ownership of the findings. Participatory methods are also often used at different stages of a non-participatory process. (See Tool 1 for a description of qualitative and participatory assessment methods.)

When to use different methods

Qualitative and quantitative methods do not exclude each other and are often best used together. For example: in a quantitative survey, qualitative methods can be used to develop an appropriate questionnaire, to gather detailed information about selected issues, and to explore the reasons behind relationships which have been discovered by a quantitative survey. Qualitative methods can also be used to identify the issues that need to be investigated more widely by a broad-based survey.

For example: The Household Economy Approach (HEA) uses a combination of qualitative and quantitative techniques to find out how different household economies operate, how many households are most vulnerable, and what sort of assistance is required to prevent vulnerable households becoming destitute after a shock to the economic system. In other words, the findings from a survey using the HEA will show both the quantity and quality of external assistance required.

Whichever method is used, it will only provide valid information if the research is carried out systematically with proper planning, execution, and analysis.

The choice of methods depends on:
- the information required
- the purpose of the exercise
- the availability of resources.

Define the information required

To define what sort of information is required:
- First clarify the problem you want to look at.
- Then draw out the questions you need to answer.
- Consider what you need the information for. How will it be used?

For example: A study was carried out by Save the Children into the acceptability of immunisation in Somalia, where mothers did not want to take their children to be immunised and programme planners wanted to increase immunisation acceptability. A *quantitative* survey could have found out:
- how many mothers accept immunisation, how many do not, and whether this is related statistically to their socio-economic status, education, age, number of children, distance from clinic, income, clan, etc.

This information might be useful for programme planning if the social or physical factors that were found to influence the mothers could be changed.

A qualitative survey was used instead. This found out:
- why mothers do or do not take their children to be immunised. It looked at their experience with immunisation and how that affects their behaviour.

The study showed that the way mothers were treated in clinics put them off. For example, they were not told enough and were scared when their children suffered from fevers after vaccination. They thought some diseases were caused by bad spirits and so could not be prevented by vaccination. From this information it was possible to change the way clinics were run and staff were trained, and it was easier to explain to mothers why immunisation is important.

(A quantitative phase of the study had been planned to see how prevalent the attitudes discovered in the qualitative study were, but this had to be cancelled because of the poor security situation.)

What is the purpose of the exercise?

Quantitative methods are more appropriate if the main purpose is to gather highly accurate and precise data (for example, in a demographic census or family enrolment, or as a baseline for future reference and comparison), or when sophisticated statistical analysis is needed. They are particularly helpful in identifying averages and correlating different factors statistically. Quantitative findings are more widely believed to be objective, and so may be needed to support requests for assistance from donors.

Qualitative methods can illuminate nuances and highlight diversity. They are often more useful for understanding an issue or situation than quantitative methods, since no statistic is self-explanatory. If the main purpose is to build links between agency staff and community members, to transfer skills in information-gathering and analysis, or to pave the way for further development activities, qualitative methods are usually more appropriate.

For example: A global review was carried out into Save the Children UK's work in social protection, welfare and inclusion of children. This was to look at how the Save the Children policy of avoiding institutional care for children, or at least minimising it, is put into practice in the field. After extensive background research at headquarters, field research was carried out in four countries, as case studies. Qualitative techniques, including semi-structured interviews and observation were used to collect information from children, parents, care-givers and local government officials. This gave useful insights into how successful the approach to child protection in each country was in serving the best interests of the child.

What resources are available?

Quantitative methods are often on a larger scale, and so more costly in terms of assets (eg, computers and vehicles), human resources (eg, paid enumerators) and time. However, well-designed quantitative surveys can be carried out quickly and it is sometimes possible to produce results straight away by using portable computers to analyse findings in the field.

Qualitative methods also require specific skills, particularly in the analysis of findings, and qualitative research can take a long time. But the methods can be used effectively for a quick assessment of a situation. In general, qualitative methods are more suitable than quantitative methods when time and resources are limited.

> **For example:** In the global review on social protection, welfare and inclusion, it might have been useful to include a quantitative component in the case studies, to see to what extent the approach used was relevant in the particular context of the country. But there were not enough resources and time to do this, and it was not perceived as a priority for the research.

Summary

- The purpose of being systematic when gathering and analysing information is to gain a balanced view about a situation and reduce bias.
- Qualitative, quantitative and participatory methods can be used, as appropriate.
- To decide which methods to use, define:
  - what information is required, how will it be used and by whom?
  - what is the purpose of the exercise?
  - what resources are available?
- "Quantitative methods work best when you want precise, statistical answers to carefully defined questions on topics which are thoroughly understood. They are powerful tools for collecting a broad range of standard information on a large population. Statistical methods give precise estimates and you can assess their reliability. This gives support to your findings and interpretations."
- "Qualitative methods work best when time and money are short. They give a rapid feel for a problem. Essential in exploring community attitudes and priorities and when dealing with sensitive topics in depth. They can give a rich understanding of community life and help set up a dialogue between planners and community." (*Social Survey Methods*, Oxfam – for full details see 'References and further reading' section.)
- Participatory methods provide an opportunity for people to analyse their own situation and reach their own conclusions.
- A mixture of methods is usually required to reach a good understanding about a situation or programme in order to make decisions about the programme.

Part 2
Practical questions

Chapter 5
Questions to consider when undertaking planning, monitoring, review, evaluation or impact assessment

Planning, monitoring, review, evaluation and impact assessment are all components of the same process: analysing work in order to learn and improve future programmes, and to inform policy and advocacy. This process is described in Chapter 1 as the 'programme spiral'. This chapter outlines a series of questions to guide the planning of any stage of the process and sets out the basic principles on which all the exercises are based. It is important to emphasise that no exercise should be seen as existing on its own, but that they should all be linked with each other and must feed in to learning and programme development, or otherwise they are futile activities.

The questions in this chapter will help determine the best approaches to take in carrying out any exercise and the methods that should be used. They focus first of all on clarifying the aim of the exercise and who it is for; then on the objectives and key questions the exercise will address; the information that is needed, how it will be collected and analysed; how the results should be presented so that they can be most effectively used; and how the exercise should be managed in terms of people to involve, timescale, budget and other resources and how best to use computers.

Chapters 6 to 9 in this section of the book consider planning, monitoring, review, evaluation and impact assessment as discrete exercises within the programme spiral. They consider in more detail, illustrated with examples, the general points raised in this chapter that apply specifically to the implementation of each different exercise. Therefore if you are planning a review, for example, you should read this Chapter 5 first and then Chapter 8. It may also be useful to read Tool 11, which discusses some of the organisational issues that need to be addressed in developing an overall strategy for planning, monitoring, review and evaluation.

Terms of reference

Everyone who is involved in planning, monitoring, review, evaluation or impact assessment should discuss and come to an agreement on the questions listed below before carrying out the exercise, although new information and views will continue to come up. Once agreed, the decisions should be written up as the 'terms of reference', which act as a plan of action for the exercise.

The terms of reference will vary in detail and flexibility according to the type and specific purpose of the exercise. However, they are always needed, whether the exercise is a formal external evaluation or a mini-review carried out as part of a programme visit by a member of the same organisation (see Tool 9).

The questions that should always be considered are as follows:

1. The aim of the exercise
Why is the exercise necessary? Why now?

2. Who is it for?
How will the results be used? In particular, how will they be used for programme development?
Who should be involved in the exercise?

3. Objectives and key questions of the exercise
What are the objectives of the exercise?
What key questions should the exercise address?

4. Information collection and analysis
What information is needed and where can it be obtained?
How should information be collected and analysed?
What indicators should be used to measure the impact and progress of the work?

5. Presenting the results and using the findings
What conclusions and recommendations are required? What outputs will be required and for whom?
How can findings be used for advocacy?
What language will reports be in?
What feedback will there be about the findings to people involved in the work?
What evaluation will there be about how the exercise was carried out?
What follow-up work will be done to help put the recommendations into practice?
How should the results be stored for future use?

6. Organisation
How will the exercise be directed and managed?
Who should be involved and what are their tasks and responsibilities?
What is the timescale?

What resources will be needed and what is the budget?
The use of computers.

Each of these points will now be considered in more detail.

1. The aim of the exercise

Planning, monitoring, review, evaluation and impact assessment are usually carried out for a variety of reasons and are expected to provide useful information to several audiences. In order to provide genuinely useful information, however, the exercise must have a focus and overall aim.

In general, monitoring and evaluation is carried out for different purposes:

- **Accountability:** to provide information on effectiveness/efficiency, to demonstrate that activities have achieved their objectives
- **Management support** : to provide inputs to the implementation of ongoing initiatives; to inform decision making processes
- **Learning:** to draw lessons on past and present activities with a view to learning why some achieved their objectives or unintended outcomes in order to plan future activities.

Table 5.1 shows how the aim of the exercise will determine its design.

Table 5.1 The aim of the exercise and design questions

Features	Accountability	Learning
Basic aim	Finding out about current and past activities	Improving future activities
Emphasis on	Degrees of success and failure	Reasons for success and failure
How many examples, projects?	Randomly selected, ideally all population	Selected on the basis of their relevance
When to evaluate	At the end of the project/ programme cycle	As project/programme develops, embedded in planning cycle
Who should evaluate?	Should be independent, hence external	Should include staff, beneficiaries, wider set of stakeholders
What kind of data?	Emphasis on quantitative data	Mix of quantitative and qualitative data but emphasis on qualitative

Why is the exercise necessary? and why now?

- Planning, monitoring, review and evaluation are expensive and time consuming for all concerned. It is important to know why you are doing the exercise at this particular time.
- Consider how the exercise will feed into other planning and policy activities, and whether it will clash with other priorities for example prior engagements of partners.

2. Who is it for and how will they use the results?

As discussed in Chapter 2, many different people may use the analysis, conclusions and plans produced as a result of an exercise. In addition, the process of carrying out the exercise can in itself be extremely useful to all those involved.

It is important to decide at the beginning how the results will be used and by whom. If the intended use of the exercise is clear, it will be more useful and less threatening (particularly in the case of a review or evaluation) for those who are the subject of the exercise. The participants in the exercise should always be intended as recipients, and means of communicating the findings back to them should be considered from the beginning of the exercise.

It is also useful to plan a follow-up exercise to see whether the findings have been acted on, and if not, why not.

3. Objectives and key questions of the exercise

What are the objectives of the exercise?

The objectives of the exercise will depend on its overall aim and who it is for. Objectives are more specific than aims and they should be measurable: it should be possible to demonstrate whether or not the exercise has achieved its objectives.

Different people may want to investigate different issues. However, it is important that the exercise has a focus, so that it can concentrate on a manageable number of issues and investigate them in depth. An overall aim and a limited number of specific objectives, agreed by all concerned, can help decide which issues should be priorities.

What key questions should the exercise address?

- Key questions should highlight areas that need special attention if the main objectives of the exercise are to be met.
- Key questions should be realistically possible to answer.

Once the questions have been formulated, it is possible to see what kind of information will be needed. This will determine the methods, timescale, personnel and resources needed. It is important to be selective and realistic about the amount of information that can be analysed. If you attempt to address too many questions, it may not be possible to answer any of them satisfactorily. It would be better to answer a few properly, while bearing the others in mind.

One way to select those questions that should be addressed is to use the following criteria:
- What resources are available: can the question be answered?
- What is the importance to the programme of answering the question?
- What is the importance to the organisation of answering the question?
- What is already known about the issue? Is it worth more research?

It is also important to be flexible, so that questions can be amended or added during the process if necessary.

4. Information collection and analysis

What information is needed and where can it be obtained?

It is often necessary to devote a considerable amount of time and resources to collecting and analysing relevant information throughout the exercise. The information needed varies according to the objectives of the exercise, but it usually includes some or all of the following:

Information about the issue the programme aims to address and its context:
- the issue itself
- the local and national context of the issue
- the rights context: what rights are being violated, who are the rights-holders and duty-bearers?
- the people who will be (or are) affected by the work
- the services that already exist and other agencies working in the area
- existing resources available locally and through other organisations and donors (including people, training, infrastructure and money)
- the lessons that have been learned from experience of work on previous initiatives or on similar programmes in other parts of the world and which might be relevant in this situation.

Information about the programme:
- the history of the work
- the policy context of the work

- information that will provide an understanding of the problems and constraints, including the perceptions and opinions of a range of different people
- how the work is carried out
- the wider impact of the work, including unintended impact.

What indicators should be used to measure the impact and progress of the work?

Indicators are usually needed to show (or indicate) whether objectives are being reached, and how effective the work is. Each indicator requires a 'means of verification' which describes how you can find out about the indicator. Indicators and means of verification can be identified by asking the following questions:
- What things would make us feel we were making progress?
- How could we find out if these things are happening?

Process indicators must be chosen to enable the monitoring of progress in carrying out activities. Impact indicators are used to monitor what impact the work is having in terms of achieving its objectives. Indicators need to provide information about the work in terms of both quantity and quality. They must also be relevant to the different people involved in the work.

While indicators are often useful, they have limitations. They are not always the best way to measure progress or impact. Nor is it always possible to monitor them in a verifiable way (see Chapter 6).

Be selective

It is important to be selective about what information is collected. It is better to collect a small amount of accurate and useful information, than a large amount of less accurate information that cannot be used.

How should information be collected and analysed?

Planning, monitoring, review and evaluation and impact assessment is a continuous process of information-seeking, interpretation and judgement. The collection and analysis of information should be as systematic as possible, with cross-checking throughout so that the reasons behind the conclusions and recommendations that are drawn from the exercise can be clearly understood (see Chapter 4). Analysis should be carried out throughout the process, as well as at the end.

When planning the exercise, you will therefore need to consider where and how this information can be obtained:

- What documentation is needed and where can it be found?
- What internet sites can be used to search for relevant information?
- What information can be obtained from interviewing key individuals, and where can they be found?
- What information is available from monitoring systems and previous reviews or evaluations?
- What information will be gathered from the field and what general approach and methods will be used?
- How will that information be analysed?
- What skills, experience, or technical support will be required to obtain and analyse the necessary information?
- What sort of awareness, communication skills and languages will be needed to gather information from different groups?
- What issues concerning child protection and ethics need to be considered when gathering information? (See chapters 2 and 3.)
- What equipment will be needed and how can it be obtained?

It may be useful to suggest methods of collecting and analysing information in the terms of reference for the exercise, but these will probably be negotiated and further developed in the early stages of the exercise itself. All methods and approaches should be designed to make sure the perspectives of different groups are considered (see Chapters 2 and 3). Different interpretations of the same piece of information need to be taken into account. It may not be possible to reconcile them, in which case the different views should be recorded in the report.

Some methods for collecting and analysing information are described in Section 3, Tools 1, 2, 3 and 5.

Review of existing documents and knowledge

Before designing methods of collecting information for any exercise, it is important first of all to collect and study any relevant existing documentation. This could include:

- internal documentation from the agency such as project proposals and planning documents, policy documents, previous reviews or special studies
- external documentation such as statistics, relevant government policy and legislation, planning documents, external studies or surveys.
- information from monitoring systems can be used for review and evaluation.

Collecting and analysing information about indicators

Information about impact and process indicators should be collected using quantitative and qualitative methods as relevant. The approach and methods used should be decided according to the objectives of the exercise, and who it is for. (See Chapter 4 and Tools 1 and 2. See also Chapter 7 on methods for collecting and analysing information for a monitoring system.) More details on analysis of quantitative and qualitative information may be found in Section 3, Tools 1–7.

When should the data be analysed?

It is important to make sure enough time is allocated for analysis when planning the exercise. Thorough analysis can take a long time, particularly when there is a large amount of qualitative information, and particularly when participatory methods are used. If the analysis is too rushed, information may be wasted or misinterpreted and important details may be missed out. But if the analysis takes too long, the results may be out of date.

Different stages of data analysis can be carried out at different times during the exercise, according to who will use the information. The most important thing is to ensure that results are available when they are needed.

Who should analyse the data? (Who will benefit from the process?)

The process of analysis can lead to a greater understanding of the data, and so a certain amount of analysis should be carried out by the people collecting it and by the people using the data to make decisions. Where large amounts of quantitative data are collected, the actual calculations may need to be carried out by people with statistical expertise.

Participatory approaches to analysis are essential where the aim of the programme is to support people to analyse their own situations, make their views heard and hold decision-makers accountable.

The process of data analysis can be a useful way of checking the accuracy of data collected, and can identify any unusual or unexpected results. This is useful for programme management.

5. Presenting the results and using the findings

If findings are not used, the whole exercise will have been a waste of time and resources. The findings should therefore be presented in a way that makes them as accessible as possible to the people who need them.

What conclusions and recommendations are required?

As a result of collecting and analysing information, it should be possible to draw conclusions that can be acted upon.

It is important to show how the conclusions have been reached. It may be useful to show how the work is viewed by different people with different perspectives. It is often more useful to show the range of different opinions and why they are held, than to present a broad agreement which may be superficial.

Include a description of the important points raised in interviews and interpretation (for qualitative results). It is useful to give a selection of examples of what people actually said in interviews, word for word, which illustrate important points. This can be the best way of conveying local views to people reading the report.

The terms of reference for the exercise should specify what kinds of recommendations are needed and who they are for. It is important that all the people who will be responsible for putting them into practice have been able to participate in drawing them up.

Where issues of power relations are concerned it is important to anticipate how these will be addressed in the short and longer term.

Recommendations are based on the conclusions and should propose:

- what course(s) of action should be taken
- how they should be implemented, by whom, and when
- what resources, or inputs, are required (including money, people, assets, training, time)
- the constraints or problems that are likely to be involved and how they can be addressed
- the follow-up that will be needed to make sure the recommendations are acted upon.

Even if this level of detail cannot be achieved, it is still important to provide recommendations for future directions and options.

What reports (or other forms of presentation) will be required and for whom?

It is best to decide at an early stage how the findings will be recorded and presented (otherwise the end result may be a long set of notes which are very difficult to edit). It may be better to develop a *report format or framework* at the beginning of the exercise. If the programme that is being examined is complex and has many components, it may be difficult to give an overview. Different ways of presenting the findings can be considered. For example, in a review of a large health programme it was suggested that it might have been better to look at themes running through the programme, rather than at individual projects.

Where clear formats are used for reports, this can help the analysis of the information and stimulate discussion about the most important issues. As a general guide, a report should be short, written in clear language, and translated as necessary. When a report is long it is vital to highlight the most essential information. It may also be possible to present some of the findings as a set of diagrams. (See Chapter 8, for a sample format of an evaluation report.)

Different methods of presenting the results can be used for different users. For example, a workshop using visual aids may be the best way of stimulating a group discussion based on the findings. Slides, photographs and/or video may help to present the findings to a wider audience. A combination of report and audio-visual methods may be most appropriate. Puppet shows, theatre, role play, diagrams, and video have all been used to help present assessment, monitoring, review and evaluation results. (See Tool 10, on presenting and sharing information.)

How can the findings be used for advocacy?

Advocacy is becoming an increasingly important component of all development programmes. The findings of planning, monitoring, evaluation and impact assessment exercises can be used for a range of advocacy activities, for example, as evidence to lobby for policy change.

What language will reports be in?

The findings may need to be presented in different languages. This can be time-consuming but may be vital if all the users are to have access to the findings.

What feedback will there be about the findings to people involved in the work?

Whenever possible, the findings should be made available to all the people involved in a project or programme, and they should have the opportunity to comment on them. This is essential if a project is to be accountable to its users.

It is also important to thank people for their help, information and time. Even when the main purpose of the exercise is to help senior managers make decisions, there should be some feedback to programme staff, partners and people who are affected by the work.

What evaluation will there be about how the exercise was carried out?

There should also be an opportunity for partners, staff and managers to comment on the way the exercise was carried out and lessons that have been learned from

the process. It is useful to include an assessment of the process in the report:
- to reflect on what has been learned from the process by all involved
- to identify weaknesses in the process and how they could affect the findings and conclusions
- to learn from the experience for future exercises.

What follow-up will be done to help put the recommendations into practice?

Once the recommendations have been accepted by all the relevant people, it may be necessary to provide support to those responsible for putting them into practice. This may include:
- ensuring all staff, including senior managers and partners, support the changes required which may include changes to working methods, job descriptions, additional resources, training, etc
- follow-up meetings to assess the relevance and effectiveness of the recommendations.

How should the results be stored for future use?

Make sure the report is filed and referenced in such a way that it will be available to:
- people working on the project in the future
- people working on similar projects who could learn from the experience
- people undertaking planning, monitoring, review, evaluation or impact assessment of similar work who would be interested in the methodology used
- people who can use the findings for other purposes, for example, research or advocacy.

6. Organisation

How will the exercise be directed and managed?

The way an exercise is directed and managed and who is involved should be determined by its main purpose and who it is for. It is essential to consider whether participatory techniques should be used and who should be consulted at different stages. In rights-based programming, people – including children – have a right to participate in decisions that affect them. It will also affect the 'ownership' of the findings and hence how effective the exercise can be in influencing decisions (see Chapter 2). Ethical issues and child protection must always be considered when children participate in the exercise (see chapter 2).

Where several people have an interest in the exercise, it may be useful to form a 'steering committee' to guide its progress. This could include, for example, the programme director, senior project staff, representatives from the community, representatives from partner organisations.

When an external consultant is employed to manage the exercise, the terms of reference need to be particularly clear, and it may be necessary to draw up a contract between the programme and consultant (see Tool 8). It is important to clarify, for example, who will own the final report, the limits to the consultant's independence, and who else should be involved in designing and carrying out the exercise.

Who should be involved and what are their tasks and responsibilities?

You need to consider who will be needed to carry out different tasks in the exercise, and make sure there is enough time to carry out each task. Table 5.2 on pages 63 and 64 lays out some points to consider as examples.

Warning
Time often runs out at the end of the exercise, leaving less time for proper consultation with all the people involved about the conclusions and recommendations. There is then a danger that the findings will not be used after all.

What resources will be needed and what is the budget?

Resources needed for a one-off exercise such as assessment, review or evaluation may include the following expenses:
- Travel: international and national, including air fares, taxis, fuel and trains.
- Accommodation and expenses while collecting information.
- Office expenses: including stationery, photocopies, use of telephone, telex, fax, and computer.
- Staff time: including external consultants, project staff, research assistants, secretarial assistance, people to enter data, drivers, translators, interpreters.
- Equipment for collecting, analysing and recording information: for example, weighing scales, notebooks, cameras.
- Workshops: including venue, materials, travel and accommodation for participants, per diems, external trainers or facilitators.

The cost of a monitoring system can be considerable. It includes a one-off cost to design the system, and recurrent costs to run it which should be included in the programme budget (see Chapter 7).

Table 5.2 Tasks and responsibilities

Tasks	Who does it? Examples of who might be needed	How long will it take? Examples of time factors
Formulation of purpose and objectives of the exercise	Main stakeholders must be involved	• Time to make sure there is agreement from different stakeholders
Writing out terms of reference	In consultation with relevant stakeholders	• Time for consultation
Recruiting, briefing and managing consultant (if relevant) and team leaders. Includes drawing up contract, providing ongoing support and supervision	Person responsible for co-ordinating exercise, in consultation with relevant stakeholders	• Time needed to identify suitable people and interview them. • When are they available? • Time required to obtain and read background material
Recruiting briefing, training and supervising staff involved, and providing on-going support	Co-ordinator, and all involved, including people collecting data, translators, administrators, data analysts	• When are people involved available? How much time • How much time is required for training, etc?
Agreeing on objectives and specific questions for the exercise	All stakeholders involved	• Time for consultation
Designing methods for collecting and analysing data, pre-testing methods, translating questionnaires and data collection guidelines	Includes researchers, trainers, support staff	• Time for designing methods, consultation to make sure methods are suitable, trying them out and amending if necessary • Time needed for training in specific techniques
Collecting information: includes reading and analysing existing records; can also include holding meetings, conducting surveys and interviews, and using participatory methods	Researchers and support staff including drivers, administrators and translators	• Consider time needed to travel, trace people for interviewing, organise meetings • Take account of public holidays, seasonal weather and activities • Consider when is the best time of day to talk to different groups of people

Tasks	**Who does it:** Examples of who might be needed	**How long will it take:** Examples of time factors
Checking data, analysing and interpreting the results. This could include checking and entering data onto computers. For qualitative analysis it includes recording and summarising findings, translating where necessary. Organising meetings and workshops	Researchers, in consultation with other people	Time needed to check and enter data (consider availability of computers, electricity supply). Analysis often takes longer than expected, especially where participatory approaches are used
Writing conclusions and recommendations	Team leader and researchers in consultation with relevant people	Time for consultation, feedback, and amending conclusions as a result
Preparing and presenting the results. This includes writing it up, editing it, photocopying, translating, organising workshops, editing video material, and distributing the results to all the people who need them	Consider who will do each of the tasks	Time needed for all these tasks. Consider timing in relation to planning exercises to ensure results are used. Opportunities to use findings for advocacy purposes
Providing feedback to all who have been involved in the exercise, for example, by organising workshops	All who have been involved	When is a good time for all relevant people?
Making sure that recommendations are acted on	What role do programme managers and advisers play?	What is period for implementation of recommendations?

The use of computers
Computers are most useful for:
- designing and producing clear reports, information collecting tools, and so on
- communications: access to e-mail, internet
- analysing quantitative data, for example, from surveys or regular record system
- recording and displaying information that is continually updated: for example, staff records and salaries, accounts, stock control, information about programme indicators.

The costs of using computers are:
- cost of buying, maintaining and updating the equipment, including voltage stabilisers and power back-up systems where necessary
- time and expertise to set up a program to do a particular task – once set up, a program often needs to be amended and modified to meet changing needs, which can be expensive
- data-entry, which is a skilled and time-consuming task.

If computer skills are not available locally, it might be better to use manual techniques for analysis, even if it takes longer.

The types of programs that can be used include:
- **Spreadsheet programs:** text and figures can be entered in tables which can be easily amended and updated. They can produce simple statistics, and graphs based on the figures. Spreadsheet programs are relatively easy to use.
- **Database programs** can be used to record and display information that is continually updated. They can search and sort information, and carry out simple statistical analysis. These might be useful for entering data collected in a survey, for accounts, or for staff records. Database programs have to be specially tailored to the user's requirements, and this needs specialist knowledge. Once tailored, data can be entered by anyone with accurate keyboard skills and a little training.
- **Management Information Systems (MIS)** are systems designed to help organisations manage their resources, plan and monitor activities and demonstrate their results and impact. They can be used for storing project information (objectives, actors involved), tracking user defined indicators, monitoring project completion rates, detailing budgets/expenditure, producing graphical display and generating reports. Such packages can provide an overview of a project or series of projects, and enable specific aspects to be pulled out and analysed. These are usually expensive and require considerable training and support. Some examples are:
  - *PROMES* – Project Monitoring and Evaluation System, has four key modules dealing with human resources, project management, financial administration and objectives/process monitoring and evaluation. *PROMES* is essentially a qualitative system and does not gather much quantitative data. Available in English, French, Spanish. Multi-user compatible. See www.promesweb.nl
  - *MER* – The MER system (Monitoring, Evaluating, Reporting) is a design, monitoring and evaluation methodology with an optional suite of software tools for information management, analysis and reporting. See www.kcenter.com/mer
  - *TeamUP-PCM* is a Windows-based project cycle management package designed for international development planning and implementation.

It has modules on stakeholder, conflict and 'tree' based analysis, planning, and performance indicator monitoring and budget tracking, as well as a logical framework matrix. Available in Spanish and English. See www.logframe.com

- The *SoNoMIS* project is a non-profit initiative to develop and provide low-cost access to flexible internet-based management information systems, focusing on organisations involved in international co-operation, sustainable development and emergency aid. See www.sonomis.org

- **Geographic Information Systems (GIS)** are able to assemble, store, manipulate and display geographically referenced information. Data can be used to project the various impacts of different environmental or other 'shocks'. GIS systems might be used for resource management, development planning or emergency response. These are usually specialised systems that require large amounts of data collection and programming, and 'expert' operation. For example:

  - *RiskMap* is a programme developed by Save the Children UK to monitor food security risk levels. It can predict the onset and impact of events such as drought on household economies. An intra-household model is now being developed to better understand the effects of changes within the household. For more information on these approaches, see www.savethechildren.org.uk/foodsecurity

- **Combined programs** can be used for specific purposes. For example:

  - *Epi-info* is a software package used to collect and analyse information from surveys. It combines database, statistical analysis, graphics and wordprocessing facilities. It is relatively easy to use and available free of charge. See www.cdc.gov/epiinfo

- **Statistics programs** such as SPSS are only really necessary when more complicated statistical analysis is required. They require specialist statistical knowledge.

- **Word processing programs** can be used to write reports.

Summary

- Terms of reference can be drawn up at the beginning of an exercise, but will usually need to be adapted as the exercise progresses and the situation changes. It is useful to reconsider the questions at different stages of the process.

- The following questions should always be considered when beginning any planning, monitoring, review, evaluation or impact assessment exercise:

- what is the aim of the exercise?
- who is it for, and how will it be used?
- what are the objectives and key questions of the exercise?
- what information is needed, how can it be collected and analysed?
- what indicators should be used to measure the impact and progress of the work?
- what conclusions and recommendations are required? What outputs will be required and for whom?
- how can findings be used for advocacy?
- what language will reports be in?
- what feedback will there be about the findings to people involved in the work?
- what evaluation will there be about how the exercise was carried out?
- what follow-up work will be done to help put the recommendations into practice?
- how should the results be stored for future use?
- how will the exercise be directed and managed?
- who should be involved and what are their tasks and responsibilities?
- what is the timescale?
- what resources will be needed and what is the budget?
- the use of computers.

Chapter 6
Assessment and programme planning

Chapter 5 suggested a sequence of questions that should be answered when undertaking any planning, monitoring, review and evaluation exercises. This chapter looks in more detail at the different stages of assessment and programme planning. If you are intending to undertake an assessment and planning exercise you should therefore use both this chapter and Chapter 5, to make sure that the important points have been covered in the terms of reference for the exercise. Other chapters are referred to where relevant.

The first part of this chapter considers the initial questions that need to be addressed in order to clarify why an assessment and planning exercise is necessary, who it is for and how the results will be used. The remainder of the chapter explains in detail the five stages that are usually involved when undertaking the assessment and planning of a programme or project: identifying the issues and problems that should be addressed; carrying out a situation analysis; producing a draft proposal for a programme that links together aims, objectives, activities and indicators for measuring progress; appraisal of the proposal; and obtaining official approval.

Designing an assessment and planning exercise

Assessment and planning (for the purposes of this book) is the process of identifying and understanding a problem and planning a series of actions to deal with it. The end result is to have a clear and realistic plan of activities designed to achieve a set of clear aims and objectives. This plan should also include indicators for each activity, as a way of measuring that the objectives are being met and progress is being achieved.

The way an assessment is carried out and who should do it will depend on its precise purpose, and what sort of approach is best suited to the circumstances.

When and why is an assessment necessary?

A formal assessment is likely to be necessary:
- before starting a new programme
- when expanding an existing programme into a new area
- when starting work with a new partner

- when changing the direction of an existing programme so that new objectives and baseline are required.

Who is it for?

An assessment may be for:
- **programme management, staff and partners**: to learn about the area and people concerned; to understand the problems affecting people, their causes and how they are already being tackled; to understand the rights which have been violated, and the obstacles to securing rights; to design a programme to support efforts to tackle them, developing objectives and planning activities; to gather information that will help to monitor and evaluate the effectiveness of the work
- **people who will be affected by the work**: to ensure the programme developed as a result of the assessment is relevant to their needs and resources; is accessible, even to the most vulnerable groups; is owned by them so that they have genuine influence over the decisions affecting them; and is therefore more likely to be effective and sustainable
- **policy advisers** : to be able to advise on good practice and learning opportunities
- **donors**: to decide whether or not to fund a programme, and to provide information that will help them evaluate the effectiveness of the work.

How will the results be used?

It is important to consider from the beginning how the assessment will be used and by whom, as this will affect how the assessment is carried out, the method(s) of presentation, and the language(s) used for presentation.

The results of an assessment may be used:
- as a basis for programme planning discussions between programme managers, staff, partners, and people who will be affected by the work
- as a funding proposal for donors
- as an initial analysis of the situation before the programme starts, to be compared with an analysis later on to show what impact the programme has made.

The stages of assessment and programme planning

The initial assessment and planning of a programme or project usually goes through the five stages described below, although in reality there is rarely such a clear sequence.

Stage 1. Problem identification
Identifying issues, problems and needs that should be addressed. Identifying opportunities for work within the country strategy and in line with the agency's principles and values.

Stage 2. Situation analysis
Needs assessment, analysis of rights and accountabilities, baseline study.

Produce project concept note

Stage 3. Programme design: how to address the problem identified
Collecting and analysing information, defining aims and objectives, developing activities that will achieve them, drawing up a plan of action, selecting appropriate indicators for measuring progress, and deciding how best to monitor and evaluate the work.

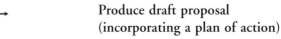

**Produce draft proposal
(incorporating a plan of action)**

Stage 4. Programme appraisal
Appraisal of the proposal by the agency to see whether it fits with the policies, principles, values and priorities of the organisation, and to see whether it is feasible.

Produce refined proposal

Stage 5. Approval and baseline studies
Obtain official approval and funding, carry out baseline study (if not already done) and start work.

Stage 1. Problem identification

The process of assessment begins when a problem or issue is identified that an agency believes can and should be addressed. In some cases, a government or NGO will present an agency with a specific proposal and request for funding, having already identified and defined the issue. In other cases, the agency has to try to understand the situation in a country, region or sector before being able to identify problems and opportunities for work.

Stage 2. Carrying out a situation analysis

It is vital to understand as fully as possible an issue, its causes and its consequences before attempting to draw up a plan of action for a programme or project to address it. Carrying out a good situation analysis is the best way to make sure that a programme is likely to achieve the desired objectives. It involves collecting and analysing information about a particular issue in its broader context in order to make a sensible assessment of what needs to be done.

The extent of the investigation required will depend on how much is already known. Sometimes it may be more appropriate to do a thorough investigation at the programme design stage.

Some of the information required is collected over time and analysed through informal meetings and discussions or through personal experience. Some of it can be gathered from existing published and unpublished documents and some can be collected using systematic research techniques (see Chapter 4 and Tools 1 and 2).

The collection and analysis of information at this stage is often directly linked to proposed work. It is needed:

- to analyse the situation in which the agency will be working
- to help establish priorities and make appropriate choices about what the agency should address and how it should work
- to understand the complexities of an issue, its causes, and how it is already being tackled
- to understand how different issues affect the groups in which the agency has a particular interest (see analysing differences, Chapter 3)
- to analyse the constraints and opportunities for an intervention (see Tool 5, SWOC analysis).

The appropriate frameworks and methods to use for this research depend on the nature and precise purpose of the investigation, whether it is important to gain a broad view of the problem, or to carry out a more in-depth analysis. It is often necessary to involve different people in the investigation in order to understand the different views of a situation (see Chapters 2 and 3).

For example, in taking a child-rights approach to programming it is important to emphasise the following areas in a situation analysis:

- Rights which have been violated and the impact of this on children
- The causes of violations of children's rights
- The obstacles to securing children's rights
- Data disaggregated by age, gender, ethnicity, ability, location, etc.
- Mapping of duty-bearers to establish the roles in and responsibilities for the provision of children's rights among individuals, organisations and institutions
- The legislative, administrative and economic frameworks
- The level of awareness of children's rights among children, the general population and decision-makers.[1]

---

1 *An Introduction to Child Rights Programming: Concept and application.* Save the Children Policy Guidelines series, 2001

For example: A situational assessment of care and protection of children infected and affected by HIV was conducted in Ho Chi Minh City by the Ho Chi Minh City AIDS Bureau and Save the Children UK. The following groups of people were interviewed to determine whether children's rights were respected: children infected with HIV (living in institutions and the community); children affected by HIV (children with an infected parent or sibling but not known to be infected themselves); caregivers and duty-bearers (including parents of infected children, institution managers and staff, health workers, and local authorities).

The questions asked of informants were based on the rights of children as promulgated in the UN Convention on the Rights of the Child. The Socialist Republic of Vietnam was the first Asian signatory to this Convention. They wanted to know whether specific key rights under the Convention were being respected.

This allowed a holistic analysis to be made of all those affected by or infected by HIV in different situations. As a result a range of recommendations were made, looking at practical and advocacy interventions/strategies.

It is important to do enough analysis in order to be able to understand the situation and to be able to develop strategies. However, it is also important to recognise the limitations on your ability to conduct a full analysis and decide which gaps in the analysis need to be filled as part of the programme strategy. An understanding of the situation of children's rights in a country, for example, should be built up over time and is not a one-off process.[2]

For example: Another framework/methodology used for situation analysis is the Household Economy Approach.[3] This has been developed by Save the Children to help find out how different wealth groups obtain food and basic needs in normal times and under stress. This understanding can be used to plan interventions which are targeted to specific needs, and do not have a negative affect on the local economy.

A further development is the Intra Household Model (IHM) which can be used to carry out poverty analysis on the different members of a household, and help predict how they will be affected by a change. For example: how will the children be affected if a parent dies of AIDS? How can child labour be addressed realistically, given the importance of the child's income to the household economy?

In some cases, research carried out in order to identify and understand a problem further is not directly linked to an existing or planned programme,

---

2 Joachim Theis, *Tools for Child Rights Programming*, Save the Children.
3 *The Household Economy Approach: A resource manual for practitioners*, Save the Children, 2000

but is undertaken as a piece of work in itself. This may be:

- to investigate more fully a sector that has been identified as a priority for the agency
- to investigate a particular phenomenon that is relevant to the work of the agency in a country
- to investigate an area or topic that is important for development work in a particular country, or generally, but which is not well understood
- to test assumptions to find out whether they are valid, and whether they can be applied more generally.

The results of this research may feed into policy development rather than directly into programme planning or management.

Some tools that can be used at this stage include: problem tree/objectives tree (Tool 6); participatory learning and action (Tool 1); surveys (Tool 2); SWOC analysis (Tool 5); stakeholder analysis (Tool 12).

Project concept note

A project concept note can be produced at about this stage to provide a broad view of what the project will look like.

> **For example:** The Department for International Development in the UK requests a project concept note with the format below for all projects over £250,000, in order to decide whether or not a full project design process should go ahead:
>
> Maximum of two pages, to include:
> 1. Project title and code
> 2. Basic information:
> - Project objectives – how do they relate to DfID's overall objectives and those set in the country strategy paper?
> - Rough cost
> - Principal project partners and recipient institutions
> - Other donors (if any)
> 3. Significant policy/design/implementation issues
> 4. Statement (drawing on 2 above) of who it is planned will be consulted during design and appraisal (and how)
> 5. Projected timetable of steps to project approval
> 6. Draft logical framework and project header sheet.

Stage 3. Programme design: how to address the problem identified

Collecting and analysing information

Once the issue that the project will address has been identified and its causes are understood, further information and analysis is required:

- to investigate in more detail specific areas in which the agency would like to work
- to identify the aims and objectives for a plan of action for the programme, and ways of measuring progress in relation to the objectives
- to consider alternative plans of action, or strategies, and compare their relative advantages and disadvantages, and the resources required to carry them out
- to see whether or how approaches which have worked elsewhere could be applied to the new situation.

Information is needed about:

- **the local and national context:** economic, political, legislative, administrative, social, cultural and physical aspects that affect the issue the programme aims to address. (In child rights programming, for example, what is the awareness of child rights amongst the general population, and among decision-makers?)
- **the issue the programme aims to address:** its relative importance, how different people perceive it, its causes and how it is being tackled already; if it concerns a violation of rights, what are the causes of the violations, and what are the obstacles to securing rights?
- **the people who will be affected by the work:** including social factors; economic activities and relationships; the roles of men, women, boys, girls, disabled people and different ethnic groups; cultural attitudes; power structures; vested interests; level of education and training; for child rights programmes what is the impact of the rights violation on different children? Are certain children discriminated against more than others? What are the best interests of the child?
- **the services that already exist and other agencies working in the area:** what roles and responsibilities do individuals, organisations and institutions have for tackling the issue? Who are the duty-bearers responsible for children's rights? What are the strengths and weaknesses in current programmes and what has been tried previously? What are the linkages between them? What are the reasons for the success or failure of previous initiatives by government or other agencies? What are the institutional strengths and weaknesses of the organisations concerned, including management capacity, technical expertise, staffing levels, etc?

- **existing resources:** available locally and through other organisations and donors, including people, training, infrastructure and money.
- **the lessons that have been learned:** from experience of work on previous initiatives or on similar programmes in other parts of the world that might be relevant in this situation.

> **For example:** In the Programme for Abused and Exploited Children (PAEC) in the Philippines, Save the Children uses the child rights programming framework as a guide in programme development. They ask their partners to broaden their analysis to include not only the description of the situation of children, but more importantly the underlying factors that have brought about this situation. They have also added the dimension of resource analysis and role/responsibility analysis which put emphasis on the accountabilities of duty-bearers in upholding children's rights.

Some of this information may already have been gathered during the problem identification stage, but a closer look at the problem and its context will be necessary now. It is important to involve all the people whose views are relevant at this stage (see Chapters 2 and 3).

> **For example:** Save the Children carried out participatory action research with migrant children and young people in cross-border areas of China, Myanmar and Thailand. This was carried out in order to gather insight into the lives of migrant children and young people, their realities, challenges and decision-making processes. They employed a participatory approach to understanding migrant children's perspectives and needs and to explore appropriate interventions.

Establishing programme aims and objectives and drawing up a plan of action

Once further information about the problem and its causes has been gathered and a specific area of work identified, aims and objectives should be set to help guide the work. A plan of action can then be drawn up, bringing together activities designed to achieve the objectives. Clear aims and objectives are essential for monitoring and evaluation, and they must be closely linked to the activities. Logical Framwork Analysis (see Tool 3) is a tool for bringing these together.

Aims are the broad long-term goals set for the work. They may be set as a result of discussions with the different people involved, especially those who will need to be actively supportive of the programme if it is to succeed. They should be based on:

- the agency's broader strategy

- the goals and objectives of government, communities and other agencies involved
- the agency's policies, principles and values
- what the agency can realistically hope to achieve in addressing the problem
- the particular right or rights to be addressed.

> **For example:** Save the Children aims to base its programmes on child rights. This means that practical action or direct intervention work should be complemented by other strategies that are directed towards strengthening institutions/mechanisms for children and building constituencies for children's rights. This should be clearly stated in the programme aims.

Objectives are more specific. They describe the change that the programme intends to bring about so that activities can be designed accordingly. They are used to focus the work, and judge what progress you are making. To be useful for programme planning and development you should be able to demonstrate whether or not you have achieved your objectives. Objectives should be **SMART**. In other words:

- **Specific**: Exactly what will change (eg, behaviour, attitude, access to resources) in whom, what proportion of the population, in what geographical area? Is the change an increase, a decrease?
- **Measurable or monitorable**: There should be some means of demonstrating that the change has occurred, quantitatively or qualitatively.
- **Achievable**: It must be achievable given the resources and organisational capacity available, in the context and under the prevailing conditions.
- **Relevant**: It should be relevant to the context and the perceptions of those involved.
- **Time-bound**: The change should take place within a specified time.

Where agencies have a particular focus, this should also be reflected in the objectives. For example, agencies working for the benefit of children should have child-focused objectives.

Different people involved in a programme may have different objectives, and these should be recognised throughout the planning, monitoring, review and evaluation process. For this reason it is important to involve all the relevant people when identifying aims and objectives (see Chapter 2).

Common problems with objective setting:

- Unrealistic objectives that are not achievable by the programme in the time available. This is very discouraging. Donors, for example, often encourage agencies to adopt more ambitious objectives which are hard to achieve in the time available. One way to address this is to plan in phases, with intermediate objectives which contribute to a more long-term objective.

- Objectives expressed as an activity. For example: "to carry out awareness raising activities about HIV amongst young people". It is possible to do the activity without changing anything. A better objective would be "Increase HIV-related knowledge in young people aged 11–18 in district X".
- Ambiguous or vague: For example "improve living conditions". You cannot tell whether or not this has been achieved.

When objectives are clear, it is possible to clarify the ultimate purpose of all the activities of a programme. It is then possible to see whether the programme is achieving anything or being effective. In practice, the process of clarifying objectives can be difficult because there are often different levels of objectives, from the specific to the more general. One way to sort out the different objectives and their relationship to the aims and activities of a project or programme is to construct an 'objectives tree' (see Tool 6, for a description of one method of identifying objectives and constructing an objectives tree).

The general principle of an objectives tree is illustrated in the example below from a Save the Children country strategy paper for Ghana. This forms the basis for a strategic, or long-term plan at country level.

Note
Objectives need to be flexible if they are to be relevant. Sometimes during the course of a programme it becomes clear that the original objectives are no longer relevant. Lessons learned from programme experience can show what the new objectives should be. One objective of a review or evaluation is often to establish new objectives for an existing programme. The important thing is to be clear about why they have been changed, and to incorporate lessons learned into future planning.

For example: Children displaced by war in South Sudan have ended up in slums on the outskirts of Khartoum, where there is no educational provision. This is because education is the responsibility of each province in Sudan, and the Khartoum authorities have refused to provide education for children from outside the province. Save the Children obtained donor funding to support the displaced communities to set up their own schools. Save the Children was to pay for teachers' salaries in the short term, while trying to persuade the Khartoum authorities, through advocacy, to take over responsibility for teachers' salaries in the long term. This was stated in the original proposal as a programme objective to ensure sustainability. However, the advocacy strategy failed, and Save the Children has decided to change its original objective and continue to provide teachers' salaries itself, for humanitarian reasons. The reasons for this change need to be clearly documented in order to persuade donors to continue funding the project.

For example: Strategic aims of Save the Children (UK) Ghana programme
Key issues identified for Save the Children in Ghana (from analysis of
strategic issues for children and young people in Ghana, and an analysis of
Save the Children's strengths, experience and opportunities in the country):

- reproductive health
- children in need of special protection
- resource allocation for basic services for children
- cross-cutting issues – gender, disability and HIV/AIDS

The first two aims are shown below:

Reproductive health aim
Reduce morbidity and mortality due
to poor reproductive health amongst
poor women, young people and other
disadvantaged community members.

Child protection aim
Children and young people (CYP) in
need of special protection, particularly
those in contact with the law, receive
adequate protection and more
appropriate treatment in keeping with
national child rights policies and laws.

Strategic objectives
1. Improved reproductive health in target
   communities through improved
   access to and use of appropriate
   reproductive health services by
   poor women, young people and other
   disadvantaged community members
2. Increasingly safe sexual behaviour of
   young people in target communities
   resulting in increased protection
   from HIV/AIDS
3. Reduction in target communities of
   the incidence of two traditional
   practices that are harmful to good
   reproductive health: female genital
   mutilation and the use of the herb
   Kalguteem
4. In all ten regions of Ghana, key
   partners, including NGOs and the
   Ministry of Health, have received
   information and advocacy materials
   and are implementing effective
   reproductive health activities

Strategic objectives
1. In target districts, children in need of
   special protection receive adequate
   protection and treatment that is in
   the best interest of the child
2. CYP who need special attention due
   to target issues of difference (gender,
   disability and HIV/AIDS) receive
   more protection and appropriate
   treatment from communities and
   other agencies
3. Community management mechanisms
   which are in the best interest of CYP
   are better understood and valued,
   resulting in their preservation for the
   the benefit of CYP

Activities
For objective 1
- Maintain through 2000 and 2001
  existing Family Reproductive Health
  Programme (FRHP) supporting projects
  throughout Ghana

Activities:
For objective 1
- Conduct baseline survey to
  understand current status of children
  in need of special protection including
  CYP in conflict/contact with the law

- Conduct evaluation of all aspects of existing FRHP projects
- Support the development of at least 20 reproductive health projects in Ashanti and Northern regions based on lessons learnt from prior experience

For objective 2: etc.

- Facilitate efforts to develop and strengthen local structures and processes responsible for child protection with particular attention to new Child Panels
- Strengthen the data collection and analysis system at district level on issues affecting children in contact/ conflict with the law

For objective 2: etc.

Plans of action

Each objective must have a clear plan of action designed to meet it, drawing together activities that address the objective and specifying the following:
- *what* activities will be undertaken
- *how* they will be carried out
- *who* will be responsible for what and when
- what resources, or inputs, are required (including money, people and assets)
- the intended result, or *output,* of each activity
- how the output will help achieve the objective.

Plans of action need to be realistic and feasible and so must take into account:
- what and who is available in terms of staff, resources, skills, management capacity, etc, locally and from elsewhere. Human resources are usually the most expensive part of an activity, and vital for its sustainability. Consider what workforce is required to meet the objectives, in terms of numbers, roles, levels. What are the skills and competencies required? Can these be developed in-house, or do they need to be recruited from outside?
- the priorities of people involved, including government officials, donors, communities, groups within communities including children, women, people with disabilities and different ethnic groups
- what assumptions are being made in suggesting that the activities will achieve the objectives
- the risks and uncertainties that could affect the success of the activities
- the risks of negative side-effects from the activities: for example, a forestry programme could damage the environment, or a project working outside existing structures could increase dependency on an external agency
- the likely cost and cost-effectiveness of the activities (see Tool 4 on cost-effectiveness analysis).

Compare different possible strategies

Consider the advantages and disadvantages of different plans of action. The same problem can often be tackled from different angles and at different levels. There may be several possible ways to achieve the same objective.

To meet more ambitious and long-term objectives it may be necessary to plan in phases, each with more short term, intermediate objectives. This can help meet donor reporting requirements.

Differentiating between objectives and activities

Objectives and activities are often confused in planning, monitoring, review and evaluation. For example, it is often assumed that a successful activity indicates a programme that has met its objectives, but this is not always true.

For example, a health education programme may increase people's knowledge of the paths of HIV transmission, but have no effect on their behaviour because of all the other factors (availability of condoms, feelings of invulnerability amongst people to STD/HIV infection, etc).

Indicators

Once clear objectives and plans of action have been identified, the next step is to establish a set of indicators, or ways of measuring (indicating) that progress is being achieved (see Chapter 5). The process of selecting indicators is described below in general terms only.

Indicators need to be set at the outset of a project or programme as part of an assessment, since the collection of information about indicators – which is part of the process of monitoring – has to be incorporated into the way the programme is designed.

The following factors are important in selecting key indicators which will be used in monitoring (see Chapter 7 for more detail):

- information that will show whether or not objectives are being achieved
- information that is required for effective management of the work (finance, staffing, logistics, etc)
- what the priority problems are for different groups involved in the work
- the data that is available and can be collected accurately in order to ensure that the information is up to date, accurate and relevant (this will depend on the skills, training and supervision of staff, and the availability of other statistics for comparison)
- whether the information will be used (the capacity for response to the information gathered depends on the availability of resources, staff skills, the decision-making structure, and the planning procedures)
- the need for comparison with other countries, the information needs of funding agencies and others (it may sometimes be necessary to resist

pressure from donors to collect information that is not useful for the programme).

Indicators may be changed over time if they are found to be too difficult to collect, or not to be meaningful.

REMEMBER: A small number of meaningful indicators which can be looked at regularly and carefully is more useful than a long list which is too time-consuming to use.

Process indicators

Process indicators show what is being done and how it is being done. Are the activities actually being carried out? Are the processes involved working, and are they helping to achieve the objectives? For example, are key partnerships developing? Are meetings being held regularly?

Indicators of changes in external circumstances (political, economic, seasonal) that could affect activities may also be needed.

Some process indicators are routinely collected for the day-to-day running of the programme. For example, clinic records will contain information about people seen, their main complaints, diagnoses by clinic staff, and the prescribed treatment.

Impact indicators

Impact indicators are needed to measure change as a result of what is done and how it is done. They are needed to assess what progress is being made towards reaching the objectives, and what impact the work has had on the different groups of people affected by the work. Impacts are changes that result from the activities. An evaluation will usually rely on impact indicators to see whether or not the programme objectives are being achieved.

Changes take place over time, and the impact indicators can help track the different stages of change, as they occur. For example, a change in attitude may be followed by a change in behaviour. Some changes may be short-term (intermediate) or longer term and more permanent. The impact can be positive or negative.

Any programme will also have a wider impact, and unintended impacts, which cannot be foreseen, and so cannot be captured by predetermined indicators. Other approaches are needed to look at these changes. See Chapter 9 for more on impact assessment.

Some indicators may be useful for monitoring both the process and impact. For example, if the objective of a programme is to raise awareness about maternal and child health in the community and to improve ante-natal and post-natal care, one impact indicator might be a decrease in maternal and neonatal mortality. A process indicator might be the number of health workers trained. An indicator for monitoring both process and impact would be to see how much health workers remember from their training six months later, and whether it has affected the way they work.

Quantitative indicators and qualitative indicators

Where the objective of the work is to achieve a quantitative change, it is usually quite straightforward to choose what to measure. It is much more difficult to choose indicators to measure a qualitative change. (It is often the most difficult part of the whole planning and evaluation process.) Both quantitative and qualitative indicators are necessary. For example, you need to know not only how many community health workers have been trained, but also how well they function.

Sometimes it is possible to find 'proxy' indicators for qualitative change. Proxy indicators measure things which represent (or approximate) changes in areas that cannot be measured directly.

For example, where the objective is to increase community participation, an assessment of the qualitative changes that are taking place in relationships and decision-making within the community is required. The number of committees formed would be a good indicator for monitoring process, but no good as an indicator of impact. Possible proxy qualitative indicators for impact might be the regularity of meetings, who is represented, who dominates the discussion, what is decided, and how decisions are put into action.

The following hints may be useful in identifying qualitative indicators:

- As a general rule, it is easier to assess behaviour than feelings, since behaviour can be observed.
  For example, if an objective is to increase people's confidence in meetings, this can be observed by the frequency with which people speak, whether they speak clearly, and whether they make their points clearly. These might be useful indicators of confidence.
- One way of identifying qualitative indicators is to ask the question, "If you (or the project) were a complete disaster, how would people know?"
  It is sometimes easier to think of indicators of failure than of success, but the same indicators should be useful for either.
- Perhaps the best way to identify qualitative indicators is through discussion and asking questions: "What do you mean by ...?"
  Even when the objectives of a programme are not really 'SMART' there must be some ways of determining what effect the programme has had. Brainstorming sessions can be a useful way to see how different people understand a concept. For example, what is meant by 'child well-being'? Once a concept has been broken down (or 'unpacked') into more specific components, it is easier to select meaningful indicators.

(Qualitative techniques are discussed in Tool 1. Examples of indicators for measuring participation are given in Tool 7.)

Linking objectives with indicators

Table 6.1 shows how monitoring question, indicator and objective should be clearly linked.

Table 6.1 Linking objectives, indicators and monitoring questions[4]

Objective	Indicator	Example question
Increase HIV related knowledge	Understanding of HIV latency period	How long is it before someone who has HIV shows symptoms?
Increase safe sex behaviour	Condom use at last intercourse (unmarried person)	On the last occasion you had sex, did you use a condom?
Harm reduction regarding injection drug use	Prevalence of needle sharing	Would you say that you (a) always share needles? (b) very often share? (c) share about half the time? (d) rarely share? (d) never share?
Reduce stigma associated with people living with HIV/AIDS	Willingness to care for someone with AIDS	If a family member or a close friend became ill with AIDS, who would care for them?
Reduce stigma attached to children affected by HIV/AIDS	Degree of rejection experienced by orphans in the school environment	Do orphans get teased at school? Why is that?

Indicators that are relevant to different people

Indicators must be meaningful and relevant to the people who will use them. Staff, managers, and different members of a community affected by a programme will all have different views of how the progress of a programme can be measured. Participatory methods may be the best way to identify meaningful indicators.

> **For example:** In a project in Malian villages supported by the agency ACORD, the people identified their own criteria for monitoring. In order to measure the effect of changes in the production of fodder, men identified the amount of milk produced by livestock, while women identified the amount of 'khundu' (a kind of fermented drink made from milk) which is good for small children.

4 Taken from *Learning to Live: Monitoring and evaluating HIV/AIDS programmes for young people*, Douglas Webb and Lyn Elliot, Save the Children, 2000

Common dimensions of change – specific indicators

One way of selecting indicators is to identify the key areas of change the programme expects to bring about: for example, economic well-being, social empowerment, women's empowerment. It is then possible to select specific indicators for those areas of change, which are locally relevant and relevant to the particular project.

> **For example:** impact assessment studies in projects in Bangladesh, India and Kenya selected different indicators to look at the same areas of change:
> • Indicators of economic wellbeing in the Bangladesh project were defined as: landholding, occupation, assets, housing status, household expenditure and consumption, food security, credit and savings, ability to cope with crisis.
> • In India the following indicators were identified:
>   Indebtedness, assets, income, savings, investment, market mobility and power.
> • In Kenya the indicators were:
>   Animal mortality rates, occurrence of periurban destitution, need for food aid, quality of diet, rate of return to investments provided through credit, law and order.

Indictors that reflect the different objectives of people concerned

Indicators must also reflect the different objectives of different people, including people affected by the work, government, and partners (see Chapter 2).

When working closely with other agencies or governments who have specific targets, indicators of those targets may need to be included in a monitoring system. This may be difficult if the targets are unrealistic. (For example, targets may relate to objectives that are not specific, they may be based on inaccurate or out of date population data, or they may be set at central level and have little to do with the reality of what is happening at district level.)

Indicators that reflect the situation of different groups

It is important to select indicators that reflect the situation of different groups within a community, including those who are least powerful. In all development work it is important to know how women, children, people with disabilities, and ethnic minorities have been affected by a project or programme (see Chapter 3). It is important to know about:
• the **involvement** of different groups in the work
• the **impact** of the work on different groups.

The effect of a programme on different groups can be positive or negative or both. This is true for both the process and the impact of the programme.

For example, in an income-generating programme for women, the process may have negative effects on girls who have to do more housework while their mother is earning income, and so have less time for school. However, the impact of the programme, in terms of increased income for the family, may have a positive effect: perhaps there is more food, new shoes, medicine when children are sick. The impact may also be negative, however, if the consequence of the mother having less time with the children affects their long-term health and development. The impact is likely to be different for boys and girls. Different children may have different perceptions about which effects are positive or negative, and why.

When selecting qualitative indicators of well-being, it is best to involve the different groups to find indicators that are meaningful to them. (See *Street and Working Children: A guide to planning*, Save the Children, for a discussion of methods for research with children: full details in references and further reading section.)

For example: Save the Children has developed a guide for good practice in child reunification programmes, based on its experience in different countries. The recommendations for evaluation include the following suggestions for developing indicators:

Process indicators need to measure whether the practices and procedures were adequate and cost-effective, or whether they could be improved, speeded up or done differently. The impact of the programme needs to be measured in terms of the impact on children, families and communities. Have families welcomed the children, nurtured them, helped them to adapt to the new separation and the reunification? Have children been well prepared? Or have families felt the programme dumped children on them against their will? Have children been made to feel like objects delivered to unwilling adults?

Possible impact indicators could include: What proportion of children have run away, suffered from malnutrition, or stopped attending school since reunification? What proportion of children feel sad, unloved and wish they were somewhere else? What proportion of children have not had family traced and not had any long-term planning done for their future? It must be the combination of good practice in procedures and good practice outcomes that will demonstrate the success or failure of the programme. And it must be the children and the communities who judge it.

Indicators that reflect changing objectives

Indicators must reflect each of the objectives at all stages of the work. For example, different indicators of institutional development such as negotiating ability, leadership, self-financing and management, may be meaningful at different stages of a programme.

Collecting information about indicators

A range of different techniques ('means of verification') are needed to measure these indicators, and cross-checking is always essential. The methods are discussed in Chapter 4 and Section 3, Tools 1, 2 and 6. Techniques for collecting information continually in a monitoring system are discussed in Chapter 7.

If you cannot collect information about an indicator, then it is not a good indicator.

See also Tool 3 for the logical framework: a way of analysing the relationship between objectives, activities, indicators, assumptions and risks.

Baseline data

Ideally, a baseline study should be carried out as part of an assessment, before work begins on the programme itself, to look at those characteristics of the population that the programme hopes to change. This can then be compared with a study of the same characteristics after the work has been in operation for some time, to see whether they have changed. The data should be disaggregated to see what impact the programme has had on different groups. Data about key population characteristics can also be collected on a continuous basis as part of the monitoring process.

Baseline data can be collected by quantitative and/or qualitative methods, depending on the nature of the indicators (see Chapter 7). A common problem with baseline studies is that they attempt to collect so much data that it cannot be analysed. Another problem is that programmes often change their areas of emphasis as they develop, so data collected in an initial baseline study may not be relevant later on. It is essential to analyse what information is required as a baseline and to be selective. Some information can be gathered while monitoring the programme (see Chapter 7) and some can be collected at the end of the programme by asking people what has changed.

It is important to be pragmatic about collecting baseline data. At early stages of project design there may not be enough resources to carry out a formal baseline study. Baseline data can be gathered during other studies that form part of an assessment and situation analysis.

> **For example:** In Laos, a study was carried out by Save the Children in the early stages of a project to improve primary school provision for ethnic minority children.
>
> The aims of this preparatory data collection and analysis was partly to establish a baseline for measuring the impact of the project. Other important aims include:
> - to explore the causes of ethnic minority children 'failures' in education
> - to clarify what are the 'real features' of high repetition rates and drop-out rates

- to establish a relationship with the communities and with partners
- to finalise the selection of schools
- to make decisions about specific features of the interventions in different sites (ie, different activities in schools with different characteristics)
- to finalise the selection of specific indicators for each main dimension of change (see below)
- to create a benchmark for the ongoing monitoring of the project
- to clarify roles and responsibilities.

In order to address all the above aims, three complementary data collection activities will be carried out before implementing the project:

1) Collection and analysis of already existing data, mainly statistical data, at the national, district and school level (to establish how the main features of the schools/areas of intervention compare with national education trends).

2) Needs assessment and situation analysis in the sites (ie, villages and schools) where the project will be implemented (to provide a more in-depth understanding of the key issues affecting ethic minority children's right to education).

3) Video baseline in some of the sites of intervention. For communication purposes (to show what the schools and villages where Save the Children works look like) as well as monitoring purposes (by establishing a visual baseline of what the learning environment and teaching practices are before and after the project).

Project proposal

A project proposal usually includes the following headings. Different donors have their own specific requirements, and it is important to use their proposal formats. Many also require a log frame (see Tool 3).

---

1. Cover sheet: name of organisation and project, location, duration, cost and author.

2. Brief summary description of project (one or two paragraphs) including: statement of the key problem that will be addressed, where project will be located, who will be affected, how long it will last and how much it will cost and how the project meets the donor's priorities.

3. Background:
- State *where* the project is located. Explain how/why these sites were selected.

- Briefly explain the social, economic and political (national/local) situation as it relates to the project.
- Explain *why* the project/programme is being proposed.
- Explain *what* the key problem/s are that the project aims to address.
- Explain *how* the project fits in with Save the Children's strategy and experience.
- Explain *how* the project fits with the donor's objectives and priorities.

4. Stakeholders, consultation and participation:

- Two main categories of stakeholders should be clearly identified in your proposal: beneficiaries (direct and indirect) and partners.
- Explain how each main stakeholder group was consulted in identification of project.
- Explain how they will be involved in project planning, implementation and monitoring processes.

5. Programme description: aims, objectives and activities

This is a detailed description of what the programme intends to achieve, and how.

The precise wording and structure for this will vary according to different donors. For example, using the logical framework it would be: goal, purpose, outputs, activities (see Tool 3).

6. Risks and assumptions: Risks and assumptions are conditions that have to exist for the success of the project, but which are not under the direct control of the project (see Tool 3, Logical framework analysis).

7. Sustainability:

Sustainability contains both financial and organisational components to explain how the programme will maintain the benefits of the programme after the end of the funding period.

- Financial sustainability: Will funds be available to continue the programme in the long run?
- Organisational/project sustainability. For example, replication, scaling up, development of institutional skills, development of individual skills.

Monitoring and Evaluation:
Indicators:

- Indicators should be developed to measure project process and impact.
- For each indicator you need to state from where the information will be gathered.
- You will need to have some baseline information, in order to be able to

set objective and realistic targets. If this is not available, you can include this as an activity to your project plan.

Monitoring:
- Explain what monitoring systems will be established.
- Explain how stakeholders will be involved.

Evaluation:
- Will the project have a formal assessment? (eg, mid-project review, end of project evaluation)
- Is this a requirement of the donor?
- Who will be involved in the evaluation? (eg, external consultants, stakeholders, donor)
- Costs for evaluation need to be included in your budget.

Budget:
A budget is a plan relating to activities to be carried out in a specified future time period. It is an estimate of how much money you will have, when you will get it, when you will spend it and what you will spend it on.
- Use a clear layout and format – present in table format which you can report against. Always follow the donor format if there is one.

4. Programme appraisal

This is the stage of the assessment process where a third party (for example, the head office of the agency) considers the draft proposal for a programme. This provides an additional opportunity to consider the proposal objectively, and hence:
- to assess the feasibility of the proposed activities
- to consider the appropriateness of the selected activities in relation to the organisation's experience, principles, values and priorities
- to question whether the costs of the project are reasonable for the expected outcome
- to question the assumptions on which a project or programme is based
- to question whether the aims and objectives as stated are likely to solve the problem.

The checklist on page 90 has been developed by Save the Children in the West Africa region to assist programme management and advisory staff in ensuring consistent assessment and support. The checklist provides questions which aim to cover core aspects of a child and gender-focused learning approach to programming.

Example of a checklist for child and gender-focused programming

SECTION 1: Strategic intent

What are we trying to achieve for children? How do we want Save the Children to be known in this country?

SECTION 2: External context

1. Is the planned work related to an analysis of the external environment? Including the political, economic, social, cultural, and environmental situation affecting the target population.
2. What are the risks in that environment that may affect plans this year? How are we keeping our plans under review?
3. What is the expected situation of HIV/AIDS in ten years' time? How is the programme addressing this?

SECTION 3: Annual country plan

1. **Major programme priorities:**
   (a) What new programmes will be starting? Which will be ending?
   (b) What other significant developments will there be in the programme this year?
   (c) What changes to the Country Strategy Paper are required and why?
   (d) What will be the main outcomes for children of this year's work?
2. **Partners:** Who are the main current or future partners
3. **Approach:**
   (a) How is child focus and child rights-based programming incorporated as an approach?
   (b) How are 'issues of diversity' (gender, disability, etc) incorporated as an approach?
   (c) What plans are there for 'mainstreaming' HIV?
   (d) Does the programme empower the activities and organisations of partners/beneficiaries ?

4. **Learning:**
   (a) What do we plan to learn from the programme this year? How does this relate to the regional learning objectives?
   (b) What do we intend to do with our learning this year?
   (c) Are there any research or publication outputs? How will the output be used, and for which audience? When and how will it be carried out?
   (d) Are any evaluations being carried out? For whom? What do we want to review ourselves?
   (e) How will the programme objectives be monitored?
5. **Advocacy:**
   (a) What are the major advocacy plans this year (outside of those already covered under 1c)?
6. **Funding:**
   (a) What are the existing commitments and gaps?
   (b) What would be the impact of a 10%–15% increase/decrease in the funding base?
   (c) Are we making the most of opportunities in the funding relationship to influence donor policy?
7. **Human resource (HR) planning:**
   (a) What are the HR objectives for the year?
   (b) Do we have recruitment and succession planners?
   (c) Are we restructuring?
   (d) What are the major HR plans for this year? Facilitation, participation, management training?
   (e) Do key managers (particularly the Programme Director) have enough time to provide strategic leadership? Or are they overloaded?

5. Approval and baseline studies

Once a programme or project has been approved, it may be useful to carry out a baseline study if this has not already been done as part of stage 2 (situation analysis).

Summary

- When designing a planning exercise, first consider who it is for and how the results will be used.

- The stages of assessment and planning are:
  - Problem identification
  - Situation analysis
  - Programme design
  - Gathering more information about the issue
  - Setting aims and objectives
  - Designing a plan of action, including a budget and resources
  - Selecting indicators and methods for monitoring and evaluation
  - Appraisal by the agency to make sure it fits with its principles and capacities
  - Approval
  - Baseline data collection.

- Note: the stages are not always in sequence. In particular, information-gathering and analysis occur at all stages, and should be a continuous process.

- Baseline data can be collected as a formal baseline study, as part of a situation analysis, or through continuous monitoring of the programme.

- Different donors have different formats and requirements for project proposals. These can be completed through carrying out the steps above.

Chapter 7
Monitoring

Monitoring is the systematic and continuous assessment of the progress of a project or programme over time. It is a basic and universal management tool for identifying strengths and weaknesses in a programme and is perhaps the most important part of the 'programme spiral' described in Chapter 1. It provides the means for constantly modifying and improving a project or programme, and the basis for evaluation and review.

Monitoring is different from other exercises, in that it is continuous and relies on a *system* rather than a one-off input by a team of individuals with a specific task. A monitoring system requires constant amendment, maintenance and support. It must be as accessible and meaningful to new staff joining a programme as it was for the people who first designed and set it up. A good monitoring system should be simple, and the points covered in this chapter should help ensure that it is clearly focused and designed in a way that is appropriate to the needs of its different users.

The first part of this chapter lists a wide range of activities that may form part of a 'programme monitoring system'. The second part – which should be read in conjunction with Chapter 5 – discusses the points that are particularly useful for designing and managing monitoring systems: defining the overall aim of the system; selecting relevant information; the collection and analysis of data; presenting and using the results; and the organisation of the monitoring system, including how it can be maintained.

Monitoring covers a wide variety of techniques and methods and applies to the management of finance, personnel, vehicles and buildings, as well as to the progress of programme activities and the way the activities are carried out.

Types of monitoring

The types of monitoring commonly used in development work are: management/ administration, finance, and programme monitoring. We will not deal with management, administration and finance monitoring in this book. Instead, the rest of this chapter will concentrate on programme monitoring.

Programme monitoring

Table 7.1 shows some of the information that could be collected for programme monitoring, where it would come from, and how it could be used. The list is not

Table 7.1 Programme monitoring

	Information to be collected	Sources of information	Use of information
Project inputs	• What is needed and where it can be found • When it is needed and when it will be available • Cost	• From suppliers • Other organisations • Government, etc	• Plan and schedule activities • Monitor costs and budget accordingly
Results of activities, project outputs	• What is being done • What is not being done but was planned • What problems have been encountered • How the problems have been addressed • How the external situation has changed • How the internal situation has changed • Any other information relevant to work of project	• Regular records of activities • Project visits • Supervision reports • Periodic reports • Meetings, workshops with staff, project partners, and people affected by the work • Staff reviews • Newspapers, radio • Informal discussion • Observation • Surveys	• Plan future work • Identify project successes • Identify opportunities to build on strengths • Identify problems and weaknesses • Plan strategy • Review priorities • Identify training needs • Identify need for further information or research, review or evaluation
Progress of programme according to objectives	• Progress towards achieving objectives • Are objectives still relevant?	• Information about key indicators • Observation • Interviews • Visits • Reports • Case studies	• Identify what works • Modify strategy and/ or objectives as necessary • Feedback • Identify need for review or evaluation • Identify need for further information or improvements in monitoring systems • Accountability to donors and beneficiaries

continues

	Information to be collected	**Sources of information**	**Use of information**
Wider impact of work	• What changes as a result of the work? • What key processes lead to the change? • What is the intended impact, what is the unintended impact? • What impact – positive and negative – has work had on different people?	• Information about key indicators • Participatory approaches used to focus on impact with people affected by the work, and those not directly affected by the work • Observation • Case studies	• Identify what works in different situations, and use this to improve work • Develop best practice • Identify what changes are most significant and long-lasting, and use this to develop strategies and policies • Lessons and skills learnt in analysing impact contribute to improved planning • Accountability to donors and beneficiaries
The way the programme is managed, style of work	• How are decisions made? • Are the people who are supposed to be involved really involved? • Do the partners/ people affected by the work/ programme staff feel a sense of ownership of the programme?	• Indicators which show degree of participation • Meetings, discussions • Observations	• Show need to change management style • Identify need to change methods to encourage more participation • Identify problems in relationship between partners/ people affected by the work/staff, and address them • Ensure people are able to exercise their rights to influence activities that affect them
Background information on target population and context	• Have there been any significant political, economic, or environmental developments affecting target population? • Have there been any developments affecting the programme? • How is the population changing in terms of the characteristics the programme is hoping to influence?	• Surveys • Sources of information about politics, economics • Meetings with other agencies, government officials • Observation	• On-going collection of baseline data which can be used to evaluate progress • Response to changing situation, rapid response to emergencies • Keep in touch with relevant work by other agencies, government

comprehensive, but is intended to give an idea of the range of monitoring activities.

In practice, only a selection of the information shown above would be collected, depending on the nature of the work and the purpose of monitoring at any particular time (see below).

Process monitoring and impact monitoring

As shown in the above table, programme monitoring should include information about the use of resources, the progress of activities, and the way these are carried out. This is known as **process monitoring**.

Monitoring should also provide information on progress towards achieving objectives, and on the impact the programme is having in relation to these objectives. This is known as **impact monitoring**. Impact monitoring should also look at impact beyond the immediate results of the work, at the intended and unintended impact, positive and negative. By looking at the **links between processes and impact**, we can understand what changes are taking place, and what are the key processes leading to these changes. For more detail see Chapter 9 on impact assessment.

All monitoring is a form of continuous self-evaluation. If it is done well, formal evaluations will be needed less often. And if a formal evaluation is carried out, the programme staff will already be familiar with their work in relation to their objectives. They will be able to participate more fully in the evaluation, and find it less threatening. The evaluation will also be able to focus more usefully on questions which have arisen as a result of monitoring. (See Chapter 8 on evaluation for more detail.)

For example: All monitoring systems should include both process and impact monitoring. Save the Children in Trincomalee, Sri Lanka, has been helping to improve the quality of education in pre-schools through sustainable teacher training. As part of the training, teachers worked together to identify indicators of education quality: how they would know if quality education is being provided. They agreed on a list of 28 indicators based on their knowledge of what was practical and relevant in the local context. An external consultant with experience in child development helped guide them towards indicators focusing on the quality of children's learning experience, particularly the relationship between them and the teacher. The teachers used the indicators to assess their own work and see how it could be improved, and then to monitor the progress of teachers they were mentoring. This allowed them to monitor changes in the quality of the teaching **process.**

Once changes had been made in the pre-schools, parents were invited to reflect on changes they had seen in their children. This was to monitor the

impact of the programme on the children's learning. Parents were asked to reflect on what their concerns had been for their children, and what changes they had noticed in them as a result of being in pre-school.

Designing a monitoring system

A 'monitoring system' is a system for collecting and using information about the progress of a project or programme. Its purpose is to help all the people involved in the work take appropriate decisions. It is not simply a means of collecting information, however. It must also be a communication system, in which information flows in different directions between all the people involved.

The essential components of a monitoring system are:
- the selection of indicators for each activity, related to objectives
- the collection of information concerning the indicators
- the analysis of the information
- presenting and communicating the information in an appropriate way
- using this information to improve the work.

It is important to draw up terms of reference for any exercise. The points below address further some of the major questions relevant to designing and managing a monitoring system that were discussed in Chapter 5:

1. Defining the aim of the monitoring system
Deciding who needs a monitoring system and what for
Setting the objectives of the monitoring system

2. The selection of relevant information
Looking at existing systems
Key indicators
Using models and frameworks for monitoring

3. The collection and analysis of data
Methods of collecting data
What training and support is needed for the people collecting the data?
The analysis of the data

4. Presenting and using the results
Feedback, discussing the findings
Using the results for planning procedures
Using the results for institutional learning
Using the results as a basis for evaluation or review

5. Organisation
Deciding who should be involved in monitoring
Involvement of people from outside the programme
Monitoring the work with another organisation
Maintaining the monitoring system: resources, training, support and supervision

1. Defining the aim of the monitoring system

A monitoring system should be designed to meet specific needs and these will vary according to the nature and aims of the work, the organisational structures of all the partner agencies and government(s) involved, and specific requirements of donors. The monitoring system needs long-term aims as well as specific objectives. The system itself can then be monitored and evaluated to see whether it is meeting its objectives, and can be adjusted if necessary. The following points must be analysed to define the objectives of the monitoring system.

Deciding who needs a monitoring system and what for

Some examples of how information can be used for different purposes are given in the tables above. Monitoring systems commonly address the following needs:

Information needed to make day-to-day decisions about the work
Managers, staff and partners use information about the progress and quality of the work and about external factors that affect it, to plan and manage work effectively. The information is needed to:
- provide an ongoing picture of progress
- maintain high standards
- make sure resources are used effectively
- plan work
- identify problems and find solutions at an early stage
- identify opportunities
- provide a record of events
- look at the 'process' of development
- look at the work in relation to child rights
- provide an information base for future evaluations
- help staff feel their work has a definite purpose.

Information needed to be accountable to donors and to our own organisation
Although different organisations and donors have different monitoring requirements, if work is monitored well enough to ensure good management, most of the information needed for accountability should also be available.

Information needed to be accountable to partners
Programme partners should be accountable to each other in order to demonstrate their joint responsibility for achieving the objectives of the partnership.

Information needed to be accountable to people affected by the work
A programme should also be accountable to all the people who will be affected by it, even when they are not actively involved in the work.

Setting the objectives of the monitoring system
When you have defined the overall aim(s) of the monitoring system and who it is for, it should be possible to draw up its specific objectives (see Chapter 5).

For example: The Programme for Abused and Exploited Children (PAEC) in the Philippines is run as a partnership between local NGOs, international agencies and Save the Children UK. The Programme's monitoring system has the following objectives:

- For individual partners: the monitoring system requires partners to regularly assess and report their progress to Save the Children. This enables them to identify achievements and areas for improvement for future planning.
- For partners as a group: to promote exchange of information, allowing partners to discuss their work and offer information and resources to other partners.
- For Save the Children: it feeds into strategic and operational planning, particularly by identifying the impact of the programme on children, families, communities, etc.

2. The selection of relevant information

Deciding what information will be useful for making decisions about an activity or programme is often the most difficult part of setting up a monitoring system.

There is always a danger of collecting too much information on every detail of a programme. The problems associated with this are:

- If too much data is collected it may not be measured or recorded accurately.
- There is no time to analyse or use a large amount of information.
- If a large amount of information is being collected regularly from the same people they may resent it.
- If information is too detailed it may be difficult to identify important trends.

A small system that works is better than a big system that does not. The perceptions of people who are affected by the work are often more useful than a large amount of quantitative data.

In order to have a small and realistic system, stakeholders need to agree on what specific areas, activities or trends need to be monitored in order to assess project development and impact. It is important to have an opportunity (such as a workshop) to agree on priorities for monitoring. Project workers often know better than anybody else what is useful to monitor.

Look at existing systems

Most programmes have some way of monitoring the work, even if this is not identified as a coherent monitoring system. For example, programme managers may use project visits, meetings and observation to gather information needed for decision-making. Analysing existing monitoring activities and their strengths and weaknesses will help to identify what information is most useful for whom, and what are the information gaps.

Identifying the monitoring questions and key indicators

The first step in deciding what information to collect is to clarify what do you need to know, and what you therefore need to monitor to give you the answers. The selection of indicators to reflect progress towards meeting objectives is discussed in Chapter 5 and in Chapter 6. Key indicators for monitoring can be selected by asking the following questions:

- **What indicators will demonstrate progress** (in terms of both process and impact) in relation to the programme objectives?
- **What indicators will help us to understand changes** that occur as a result of the work, and what processes have contributed to them?
- **What are the priority problems** or key aspects of the work?
  It is difficult to select key indicators, particularly in a large programme or project, but this can be made easier by first identifying the key aspects of a programme, or the priority problems that are being tackled. It is then possible to formulate the questions that need to be answered in order to find out how well the programme is working. The key indicators may need to be changed as the programme progresses and new areas of work develop.

For example: In HIV/AIDS programmes for young people, the following key questions about process should be covered by a monitoring system:
- Have we defined the target population and do we know how many there are?
- Are we actually reaching this population?
- Are we spending enough time with the target group?
- Are the methods we are using appropriate in reaching them?
- How cost-effective and sustainable is the project?

- How integrated is the project with other activities?[1]

- **What information can be collected accurately?** This will depend on:
  - what information it is actually possible to collect regularly
  - the skills, training, and supervision of staff
  - time available for staff and other project participants
  - the possibility of standardising collection techniques for qualitative and quantitative information (see Tool 7, for an example of a set of questions as indicators for measuring progress on increasing group self-reliance)
  - the availability of relevant data if the indicators used are to be calculated using information from other sources. (For example, if you want to calculate rates of immunisation coverage, are reliable statistics on the population available?)
- **How can the information be analysed and interpreted?** This will depend on the analytical skills of programme staff and management and the opportunities and support for regular analysis.
- **Will the indicator provide information that can realistically be used?** This will depend on the decisions and action that people can take, given the resources available, including material resources and staff skills. The ability to take action may also depend on the existence of assigned responsibilities, and good communication between different levels of the organisation (for example, between field and headquarters).
- **What planning procedures are in operation?**
  The kind of indicators that can be used will also depend on the existing procedures for planning and making decisions. The way decisions are made will influence the selection of key indicators, and whether qualitative or quantitative information is most useful.

For example: The Thardeep Rural Development Programme is working in a number of areas including social mobilisation, micro-credit, income generation, sustainable land use, primary health, nutrition, education, human resource and gender development, and responding to emergencies. Over the years there has been a pronounced shift towards rigorous monitoring and evaluation. The monitoring system for field-based activities is based on regular joint monthly meetings of all staff in which staff present and discuss reports, case studies, financial aspects and relate them to objectives and planned outputs. The field staff maintain field diaries, the observations made therein are well documented and reviewed at forums on different

[1] *Learning to Live: Monitoring and evaluating HIV/AIDS programmes for young people*, Save the Children UK, 2000

levels in the programme, where information is shared and input is sought from the stakeholders to bring about improvement in the programme. Often the feedback is fed into future planning and strategic programme revisions.

- **What are the information needs of funding agencies?**
  When working closely with government or other agencies, there may be some pressure to collect information that is required by international organisations. These may coincide or conflict with the information needs of the programme itself.

Using a framework to identify indicators

Frameworks and models can be developed to help identify key indicators, particularly for impact. For example, see Tools 13 and 14.

3. The collection and analysis of data

Methods of collecting data

There are many different methods of data collection. A combination of methods should always be used so that data can be cross-checked. See Chapter 4 for a discussion of methods for the systematic collection and analysis of information, and Tools 1 and 2 for more details on surveys and participatory assessment.

Possible methods for collecting data at specific points during monitoring include:

Surveys with set questionnaires
Survey samples can be selected to compare populations affected by the work with people who are not affected by the work, or to compare current data with the results of a baseline study carried out before the work began. Regular surveys can be used in a monitoring system to collect information about key indicators to see how the target population is affected by a project or programme over time. (See Chapter 4 for the use of surveys and Tool 2, for more details of methods, strengths, weaknesses and prerequisites for success.)

Participatory methods
Participatory methods, including those discussed under PLA in Tool 1, can be useful for finding out how the different people involved in a programme, including the people affected by the work, view its progress. Ways of establishing a participatory approach throughout the monitoring system are discussed below under 'organisation'.

Measuring skills and knowledge

The skills and knowledge of trainees can be assessed to measure the effectiveness of activities designed to train or teach people or to influence their attitudes or behaviour. Methods for this include:

- written, oral or practical tests: simple tests to see whether someone knows something or can do something, and more difficult questions which find out whether someone understands the reasons for doing something
- role play and games
- demonstration of a particular task
- observation of normal practice using a checklist.

Possible methods for collecting data regularly for a monitoring system include:

Regular record-keeping: forms and diaries

Some information about activities is recorded on a regular basis. Forms and set formats are often used for recording quantitative and qualitative information. The following factors are important:

- Good form design will facilitate the accurate recording of information.
- Clear instructions on how to use forms should always be available. Instructions should include clear definitions of terms used on the forms.
- The form should contain enough information to be useful to the people collecting the data.
- The people collecting the data need to understand how the information will be used.
- The information needed to complete the forms should be available without too much extra effort.
- The format should be the same in the different forms and registers used.

Other methods of regular record-keeping include:

- Diaries to record activities (especially useful for recording qualitative information)
- Observation using checklists.

Supervision checklists and reports

The collection of data during supervision meetings provides an opportunity to discuss the information as it is being collected. This can be useful for both supervisors and those being supervised. Checklists and set formats can be used to ensure that information about key indicators is collected.

Project visits

Visits by project managers, advisers and staff from other projects are common monitoring activities. Their reports can be useful monitoring tools, since they offer a particular view on the progress of the work. These reports can be made more relevant if staff are already monitoring their work and have identified objectives and indicators clearly. If field staff prepare outlines of the aspects of the work they would like the external personnel to assess, it also helps to make the reports more relevant to local problems (see Tool 9, Programme or project visits).

Case studies

Case studies can be used to examine the impact of a programme on a particular group, for example selected households. A checklist can be used to ensure certain questions are addressed, without being restricted only to predetermined indicators. It can be a useful way of looking at unexpected outcomes and indirect effects of a programme, and to see how other factors have contributed to any changes in people's lives.

For example, this approach has been used to monitor the impact of microfinance programmes on households. The selection of households for case studies needs to be systematic to avoid bias. In order to trace any long-term changes caused by the programme, there also needs to be some means of following up information on all members of the original family if they later move away.

Spot checks: periodic studies into a particular aspect of the work

Selected activities may be monitored in detail over a specific period. For example, all staff could fill in activity sheets every day for several weeks to assess the effectiveness of their use of time. This can be a useful exercise leading up to a more formal evaluation, since it gives staff and participants a clearer idea of what they are doing, especially if they do not usually keep regular records of activities.

Any monitoring system will consist of a range of methods.

For example: The Programme for Abused and Exploited Children (PAEC) in the Philippines – in which Save the Children works with several partners – uses the following methods for collecting, analysing and disseminating findings:

- quarterly reports
- feedback from children and other stakeholders
- observation of activities
- discussion with programme team of partner organisations
- discussions with programme team (away days, country review and planning meetings)
- partners meetings and documentation of meetings
- copies of monitoring visit reports of Save the Children project officer sent to partners

- workshops with groups of partners around a specific issue/topic/theme
- production of research output that documents experiences/learnings
- external evaluation.

What training and support is needed for the people collecting the information?

Continuous support and supervision are all essential to ensure data is collected accurately, and to ensure that people understand the use of the information they are recording (see Tool 11).

The analysis of data

Analysis refers to the way the information is interpreted and how the meaning of the results is assessed. Chapter 5 considers different methods of analysis, who should carry them out, and the use of computers. In a monitoring system, analysis can be done continuously, periodically, or irregularly, depending on the use of the information.

Analysis often takes the form of meetings where the findings can be cross-checked and discussed in the most relevant forums, with the relevant stakeholders. For example, the analysis can be by sector or by locality. The most important thing is to ensure that the analysis is accurate and relevant, that it is understood by the people using the findings, and that results are available when they are needed.

4. Presenting and using the results

Feedback, discussing the findings

It is important to provide opportunities to discuss the findings with all the people who are interested, including the people affected by the work. Some ways of presenting the results of monitoring exercises are discussed in Chapter 5.

Using the results for planning procedures

If monitoring information is really going to be used to improve the quality of the work being carried out, it must be incorporated into existing planning procedures, or planning procedures should be developed specifically to use the information.

For example: In a Save the Children-supported rural development project in Pakistan a monitoring system has been developed as part of an overall 'monitoring, review and planning system'. This ensures that planning is based on the information from monitoring through a series of monthly and six-monthly meetings between staff, managers and stakeholders.

Using the results for institutional learning

Monitoring systems are a way of analysing project experience. The results of this analysis can be used by the agency and other organisations in making informed decisions about future work. They can also be shared with others, inform policy, and be used for advocacy purposes.

Using the results as a basis for evaluation or review

Monitoring provides a continuous assessment of progress, but at certain times it is useful to undertake a formal evaluation to look in more detail at the impact of the work, from a more objective viewpoint. A review can also look in more detail at certain aspects of a programme which have been identified as problem areas through the monitoring system (see Chapter 8).

5. Organisation

Deciding who should be involved in monitoring

Participation in monitoring: principles and methods

The purpose, tools, strengths and weaknesses of participatory planning, monitoring, review and evaluation are discussed in Chapter 2. Participatory monitoring means that the information used for monitoring is chosen, recorded and analysed by all those involved in and affected by a project or programme. It is particularly important for community-based programmes.

The basic steps in establishing a participatory monitoring system are:
1. Discuss the reasons for monitoring so that people can decide whether it will help them.
2. Discuss and review programme objectives and activities, to make sure everyone understands what they are trying to achieve.
3. Develop monitoring questions: what do we want to know, and what do we monitor to give us the answers?
4. Select the indicators to answer the monitoring questions.
5. Decide how the information will be collected.
6. Decide who will do the monitoring, since this may require people with particular skills, and will also require people's time.
7. Analyse and present the results at meetings, displayed as diagrams, etc.

Involvement of people from outside the programme

All the people directly involved in a project or programme should be responsible for monitoring. A monitoring system must be useful for them. However, it is often helpful to have assistance from an outsider who may have a more objective view of the work.

> **For example:** In Sri Lanka, an external professional worked with groups of teachers to develop indicators which were based on an understanding of child development (the consultant's input) but practical and relevant in the local context (the teachers' input). Once changes had been made in the pre-schools, the community was asked to participate by reflecting on the changes they had seen in their children.

(See Tool 8, Using consultants.)

Monitoring the work with another organisation

When it is necessary to monitor a programme carried out in partnership with another group or agency, this should be done using methods that will provide them with information that is useful for their own purposes. (See also Chapter 2, for issues to consider when working with partners.) Partners should participate in developing the monitoring system to make sure it is useful for them, and not just a means of being accountable to donors. Many partners will have already developed monitoring systems which can also provide the information the donors require.

> **For example:** For PAEC in the Philippines, Save the Children has developed a monitoring system through discussions amongst team members, with partners and evaluators. Decisions about what information to collect were based on past experiences, programme requirements, and the logical framework which was developed at the proposal stage. Indicators were selected in consultation with partners, the team, and Save the Children's London office.

Maintaining the monitoring system: resources, training, support and supervision

The cost of running a monitoring system can be considerable (although it is also possible to have a cheap system). It should be carefully considered and included in any programme budget. The cost comprises:
- the cost of designing the monitoring system: this includes staff time, workshops, training, and may include hiring outside consultants or trainers

- staff time in collecting and analysing information
- the resources needed to print and distribute forms for data collection, and provide other materials as necessary
- continuous support and supervision for data collection and analysis
- training of managers to promote effective use in planning and policy development
- supervision needed to keep system standardised
- modification of the monitoring system as necessary.

Summary

- Monitoring is the continuous assessment of the progress of a programme over time.
- Process monitoring and impact monitoring are both needed to show what changes are taking place, what processes lead to the changes, and how the programme can be improved.
- The questions to be addressed when designing a monitoring system concern:
  - its aim: who it is for and why
  - what questions it needs to answer and which indicators will help answer the questions
  - what information should be gathered
  - how the information should be collected and analysed
  - how the results should be presented and used
  - organisational issues: who does what, how much it will cost
- Selecting a manageable amount of relevant information is key to monitoring and depends on the priorities of the work.
- A combination of methods for collecting and analysing information can be used.

Chapter 8
Review and evaluation

This chapter begins with an overview of review and evaluation and a brief analysis of their differences and similarities and how they link with impact assessment. The main focus of the chapter is on how the principles and questions contained in Chapter 5 can be used to plan a review or evaluation exercise. Other parts of *Toolkits* are also referred to where relevant.

The role of review and evaluation, and the difference between them

Review

A review is the assessment at one point in time of the progress of a project or programme. The basic purpose of a review is to take a closer look at a project or programme than is possible through the process of monitoring. Reviews can be carried out to look at any aspect of a project or programme, and can use a range of criteria to measure progress. Appropriate management decisions can then be taken. Regular reviews can also be carried out as part of a monitoring system. A review can be formal or informal, broad or in-depth, and can be carried out internally (by programme staff) or by outsiders.

Evaluation

An evaluation is the assessment at one point in time of the impact of a project or programme and the extent to which stated objectives have been achieved. In other words, has there been any change as a result of the programme, and what processes have contributed to the change?

The following are necessary to carry out an evaluation:
- Clear, measurable objectives
- Some way of showing what progress has been made towards achieving the objectives, often indicators
- Information about the indicators that can be used to see whether there has been any change as a result of the work. This could be from information collected as baseline data or gathered over time by a monitoring system.

The relationship between review, evaluation and impact assessment

In practice, evaluation and review overlap. An evaluation is usually more formal and more rigorous, involves more data and bigger samples than a review. It often takes place towards the end of a project and concentrates on past experience. Its purpose is to analyse what has been done and build on that. An external person is often involved to help validate the findings. A review is more broadly defined, usually less formal, and often determined by internal requirements.

'Impact assessment' (see Chapter 9) focuses on the more long-term and wide-ranging changes, and the extent to which the work has brought about significant changes in the lives of the people and the communities in which it is based, beyond the immediate results of the programme. In other words, some form of impact assessment should be part of all monitoring, review and evaluation. The particular approaches and types of analysis required in assessing long-term impact are examined in Chapter 9.

The emphasis should always be on using review and evaluation as a learning process, a way of examining a project or programme to see how it can be made more effective. Any review or evaluation should be 'critical', in that it should look carefully at the performance of a project or programme to see how it can be improved. But it should not be seen as a judgement in a negative sense, and it should not be a threatening exercise for programme staff, since this will make it unlikely that the results will be accepted and used. In practice, people always feel threatened by a review or evaluation. Their anxieties may be lessened if they are involved in discussions about the purpose and design of the exercise from the beginning, and can participate in the review and evaluation process.

Important questions to consider when carrying out a review or evaluation

Terms of reference should always be drafted before carrying out a review or evaluation, whether it is formal or informal, to clarify the points covered in Chapter 5. These are:

1. **Purpose and aim**
   Why is it necessary?
2. **Who is it for?**
   How will the results be used?
3. **Objectives and key questions**
   What are the objectives of the review or evaluation?
   What specific questions should it address?
4. **Information collection and analysis**
   What information is needed to answer these questions?

Where will the information come from?

What indicators can be used to measure impact and progress of the work?

How should information be collected, analysed and presented?

5. **Presenting the results**

What are the conclusions and recommendations?

How will the findings be recorded and presented to different users?

What feedback will there be about the findings and about the process to people involved in the work?

How should the findings be stored for future use?

6. **Organisation**

How will it be directed and managed?

Who should be involved? What are their tasks and responsibilities?

What is the timescale?

What resources will be needed?

1. The purpose and aim

The reasons for carrying out a programme evaluation or review are very similar.

Some reasons for carrying out a programme **review** are listed below:

- To assess the progress and impact of a project or programme when a formal evaluation is not necessary.
- To clarify the objectives of a project or programme that has been running for some time.
- When a major decision has to be made about the future direction of a project or programme, to define what the different options are, and the implications of each in terms of resources, constraints, and consequences.
- To identify key issues and problems which need to be addressed.
- When specific problems have been identified and need to be investigated before they can be tackled.
- To get feedback about a project or programme from partners and people affected by the work, and provide an opportunity for them to participate in analysing the work and planning its future.
- When a broader strategy is being reviewed and it is important to see how individual programmes fit in with it.
- When a project or programme has been finished, or handed over to another agency.
- When lessons learned from work experience need to be analysed to help formulate policy and guidelines for future work.
- To review a project or programme in the light of changing external circumstances, such as a change in government policy.
- As a staff development exercise.

For example: The mid-term review of the community-based rehabilitation programme (CBR) supported by Save the Children in Zanzibar was carried out in March 2001. The pilot CBR programme had been evaluated in 1995, and the extended CBR programme had been under implementation for four years. The purpose of the review was to assess progress against objectives in order to determine the direction of the programme during the remainder of its stated time-frame and beyond.

Sector review

A review may also be carried out to look at an agency's work in a particular sector within a country, in a region or globally. Reasons for this sort of review may include the following:
- To draw lessons from programme experience in order to formulate policy or guidelines for future work in that sector.
- To contribute to a broader strategy by looking at the past and present situation and identifying strategic issues in a particular sector.
- To identify links between similar work in different countries, and to see how they might learn from each other's experience.

For example: Save the Children is carrying out a global review of social protection, welfare and inclusion. The main objectives of the Review are:
- to assess the impacts of Save the Children's policies, programme activities and advocacy strategies in social protection, welfare and inclusion
- to learn from the experiences of examples of real projects and activities in this field
- to apply what has been learned to improving Save the Children's work in social protection, welfare and inclusion
- to give a better focus to policy objectives and Save the Children's global portfolio.

Evaluation

Evaluation may be necessary for the same reasons as review, but it implies a more formal judgement. It can be used to assess the effectiveness and impact of an experimental or pilot programme to help decide whether it should be expanded or modified; and to assess whether the progress and impact of a project or programme is likely to be sustainable in the long term, and what could affect the sustainability.

An evaluation should **not** be carried out for the following reasons:
- to justify a decision which has already been made for other reasons, for example, the decision to stop funding a project or programme

- to assign blame for a problem which has arisen.

In these cases, some kind of investigation may be necessary, but it is not an evaluation.

Evaluations can contribute to decisions over funding, but such decisions should not be the reason for an evaluation. People are unlikely to have a positive attitude towards evaluation (or any kind of critical analysis) if they know that funding may be withdrawn as a direct result of the findings.

When is an evaluation necessary?

An evaluation can be carried out at different times in the life of a project or programme. The timing will depend on the purpose, audience and use of the evaluation. An evaluation of a project or programme may be needed:

- to clarify its objectives and assess their relevance
- to assess how effective the work is and what progress it is making towards achieving its objectives
- to find out what impact it is having
- to see how efficient the work is, in terms of using resources
- to look at the long-term implications – is the work sustainable?

It is important to consider evaluation when first planning a project or programme. For some objectives it will be necessary to plan the work so that the impact can be evaluated: for example, by introducing an intervention in stages with periodic surveys to assess the impact. This may be especially worthwhile for interventions that are experimental.

> **For example:** The Aids Awareness Group (AAG)'s project on 'Health promotion in adolescents for HIV/AIDS prevention' in seven schools in Lahore, Pakistan, has been supported and funded by Save the Children UK since its inception in May 1999. Another organisation has recently started to fund AAG's activist's training, and Save the Children has started to support a similar project in Karachi. Because of the innovative nature of the project in Pakistan, it was thought important to have a mid-term evaluation to see if there were any recommendations from the various stakeholders as to whether changes should be made. The evaluation team included young people who used 'Theatre for development' (TfD) techniques to assess the effectiveness of the project in raising awareness of HIV/AIDS prevention. (See below for more details on how this was used; Tool 10 describes TfD more fully.)

> **For example:** In 1999 an evaluation was carried out to evaluate the support which Save the Children UK has provided to community-based projects in

Northern Ireland. This was done because Save the Children UK as a whole was shifting its focus from development to child rights. The evaluation was carried out so that Save the Children could learn from its experience of providing support to community projects, and use this to inform and develop its new rights-focused approach. The evaluation also had a role in documenting some of the important work that was carried out during the previous phase of Save the Children's development. The evaluation provided useful indicators of Save the Children's strengths in developing relationships with groups in terms of style or ethos of support. But it evaluated Save the Children's work solely from the perspective of the community groups, and not in terms of achieving Save the Children's aims and objectives. For example, it did not show how effective Save the Children was in promoting a culture of children's rights in partner organisations.

The evaluation itself was not as useful as had been hoped, but a critical analysis of the evaluation carried out afterwards by programme staff was extremely useful. It was an essential component (along with other strategic planning processes) in developing a future strategy for the community support programme.

2. Who is it for and how will they use the results?

It is essential to know who the review or evaluation is aimed at when deciding who will be involved in managing and carrying it out (see Chapter 2). It is also essential to clarify how the results will be used. If this is not agreed by all the potential users at an early stage, there is a danger that the findings will be ignored and the whole exercise will be a waste of time. The emphasis should always be on learning, and feeding the results back into future policy and practice.

Review and evaluation results can be used to:

- improve future work, by providing a framework for discussion between people affected by the work, staff, managers, partners and donors about how the work should develop
- inform decision-making about the specific project or programme reviewed or evaluated
- inform policy development in the country and globally
- provide evidence for advocacy, to help influence governments, partners and other organisations
- share learning across programmes (as a document that analyses the experience of a particular kind of work)
- improve monitoring and evaluation: the methods and indicators used in an evaluation can be used to set up or adapt monitoring systems to provide an on-going analysis of progress and impact
- as a source document for subsequent reviews and evaluation.

3. Objectives and key questions

These must be clearly defined before starting the review or evaluation. When there are several objectives, there should be clear priorities. If a review has too many objectives it may be difficult to analyse all the information.

Review objectives often include the following:

- To review the agency's involvement in a project or programme: how and why has the work developed over time?
- To review programme objectives: are they clear? should they be changed?
- To review the relevance of current activities: are they the best way of achieving the objectives? what are the alternative options?
- To assess the performance of activities: are they being carried out effectively and according to principles of good practice? how could they be improved?
- To assess the effectiveness of work: what is the progress towards achieving objectives? what is the impact of the programme on the different groups affected by the work?
- To improve monitoring and evaluation: identify indicators and design or refine a monitoring system.
- To consider the cost-effectiveness of the work.
- To review external factors influencing the work including: government and/ or policy changes; economic and social changes; changes in the policy and practice of international organisations.
- To look at a particular factor that is relevant to the work, for example, the situation of children in a country.

Possible **evaluation objectives** include:

To find out:

- whether the programme is making progress towards achieving its objectives
- what the impact has been on the people (men, women, boys and girls) who are supposed to benefit from the work: has the work helped to improve their well-being as stated in the original objectives? Has the work had any undesirable effects on people?
- how the situation of the target population has changed due to external factors, such as political changes, other development activities or natural disasters
- who has benefited from the work? How have the benefits of the work been distributed to different groups?

To assess:

- whether the impact, if there is one, is due to the work or to other factors
- whether the aims and objectives are still relevant, and whether there is a better way of achieving the objectives
- whether the work is being carried out efficiently, and what the major problems and constraints are

- the cost of the work, whether this is reasonable in the context, and whether resources are used as effectively as possible
- how changes in the situation of the target population will affect the impact and relevance of the work
- whether the work is sustainable, and what factors will affect its sustainability.

To make recommendations on:
- how the programme could be improved
- how the aims and objectives should be modified or revised
- how the work can be monitored and evaluated in the future
- how the work could be made more cost-effective.

What key questions should the review or evaluation address?

Once the purpose and overall objectives of the review have been determined, it is possible to formulate key questions which need to be addressed. Some basic principles for selecting specific questions are explained in Chapter 5.

For example: The main objective of the evaluation of the Save the Children US Revolving Loan Fund in West Bank and Gaza was to measure the impact of the loan programme on borrowers, their businesses and their families; to measure the programme's effectiveness; and to make decisions about the future of the programme. (Initially it was planned also to evaluate the impact of the programme on the communities and the economy of the whole area, but this was abandoned since it was found to be unrealistic to assume that a programme of this size had produced any measurable results in this respect.)

The following key questions were identified to determine the main themes of the evaluation and to focus discussions among the participants during all stages of the evaluation: from designing data-gathering tools to the final analysis of the collected information.

Impact on businesses:
- What kind of borrowers does the loan programme reach?
- What changes have occurred in the assisted businesses since receiving a loan?
- To what extent does the loan programme increase the income of borrowers?
- In which cases does the programme create indebtedness rather than wealth among borrowers?

- To what extent does the loan programme create employment opportunities?

Impact on families:
- How is the borrower's family affected by the loan?
- In projects which are profitable, does the success of the business have a beneficial impact on the borrower's family?

Loan repayment:
- What does the repayment rate depend on?
- From which sources do the borrowers repay?
- How can loan repayment rates be improved?

Programme management:
- How cost-effective is the loan programme, and how effectively is it managed?
- How do the borrowers perceive and evaluate the programme?

4. Information collection and analysis

What information is needed to answer the key questions and where can it be obtained?

Once the questions to be answered by the review or evaluation have been clarified, it should be possible to define what information is needed and where it can be obtained. It is important to consider this when designing the review or evaluation, since it will determine the methods, timescale, personnel and resources needed. It is discussed in Chapter 5 (and see also Chapter 4 and Tools 1 and 2). A combination of different methods should always be used to ensure that the data has been cross-checked.

Evaluation is specifically looking at impact, so indicators for measuring impact and progress towards achieving objectives are essential. The indicators should be able to demonstrate changes which reflect the impact of the work. (See Chapter 6 for more detail on objectives and indicators.)

For example: Save the Children's global review of social protection, welfare and inclusion used case studies from four countries to provide a representative picture of range and type of work carried out by Save the Children in this field. The case studies provided an opportunity to look at the processes, outcomes and impacts of the work, and to help assess the extent to which Save the Children's policy is in line with actual practice, and what are the gaps between policy and practice.

The methods used were:

- **focus group discussions**: with children and young people, Save the Children field staff, other staff, and other stakeholders (eg, government officials)
- **structured interviews** with individuals from same groups as above
- **video diary**, observing and documenting how work is actually carried out
- **role playing**, games and simulations to get children to tell stories about their own lives in their own words
- **content analysis** of relevant documentation
- **baseline surveys**: statistical analysis on key variables over time
- **reflective session**: debriefing with key staff on case study events.

For example: The mid-term evaluation of 'Health promotion in adolescents for HIV/AIDS prevention in schools' in Pakistan was carried out primarily by child evaluators who used the Theatre for Development method (see Tool 10). It was felt that this would allow child evaluators to express their concerns about personal health, and by performing this to other children and teachers it would open up issues for the discussion groups that followed with the audience. Two groups of children performed to six of the seven schools in which the HIV/AIDS training was carried out. The issues were then discussed in groups, with facilitators and rapporteurs. (Adults acted as rapporteurs but were sometimes asked to leave the groups so that children, especially girls, would feel able to open up and discuss issues more freely.) This approach helped to show what impact the health promotion activities had had on children in schools, and whether it was addressing the issues that were most important for children.

Evaluators also met with principals and teachers from the schools, and with a few parents (but this was limited due to lack of time).

Analysis

The analysis of the information is the key to a review or evaluation. If it is to be accurate and useful, it is important that the interpretation of information is not influenced too much by the personal view of the evaluator(s). Analysis should take into account the different perspectives of different people involved.

For example: There was considerable dispute about the conclusions and recommendations of an evaluation of a disability programme in Fiji, because it was felt that interpretation of interviews with staff and government officials did not accurately represent the content of the interviews, but was more a reflection of the evaluator's own opinions.

An evaluation is looking specifically for the impact of a project or programme. When analysing findings it is important to consider the long-term aims of the work, as well as the short-term objectives. It is possible that something that fails in the short term may be beneficial in the long term. (See Chapter 9 for more on assessing long-term impact.)

Common frameworks can be used to help analyse information and bring it together.

For example: Save the Children's global review of social protection, welfare and inclusion used a 'case study pro forma' to help analyse information gathered from the case studies. The data gathered in each of the four case study countries, using the different techniques listed above, was summarised in a common format, so it could be more easily compared.

The headings on the pro forma were:

1. Field work carried out (numbers, settings, type of informants and techniques)
2. Characteristics of the case study environment (cultural and social environment, role of children in society, legislative environment, key problems experienced by children)
3. Organisational context in which Save the Children's work in this area is carried out (project setting, type of service delivery, type of children targeted, type of outcomes, care arrangements, participation structures, financial operation)
4. Initiating circumstances and evolution (reasons for starting, key actors, how it has changed)
5. Outcomes and impacts (overall success, main reasons for success or failure, main problems, lessons learned to improve success in the future, how can impact be assessed?)
6. Innovation and lessons (what aspects are innovative? What examples of good practice can be learned? What policy implications can be drawn?)

Issues concerning the analysis of information are discussed in Chapter 5. These include analysis methods, deciding who should analyse the data collected, when they should do so, and the use of computers.

5. Presenting the results

See Chapter 5 for a discussion of questions to consider in order to decide on the best methods for presenting results.

Sample evaluation report format
The following suggested list of contents is given as an example of a report format. It is rough guide for an evaluation report. The way of organising a report will depend on the particular exercise, and the contents will also vary.

Front cover and title page
- title, name and location of project or programme
- names of those who carried out the evaluation
- names of partners involved in the work
- brief purpose of evaluation
- dates of evaluation
- date report was completed

Acknowledgements
- communities, advisers, team members, funders

List of contents
Executive summary
- A brief one- or two-page overview of the report, including the purpose and objectives of the evaluation, who it was for, how it was carried out, where and when, major results, conclusions and recommendations. This should be written last. Emphasise the most important points.

Background information
- Including how and why the project or programme began, and how it has developed; its main objectives and how these have developed; how the context of the work has changed over time; the main activities and resources.

Purpose of the evaluation and methods chosen
- Explain the purpose of the evaluation and intended audiences. What are the objectives and key questions the evaluation hopes to answer?
- What evaluation methods were chosen and why? What were the main constraints (such as staff and other resources, political context)?
- Samples of the methods used, such as questionnaires, can be included in an appendix.

- Who was interviewed, where, and why were they chosen?

Outcome of using the methods
- Where and how were the evaluation methods developed and tested before use?
- How was the information collected and by whom, and which methods were used?
- How reliable and valid did the methods prove to be?
- Include any timetable or schedule in an appendix.
- Include information about how staff and participants were trained to use the methods, if appropriate.
- Also mention unintended results, if appropriate.

Results and discussion
- Summarise findings under headings.
- Wherever possible use maps, tables and diagrams, and interpretation of qualitative findings.
- Include examples of what people actually said in interviews, if appropriate, as this can be revealing.
- Briefly describe the methods used to analyse the information.

Conclusions
- Conclusions present a summing-up of the answers to the original questions, without repeating facts presented in the results and discussion.

Recommendations
- This may be the only section some people read.
- Recommendations should be given in order of priority.

Appendices
- This should include detailed information referred to in other sections, for example, details of methods used, questionnaires, timetables and schedules.

(Adapted from *Partners in Evaluation* by Marie-Therese Feuerstein – for full details, see references and further reading section.)

6. Organisation

The way the exercise is organised and who is involved will have a great effect on whether the recommendations are followed. Chapter 5 looks at questions concerning different ways of managing the review or evaluation.

For example: The review of the community-based rehabilitation (CBR) programme in Zanzibar was led by a consultant with expertise in CBR. There was a core team of the Chairman of the UWZ (Zanzibar association of the disabled), the CBR programme co-ordinator, the CBR programme manager, and the UWZ development officer. The extended review team consisted of staff and volunteers from the CBR programme, a young disabled woman, a local district social welfare officer, and the parent of a disabled child. The different team members brought a wide range of experience, and helped to make sure the different views of stakeholders were properly represented. The review was undertaken in a participatory way as far as possible.

For example: The Save the Children health programme review in Nepal was led by a consultant. The review was expected to have a major influence on the future of the whole Save the Children country programme, so it was vital that all the relevant staff were closely involved in its design, implementation and analysis. Managerial and technical staff from the main country office and project offices participated in planning and conducting the review and in formulating conclusions and recommendations. The regional office provided technical advice and support as appropriate.

The involvement of most of the staff had many positive aspects: it helped staff to develop their critical abilities; they learned more about the programme; and they had an opportunity to look at areas of particular interest to them. The process raised awareness of existing documents. It also made everyone involved think clearly about the health programme objectives, especially the long-term objectives. It helped to develop a sense of responsibility, and resulted in prompt implementation of the review recommendations. It is hoped that this will be reflected in better ownership of future planning in the programme.

The main problem was in underestimating the time it takes to engage staff in a participatory process. More time was needed for people to digest written information and then discuss it. There was to have been an advisory committee to help monitor the review progress and act as a sounding board. This did not get off the ground but would have been useful to help clarify what was required of the findings by different potential users.

Using external reviewers and evaluators

The importance of involving the relevant people, and the relative advantages and disadvantages of insiders and outsiders are discussed in Chapter 2. See Tool 8 for a sample consultant contract and strengths, weaknesses and prerequisites for success of using consultants. See Tool 9 for strengths and weaknesses of visits as a tool for monitoring and review, and for prerequisites of a successful visit.

It is important to brief outside reviewers and evaluators who are not familiar with the country or situation and provide them with sufficient background information. A particular advantage of external reviewers and evaluators is that they need basic information and may ask the sort of fundamental questions that are quite helpful to people immersed in the programme.

Peer evaluators – people who work in similar programmes within the same organisation or from other organisations – can often be a good choice. They understand the issues from an insider's point of view, but do not have vested interests in the particular programme being evaluated.

The role of the reviewer or evaluator

The role of the reviewer(s) or evaluator(s) will depend on the approach used. They may be expected to act as an independent and objective 'judge', or more as a facilitator for a learning and developmental experience.

In any case, if the review or evaluation is to be a useful and non-threatening exercise for the staff and people who are affected by the work, it is important that there is close cooperation and a sense of partnership between those evaluating and those who are effectively being evaluated. The internal and external reviewers or evaluators will inevitably have a different approach to the exercise, and it is particularly important to clarify and articulate objectives.

See Chapter 5 for a summary of the relative advantages and disadvantages of internal and external evaluators.

Combining external and internal

It is often useful to combine internal and external reviewers/evaluators.

For example: Save the Children's global review of social protection, welfare and inclusion was led by an external institution, with an internal reviewer. The external reviewers defined the evaluation methodology, examined existing documentation, and interviewed key people to get an overview of the relevant programme work across the world. Based on this, they then selected four countries as case studies to represent different contexts. The internal reviewer/coordinator collected data from the case study countries with the external reviewers. He knew the contexts and the people, and gave the outsiders credibility in the field. This hugely improved their access to people and information.

Timescale and resources

Issues concerning the timescale and resources of a review or evaluation are discussed in Chapter 5.

Summary

- A review is an assessment at one point of time of a project or programme and can look at any aspect of the work. An evaluation looks specifically at progress in relation to objectives and impact.

- **Checklist of the review or evaluation process**
  At the planning stage decide:
  - why are you doing it?
  - for whom?
  - what is to be reviewed?
  - by whom?
  - how will it be managed?
  - when will it be done?
  - what are the resource implications?
  - how will the results be used?

  Design the review/evaluation:
  - state what is to be reviewed/evaluated
  - choose and design methods
  - choose measurements and indicators
  - choose methods for recording, disseminating and storing findings

  Action:
  Collect information
  - what? (facts, quantitative and qualitative data)
  - how? (questioning, observing, reading)

  Analyse your findings:
  - interpret information
  - assess results

Judge your results:
- decide on the value of the results

Present your findings:
- validate your analysis and judgments
- decide on format of final report and/or presentation

Using results:
Ensure the results will be used:
- agree on recommendations
- make relevant changes

Feedback:
- review needs and design of the evaluation or review

Store results so they are accessible.

Chapter 9
Impact assessment

Introduction

What has changed as a result of a programme and what difference does it make in people's lives? Development practitioners and donors have begun to focus more and more on this question. This chapter discusses impact assessment as a particular type of analysis looking at lasting changes that happen as a result of development work, beyond programme activities and immediate results. This kind of analysis is still at a relatively early stage of its evolution, and practical examples from the field are comparatively new. This is reflected in this chapter, which presents the current stage that thinking and practice within the work of Save the Children has reached.

Impact assessment is not a separate exercise, but can be a focus of any monitoring, review or evaluation. This chapter examines the different ways of understanding and analysing change in relation to development programmes, which can then be applied to monitoring and evaluation activities.

Structure of the chapter

The first section is mainly theoretical and gives an overview of what is meant by the term 'impact assessment' and how it fits into a programme cycle. It goes on to discuss the nature of change.

The second section of the chapter moves on to the practical means of carrying out a study focusing on impact. Following the principles outlined in Chapter 5, it stresses the importance of defining the aim of the exercise, clarifying how the results will be used and by whom, and discussing who should be involved.

The third section considers ways of drawing up objectives and key questions for the exercise. It is then important to decide on indicators that will reflect the changes that are expected, both positive and negative, remembering that these will not address the unexpected changes.

The fourth section looks at ways of collecting and analysing information.

The final section discusses the methods and organisation needed for collecting evidence of change.

1. What is impact assessment and how does it relate to planning, monitoring, review and evaluation?

Planning, monitoring, review and evaluation focus on the processes and direct results of a project or programme. Building on these, 'impact assessment' often focuses on longer-term and wider-ranging changes beyond the immediate results of the work.

> **For example:** As a result of a project providing displaced children with their identity documents, a child receives her birth certificate (project result). As a result, the child is able to go to school and receive an education (a longer-term impact).

'Impact' can be defined as the extent to which a project or programme has produced significant *changes* in the lives of children, young people and their communities. It is therefore more than the immediate, predicted outputs of an intervention (project or programme) and much more focused on the implications of work in the medium and long term. This crucially should include examples of expected, unintended, positive and negative impacts.

All planning, monitoring, and evaluation activities should consider the implications of a programme, although this should not mean under-estimating the importance of direct, short-term outputs and results. On the contrary, assessing long-lasting changes is impossible without a good understanding of the intermediate steps and processes leading to change. It is important that impact assessment is embedded in all stages of the programme spiral (see Chapter 1).

The nature of change

Impact assessment is about understanding and assessing change. What are the implications of our actions? What changes are significant? What is the broader context of change?

For many years development planning models have been associated with a linear notion of change, which assumes input A leads to output B and an outcome or impact C.

$$A \longrightarrow B \longrightarrow C$$

But now non-linear models of change are considered closer to the reality of development interventions:

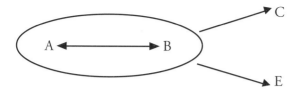

This shows how the context of inputs and outputs (A and B) affects the resulting changes. These can be expected (C), unexpected (E), positive and negative. According to this model, change is brought about by a combination of specific events, people and conditions present in a given situation, as well as by the project or programme undertaken.

The nature of change varies in different contexts. Some change is gradual and some is sudden and unpredictable – such as a coup d'état, an earthquake, or currency speculation. Some sudden change is local and some international changes will affect the project context.

The nature of change is important for the purposes of impact assessment, as it shows that development and change are the results of wider processes that are the product of many social, economic, political, historical and environmental factors – including power struggles between different interest groups. Understanding these processes is important, if the changes brought about by a given project or programme are to be properly situated in their broader context. (See the models of change below.)

2. Carrying out a study that focuses on impact

Why focus on impact? What is the aim?

A study that focuses on impact usually looks at the processes and results of the programme, and then builds on this to understand what the impact is or would be. Long-lasting change is often the result of lengthy processes of development. But significant change or progress towards long-term change can also be detected in the short term.

As in any evaluation, the aim and the resources available need to be clarified and agreed (see Chapters 5 and 8 for drawing up aims for an evaluation), as different stakeholders may have different expectations of these. If is often useful to have an introductory workshop to discuss what the different interest groups mean by impact. This can help create a shared understanding of the process and help decide which areas of change to focus on.

Difficult issues that may need to be raised at this stage include how the results may or may not influence future funding. It is difficult to have a proper mutual learning exercise if future funding depends on a successful outcome.

It may also be necessary to clarify what is meant by impact assessment in relation to other focuses in evaluation or review.

As well as for accountability to all stakeholders, impact assessment can be useful for improving future practice. By focusing on impact, questions are asked about what changes as a result of a piece of work, and what key processes lead to such changes. This can help to demonstrate what works in different situations and why, so that a project can improve its work and develop best practice.

Impact assessment requires an honest and self-critical approach and a learning culture with good and trusting relations between partners.

> **For example:** A study of two programmes focusing on working children in Pakistan looked at the *significant changes* the project set out to bring about in the lives of the children and families it touched, and at the main lessons learned through the particular approaches taken to the problems faced. The aims were:
> - to share experience and understanding on child labour issues, so that working children and their families will benefit more from future interventions
> - to provide an overview and analysis of the strategies used to combat child labour through the project, and to assess whether the project achieved what it set out to achieve and, indeed, if it resulted in meaningful and lasting changes in the lives of children and their communities
> - to determine principles which will guide future work on child labour so that the project can best protect children's and young people's rights.

How will the results be used?

(See Chapter 5.)

The answer to this question needs to be clear so the exercise can be designed accordingly. In particular it can be used by:
- **beneficiaries:** to be involved in analysing what changes have taken place, what different factors have combined to bring about changes, and how the changes affect different people. This is also crucial for identifying unintended or potentially negative impact.
- **programme management, partners, local people:** to look more widely at change in people's lives, and how different factors combine and interact to bring about change. This can support decision-making, and provide a basis for stronger partnerships in the future.
- **NGOs, governments, donors:** longer-term perspective gives a broader view of the role of NGOs in different contexts, and can be used for long-term planning and policy development;

For example: Save the Children is developing a framework for global impact monitoring. The basic procedure is to hold impact review meetings, and complete country impact reports. By summarising at different levels the impact of the global strategic plan and progress towards meeting its objectives, the aim is to improve institutional learning by feeding back into strategic policy and planning processes.

- **by programmes and partner organisations**: to provide meaningful evidence to support policy and advocacy work.

For example: In Sialkot, Pakistan, Save the Children monitored the impact of changes in the football stitching industry on children involved in the industry and their families. The findings of the impact assessment were published in a quarterly report that was distributed to all agencies involved in the work, including those responsible for developing national and international policy regulating child labour.

Who should be involved?

See Chapter 2 for general principles about who should be involved and why. The people who need to use the results should be in a position to learn most from the process of analysing impact.

You need to consider:
- triangulation and cross-checking, making sure the voices of all relevant stakeholders are heard and taken into account;
- rights – who has the right to be involved?
- Future practice – whose learning from the experience will feed in to improved programme design in the future?

When looking at impact on children, it is vital to make sure that they are directly involved in defining change and how it affects them (see Chapter 3).

For example: The social monitoring programme in Sialkot, Pakistan, assesses the impact of changes in the football stitching industry on children and their families. It uses a combination of quantitative and qualitative research methods to monitor changing trends of child labour through social indicators. It uses PLA approaches (see Tool 1) to find out the perceptions and real needs of the people, including boys and girls involved in the industry. One part of the research focused on how football stitching affects children's study and leisure time. Another focused on the effectiveness of the education programme being implemented for working children in the project area.

Since we are also looking at unintended impact and wider consequences, it is also important to involve people not directly affected by the project – for example, children from the same community but not involved in the project, parents and teachers.

3. Clarifying the objectives and key questions of the exercise

(See Chapter 5.)

Define a model of change

In order to measure change you need a view of how it comes about, so you know what to monitor and review at different stages. All development processes make assumptions about how change comes about. Sometimes these assumptions are made explicit, but often they are not. Different stakeholders may have different assumptions about how change happens, and which changes are significant.

It is important to make explicit different stakeholders' assumptions about how change happens, so that they can be taken into account and challenged in an impact assessment exercise. This process of questioning change and how it comes about has been found to be extremely useful. It can have an impact on the programme, by making managers and staff think more critically about what they are doing.

One approach is to define a clear model about how change occurs – but as a model is a simplification of reality it must be a good one, and it must fit the situation:

> **For example:** The Household Economy Approach (HEA) was developed over many years by Save the Children as a method that could indicate the likely effect of crop failure or other shocks on future food supply to poor households. The approach used in HEA is to model the most likely chain of events linking a shock (such as crop failure) and the outcome at household level. The model is based on a detailed analysis of how households normally obtain their food and other income, and how these strategies are affected by different kinds of stress. The approach was used in Ethiopia to identify the changes in household food economy that can be attributed to food aid since May 1999. It enabled an assessment to be made of the impact on food aid on food intake, assets and economic activities of poor households. The approach is also used to look at essential non-food items and can be used to target interventions. It may be possible to apply the basic model to other situations, for example, urban poverty analysis. But more work needs to be done to make sure it fits satisfactorily.

Table 9.1. Hypothetical theory of change for community-building

	Early activities	Early outcomes	Intermediate outcomes	Long-term outcomes
Community level	• Inform public about initiative • Mapping of neighbourhood resources and needs assessment • Neighbourhood newsletter	• Large no. residents come to meetings • Neighbourhood assets mapped and priority problems identified • etc	• Residents' attitudes about neighbourhood shifting to indicate "it is getting better" • Fewer negative events – graffiti, litter, etc	• Residents believe this is good neighbourhood to raise children • Intergroup relations harmonious • Improved outcomes on income, education, crime, physical infrastructure, health and well-being • etc
Organisations/ institutional	• Formation of multi-institutional governing entity for initiative	• Governing entity well functioning with: good leadership, management, etc	• Visible projects successfully implemented, etc	• Neighbourhood projects have provided reform in public and private institutions outside neighbourhood etc
Personal network/ family	• Mutual support groups formed, eg, alcohol abuse	• Residents know more neighbours names and faces • Increased resident participation on boards • etc	• Increased number informal associations • Neighbours more willing to ask each other for help • Vulnerable populations well cared for	• Residents feel comfortable acting when neighbour does something wrong (eg, children misbehave) etc
Individual	• Leadership development programmes	• Residents training in conflict resolution, etc	• New non-traditional leadership emerging in neighbourhood activities	• Residents running most of the significant civic, cultural, economic, social and political institutions in the community

Source: Connell J and Kubish A, (1998) 'Applying a theory of change approach to the evaluation of comprehensive community initiatives: progress, prospects, and problems,' in Karen Fulbright-Anderson, Anne C. Kubisch & James P. Connell (Eds.) *New Approaches to Evaluating Community Initiatives: Vol. 2, Theory, measurement and analysis* (pp.15–44). Washington: The Aspen Institute.

Another approach is using problem trees (see Tool 6) to examine the relationship and links between different causes of a key problem, to see how changes in environmental factors, community factors and individuals may interact. This then shows where you might start looking for change and impact.

A third approach is to use a matrix to show how change occurs at different levels, and as part of a process, over time. For an example of this see table 9.1 (page 131). This example is taken from a community-building project, but a similar approach can be used in other situations.

Developing key questions: what areas of change should be assessed?

Once the model for change has been made explicit, the next step is to define the areas or kinds of impact to be assessed. It is not possible to look at all the areas included in the model, so those areas most relevant for the purpose of the exercise need to be selected. This then helps identify key questions and indicators (see Chapter 5). There is no single way to do this. The following examples show how different areas have been selected in different situations:

For example: The Children First project in Jamaica developed a problem tree to identify the causes and results of 'risky sex' (see Tool 6). From the problem tree, the project was then able to work out its impact indicators, based on the causes of risky sex and the unwelcome results. To reach this objective they had to ask what behaviour the project was trying to encourage and prevent. They grouped the resultant indicators into four categories:
  1. Contextual changes: such as a reduction in poverty of the target groups
  2. Intermediate impacts: increase in knowledge of condom use
  3. Behavioural outcomes: increase in condom use
  4. Long-term impacts: reduction in unwanted pregnancies.
(Webb D., *Learning to Live*, Save the Children 2000)

For example: The matrix below was adapted by Save the Children to help focus discussions about impact with partner organisations. It provides a framework to focus on the dimensions of change which have been identified as priorities (see page 136). Change and impact are looked at as part of a continuum of activities and results, not just the end point. Different examples of programme work can be put in the matrix to show how changes occur in the different dimensions. More discussion and evidence is then needed to explore the actual impact or process of the work.

The example below refers to work on juvenile justice in Honduras. It was developed by a group of different stakeholders. In the example, the approval of a new law was identified as a significant example of impact of Save the Children's work, but it cannot be considered as the end of the process, as it will only have meaningful impact in the lives of children and young people when the law is translated into practice. (See also Tool 13 on evaluating advocacy for more examples of frameworks to help analyse change.)

Table 9.2. Dimensions of change in juvenile justice work in Honduras

Dimensions of change	Early activities	Early outcomes	Interim outcomes	Impact
1. Wider impact on policy and practice	Exploratory research study on juvenile justice and gangs	Needs assessment with young people in conflict with the law or involved in gangs indicates need to strengthen the normative framework for rehabilitation	Violence and gangs included as themes in the political campaign Public opinion mobilised on issues of violence, juvenile justice and gangs	The law on social rehabilitation approved by national congress BUT need to develop a programme for supporting the rehabilitation measures provided by the law
3. Improved participation	Consultation and participatory workshops with children and young people as part of the research process	Visions and opinions of young people are promoted and evolve through the study		
4. Collaborative working		Co-ordination and partnership between Save the Children and ACJ (principal partner)	Collaboration between several organisations of state and civil society (larger network)	Creation of network 'Movimiento por la Vida y por la Paz'

For example: An Oxfam study in Pakistan explored the impact of a number of micro-projects. It started from the assumption that human development or well-being is multi-dimensional. The approach they adopted was explicit about what these dimensions are, in order not to miss important elements, and in order that the study focus on the ends of development, not just the means. These dimensions are:

- life (which encompasses health, nutrition, security and so on)
- knowledge
- excellence in work and play
- relationships

- beauty/environment
- inner voice/peace
- religion
- empowerment.

Discussions were held during project visits to see what changes had taken place in each of the dimensions, and to what extent these were a result of the project.

Impact of advocacy

(See also Chapter 11.)

There are particular issues and challenges concerned with assessing the impact of advocacy. This may usefully be looked at in terms of intermediate outcomes and long-term impact, as in the first example above. A number of frameworks have been developed to help clarify the focus of impact assessments of advocacy work. See Tool 13 for details.

Impact on whom?

It is important to consider how changes in the lives of children will eventually affect the lives of their children, and how this will eventually have an effect on broader society. Depending on the purpose of the impact assessment, and the areas of change to be looked at, the impact may be on: individuals, households, groups, community, organisations, institutions, society in a broader sense, or ideas.

It is always important to consider how impact is affected by gender, age and disability (see Chapter 3).

For example: The Thardeep Rural Development Project (TRDP) works in the Thar desert of Pakistan. A key part of its programme is to provide micro-financing services to poor and vulnerable communities, many of whom are trapped into exploitative relationships of indebtedness to contractors. As a result, many children are exploited as workers in the rug industry. A qualitative impact assessment has shown that the project has successfully reduced the extremely exploitative dependency of weavers' families on contractors for credit. TRDP carpet loan children have increased chances to go to school.

Boys, though, have gained more than girls. Some of the girls we met said that they go to school, but when they were asked to draw a time-chart for their day, they didn't leave any space for schooling. Other girls say they go to school, but on further questioning, state that they don't go at the same time as their brothers, they go later, when they have finished the household chores.[1]

Indicators

See Chapters 5 and 6 for a detailed discussion of indicators.

Types of indicators and areas of change

It is important to agree on the main areas where change is expected to happen. These can be defined as categories, areas or dimensions of change. For example, impact assessment studies often examine the following three categories of change in people's lives:

- **Material wealth:** This includes assets (land, cattle, housing), income, credit and savings, occupational status, wages, expenditure, food security and quality of diet, dependency on money-lenders or food aid.
- **Social well-being or human capital measures:** These refer to health status and more specifically infant and child mortality, water and sanitation, and education (literacy, school attendance, drop-out rates).
- **Empowerment or political capital measures:** These include ownership and control over assets, perceptions of well-being and quality of life, participation in decision-making and public institutions, access to public resources, dependency and mobility, family-planning rates as a proxy indicator for women's empowerment.

For example: Save the Children has developed a guide for good practice in child reunification programmes, based on its experience in different countries. The recommendations for evaluation include the following suggestions for developing indicators:

Process indicators need to measure whether the practices and procedures were adequate and cost-effective, or whether they could be improved, speeded up or done differently.

- The impact of the programme needs to be measured in terms of the impact on children, families and communities.
- Have families welcomed the children, nurtured them, helped them to adapt to the new separation and the reunification?
- Have children been well prepared?
- Or have families felt the programme dumped children on them against their will? Have children been made to feel like objects delivered to unwilling adults?

---

[1] Taken from Crawford, S. *Impact Assessment: Project on child labour in the carpet industry of the Thar Desert*, Save the Children UK/Thardeep Rural Development Project, 2000

Possible impact indicators could include:
- What proportion of children have run away, suffered from malnutrition, or stopped attending school since reunification?
- What proportion of children feel sad, unloved and wish they were somewhere else?
- What proportion of children have not had family traced and not had any long-term planning done for their future?

Another example is the five dimensions of change used by Save the Children to look at changes resulting from its programmes at different levels. These are used as a common framework to monitor regularly the impact of programmes at different levels and to analyse impact trends and gaps:

Common dimensions of change of Save the Children's work

1. Changes in the lives of children and young people
Which **rights** are being better fulfilled? Which rights are no longer being violated?

2. Changes in policies and practice affecting children and young people's rights
Duty-bearers are more **accountable** for the fulfilment, protection and respect of children's and young people's rights. Policies are developed and implemented and the attitudes of duty bearers take into account the best interests and rights of the child.

3. Changes in children's and young people's participation and active citizenship
Children and young people **claim their rights** or are supported to do so. Spaces and opportunities exist which allow participation and the exercise of citizenship by children's groups and others working for the fulfilment of child rights.

4. Changes in equity and non-discrimination of children and young people
In policies, programmes, services and communities, are the most marginalised children reached?

5. Changes in civil society and communities capacity to support children's rights
Do networks, coalitions and/or movements add value to the work of their participants? Do they mobilise greater forces for change in children and young people's lives?

Different aspects of these dimensions are important in different situations, and may be expressed in different ways. It is possible to use the different dimensions as a starting point to develop locally relevant indicators.

For example: In three impact assessment studies of three different projects, the same key areas of change were identified (material wealth, social well-being and empowerment). The different projects then went on to identify specific indicators under each area, which were relevant to them. One of the common areas of change was women's empowerment, for which different and context specific indicators were identified:

Table 9.3. Indicators of women's empowerment

BRAC (Bangladesh)	Proshika (India)	Wajir (Kenya)
• Involvement in income-generating activities • Ownership and control over assets • Perceptions of own well-being • Economic dependence on husbands • Mobility	• Access to public resources • Participation in local institutions	• Perceptions of changes in quality of life

Participatory approaches to developing indicators are more likely to demonstrate impact that is significant to those involved.

For example: Adult staff of Save the Children had traditionally identified impact indicators themselves for their child-to-child health and hygiene programme in Nepal. However, in this case children were asked to identify indicators, using participatory methodologies. Having spent time with adults talking through the process, the children were invited to draw pictures or write stories representing the differences in their hygiene before and after the implementation of the project. From this, and from focus groups, they were able to identify differences in practice and attitude, and therefore the indicators of change.

The children identified more focused indicators and a greater number of them than the adults. For example, the staff indicators included personal hygiene and school environmental hygiene, while the children suggested punctuality in class, use and condition of the toilet, and the quality and location of the drinking water. Their indicators will allow a more effective monitoring of the impact of future child-to-child projects.

It is usually necessary to change, update and reformulate indicators as the work progresses.

Capturing unexpected impacts

Indicators can only capture expected change and will only reflect those areas of change that can be made explicit or are agreed upon by key stakeholders. This leaves out situations where unexpected change occurs, or areas of change that have not been agreed or are left hidden by one or more stakeholders.

What kind of change is captured by predetermined indicators?

	Expected	Unexpected
Agreed	Yes	No
Not agreed	No	No

So it is important not just to rely on predetermined indicators to assess change. This is particularly true in impact assessment.

> **For example:** In the Oxfam case study on page 133, the impact assessment study used the dimensions of human well-being described above. The study focused on the degree to which different projects produced changes in these dimensions, and which ones the beneficiaries considered the most important. This was done without any prior judgement about the relationship between the dimensions, nor about the relationship between the project and its stated objectives.

Capturing unintended impact is a question of looking for changes that have happened that were not planned. In other words, looking for changes or results that were not part of the programme objectives or processes. In order to capture unintended impact, it is therefore important not to limit the questions to 'Have we achieved our objectives?' but rather, 'What has changed in people's lives?'

> **For example:** In Liberia a child reunification programme placed separated children in communities, but one negative and unintended result was that some of these became more vulnerable and were recruited as child soldiers.

Capturing negative impact

This is often difficult to do, given the pressure to demonstrate success. The Oxfam study in Pakistan (see page 133) states in its methodology: "There will be positive and negative impacts. There are negative impacts even of very good activities. It is nothing to be embarrassed about. For example, if a woman gets married she spends less time with her parents; if I have a good job I have less time to drink tea with friends" (Roche, 1999). This is increasingly recognised as part of the development process. Similarly, some Save the Children programmes have found that work aimed at improving the conditions of children in care, for example, in China where Save the Children supports small family homes for abandoned children, may result in more families abandoning their children, as they feel that they would be adequately looked after.

4. Information collection and analysis

(See Chapter 5.)

Information about impact can be collected from a wide range of people depending on the purpose and scope of the exercise. The type of participation can vary. In some cases they may be involved in reconstructing project histories, in determining and verifying indicators, in defining what was meant by change, in the design stage, and in the analysis and feedback stages (see also Chapters 2 and 3).

In addition to the groups identified in Chapters 2 and 3 other groups to involve include:

- **Non-project respondents:**
  Individuals who have not been involved in the projects assessed but have similar characteristics to those whom the projects seek to support. They may be interviewed as control groups (see Attribution on page 141).
- **Excluded and drop-out groups:**
  Some intended beneficiaries of a project may be excluded from it, or be disadvantaged by it. Their views are important, particularly in understanding negative impact.
- **Project staff and partners:**
  This is good for capacity-building and ownership of the process but there is a danger that they may feel anxious about their jobs, reputations, future funding, and possibly obstruct or manipulate findings.
- **Donors:**
  Donors may be involved directly, for example, in agreeing the terms of reference or scope of the impact assessment, or attending introductory workshops. Even if they are not involved, their unseen presence affects the study design and implementation. This particularly affects the selection of the impact assessment team, which projects are selected, and the degree to which independence and 'objectivity' are sought.

5. Carrying out a review or evaluation that focuses on impact: methods and organisation

Who should carry it out?

The relative advantages of insiders and outsiders in carrying out a study focusing on impact are the same as for any evaluation or review (see Chapter 8). The critical requirement for the person leading or facilitating the study focusing on impact is the ability to see the broader implications of the work.

Sampling

(See chapter 4.)

For impact assessment it is particularly important to select samples that will reveal unintended as well as expected changes. The size of the samples will depend on how wide and how deep the analysis needs to be. A small sample will allow a greater depth of impact analysis. A larger sample will demonstrate how wide is the impact.

Case studies are often used to look at impact. It is a useful way to test the model of change, its relevance, and its limitations, and to analyse it in considerable depth. But it is not possible to generalise from case studies, unless a wider survey is then carried out to test the findings.

Timing

(Issues concerning timescale and resources are discussed in Chapter 5.)

Consider seasonal issues and the time of day. People's answers will vary according to the time of year, and their availability will be affected by it. This can be significant if you are comparing the situation before and after an intervention, and need to go back to the same group. It is important to consider how the impact assessment will relate to planning, or learning opportunities (see the diagram in Chapter 1).

> **For example:** Save the Children's global impact monitoring process includes an annual workshop in each country to assess the impact at country level, which will then feed into the organisation's existing cycle of regional planning meetings.

Where there is no baseline

To measure change there has to be some starting point. What was the situation like before? In theory, if a baseline study has been carried out at the beginning of the work, a similar study can be carried out to see what has changed. However, in practice baseline studies are quite rare, and where they have been carried out they have often looked at factors which seemed important initially but have become less relevant as the programme has developed. If a baseline is not available:

- Use project documents and records: for example, reviews, situation analyses, case study reports, monitoring information.
- Use information from other organisations: including statistical records

from local government departments such as tax, education, land use, crime. This may be time-consuming to collect and it may not be possible to compare if the way the information has been collected has changed over time.

- Gather baseline information from key informants: asking simple questions of key informants that compare different years, or the situation before and after a project intervention can be useful. Quantitative and qualitative information can be provided quickly (see Tool 1 PLA).

- If there is no baseline, it is still possible to compare the situation before and after an intervention, using needs assessments and responsibility analyses (see Chapter 6).

Attribution

It is unlikely that you will be able to prove that a certain effect is attributed to a particular cause or that it was the result of a particular agency. It is more a question of understanding how your activities work over time in combination with others to produce certain effects.

Different approaches that can be used to deal with attribution include:

- *Control groups.* This requires a comparison between a population that has been targeted by an intervention and one that has not. Ideally the assessment should be done before an intervention and again afterwards, to see whether there is any difference between the two populations. In practice this is difficult to carry out. There are so many variables that can cause differences between two populations, it is difficult to establish the particular cause. There are also ethical considerations with carrying out research with a community that is going to see no benefit from it.

- *Non-project respondents.* Ask both project beneficiaries and non-beneficiaries to recall their situation from a date before the intervention occurred, and compare this to their current situation.

For example: Oxfam in Kenya asked households in project and non-project sites to score out of ten their quality of life and ability to withstand drought, ten years ago and now. The responses showed a marked difference between project sites, where people perceived things to be improving, and non-project sites, where people perceived things to be getting worse.

There are still problems in being able to attribute differences precisely to specific variables, and find strictly comparable groups. There also may be difficulties persuading people to spare time for an interview when they have had no direct interest in the project, or they may wish to exaggerate their needs. If non-project respondents are groups that the NGO is planning to work with in the future, then some of the ethical dilemmas associated with this approach are lessened, and data gathered can be used as a baseline for that group.

- **Using secondary data and other key informants.** Secondary data from relevant government departments, research, etc may show up trends throughout the region due to broad economic, environmental, political and social phenomena, and changes which seem to occur only in the project affected area.
- **Look for other explanations.** Deliberately explore other possible explanations for an observed change or difference between various populations or groups. Although it is difficult to apportion the degree to which project or external factors contribute to a given change, it is important to explore possible alternative explanations for observed changes.

Cross-checking

This is essential in any study – see Chapter 4 for an explanation of how this can be carried out. The evidence of impact needs to be cross-checked to enable a valid judgement to be made. The views of different stakeholders should be gathered, possibly using a range of different methods. Cross-checking exposes bias, specific interests and power relations. It also reveals contradictions which may or may not be easily explained.

Cross-checking can be done in the following ways:

- Using different methods to look at the same thing: for example, observation to check if there are discrepancies between what people say and their actions, quantitative surveys to see how prevalent are changes identified using qualitative methods. Mixing qualitative and quantitative methods is vital. Consider which sequence of methods makes most sense.
- Using different researchers to collect data and compare results. This can help reveal their different biases and their own influence on the responses findings.
- Asking different informants the same questions, for example, men, women and children will each reveal different answers. This can also reveal important differences in priorities.
- Comparing information from different sources, for example, government officials and local records can show up differences, and also show how accurate information is.

Summary

- A review or evaluation can be designed to focus on lasting changes and wider impact, beyond the immediate results of the programme.

- The purpose of this study is accountability and learning: to demonstrate past impact and improve future programmes.
- In order to understand and measure impact, you need a model of change. This enables you to develop key questions and indicators to look at what change has taken place, and what processes have led to it.
- Indicators can be selected to look for expected impacts. Unintended impact can be captured using more open questions to find out what has changed in people's lives.
- A range of methods can be used for collecting evidence of change.
- Cross-checking evidence is essential to make sure the judgement of change is valid.
- There are different ways to compare before and after. A baseline study is one way.
- It is hard to prove attribution, but it is possible to understand how activities work over time to produce effects.

Chapter 10
Planning, monitoring, review and evaluation in emergency situations

Introduction

The processes of planning, monitoring, review and evaluation are as essential for work in emergencies as they are for longer-term development work. They are needed to help ensure that good decisions are made in planning and managing emergency programmes, and to learn from experience to improve the quality of future work.

On the whole, the principles and approaches discussed in earlier chapters can be applied to emergency work, but there are some aspects of emergency situations that have special implications for planning, monitoring, review and evaluation. To cover all the issues that are relevant in emergencies you should read this chapter together with Chapter 5 and the relevant chapter on planning, monitoring, review or evaluation. References are made to other chapters where relevant.

This chapter begins with a brief overview of the SPHERE Project. The rest of the chapter focuses on the issues of particular importance in the planning, monitoring, review and evaluation of emergency situations: the constraints and compromises that may be placed on emergency work; identifying specific aims and objectives; identifying key questions and indicators; deciding on ways of collecting and analysing information; and presenting the findings.

There are many different types of emergency. Some have natural causes and some are caused by humans. 'Sudden onset' emergencies include cyclones, floods and earthquakes. 'Slow onset' emergencies occur when a bad situation gradually gets worse. These may include food shortages that become famines, civil unrest that deteriorates into war, and large-scale movements of people into refugee settlements (although all of these may also happen suddenly). It is not possible to go into detail here about the different types of emergency, and the most appropriate form of planning, monitoring and evaluation for each. Only the general issues that are relevant to all emergencies will be discussed.

SPHERE Project

An important development since the first edition of this book is the 'SPHERE Project: Humanitarian Charter and Minimum Standards in Disaster Response'.

The purpose of this is to increase the effectiveness of humanitarian assistance, and to make humanitarian agencies more accountable, especially to those they seek to assist. It is an essential tool for planning, monitoring, review and evaluation, as it can be used to set objectives and indicators for disaster response.

The Humanitarian Charter is based on international humanitarian, refugee and human rights law. It affirms the fundamental importance of the following principles:

- the right to life with dignity
- the distinction between combatants and non-combatants
- the principle of refoulement (that no refugee shall be sent back to a country where they would be in fear of persecution).

The roles and responsibilities in relation to these principles are laid out concerning the legal obligations of states and warring parties, humanitarian agencies, the International Committee of the Red Cross, and the United Nations High Commissioner for Refugees.

The Minimum Standards aim to quantify these requirements with regard to people's need for water, sanitation, nutrition, food, shelter and health care. They are based on a wide range of humanitarian agencies' experience of providing humanitarian assistance.

(See Tool 14 for a summary of the SPHERE minimum standards.)

Participation in emergencies

"An emergency is a crisis situation that overwhelms the capacity of a society to cope using its resources alone" (Save the Children working definition).

It is important to recognise that people who have been affected by the emergency are a resource, not a crowd of helpless victims. The affected population is usually made up of different communities from a variety of areas and different social, economic and ethnic groups. They may be displaced or still in their own homes. Communities will have been severely disrupted but they will be trying to adapt to their new situation, reorganising themselves and their resources, human and material. It is the task of relief agencies to participate in that reorganisation and to support it. This means that it is vital for communities themselves to be involved in all planning, monitoring, review and evaluation exercises.

SPHERE sets out a minimum standard for participation:
The disaster-affected population has the opportunity to participate in the design and implementation of the assistance programme.
    Key indicators:
- Women and men from the disaster-affected population are consulted, and are involved in decision-making that relates to needs assessment, programme design and implementation.
- Women and men from the disaster-affected population receive information about the assistance programme, and have the opportunity to comment back to the assistance agency about the programme.

For community involvement to be successful, it is important to understand the social and political structures of the affected population. It is also important to cross-check information using different sources and to accept that where relief supplies are limited, people affected by an emergency will probably try to influence agencies to gain more assistance for themselves and the people they represent. The participation of children is also very important (see chapters 2 and 3).

The issues of particular importance in assessment, monitoring, review and evaluation of emergencies are discussed in this chapter under the following headings:

1. Constraints and compromises

Ways in which the conditions of working in an emergency situation affect the process of planning, monitoring, review and evaluation. These include:
- shortage of time and rapidly changing situations
- the need for short- and long-term objectives
- co-ordinating work with different organisations
- managing large resources: problems of communication and access
- cross-border operations: working in areas of disputed sovereignty
- initial shortage of staff and resources
- serious consequences of poor decisions, resulting directly or indirectly in unnecessary deaths.

2. Specific aim and objectives

Specific aim and objectives of planning, monitoring, review and evaluation in emergencies (including disaster preparedness and relief programmes).

3. Key questions and indicators relevant in emergencies

Mortality, morbidity, water and sanitation, nutrition, food aid, shelter and site planning, health services, livelihood, psychological well-being, child protection, education.

- Underlying causes of a problem
- Who is affected, where and how?
- Efficiency of the work
- Principles and values
- Performance and effectiveness of the disaster response.

4. Methods of collecting and analysing information in emergency situations
These include:
- review of existing information
- rapid appraisal methods
- quantitative surveys
- information systems.

The application of these methods in emergencies, and their strengths, weaknesses and prerequisites for success are all discussed in brief.

5. Presenting findings
Methods include:
- feedback to communities
- oral briefings
- reports (a sample format for an assessment report is provided)
- information and communication (a sample format for a situation report is provided).

Tool 14 provides frameworks for: water/sanitation; nutrition; food aid; shelter and site planning; health services; education; child protection.

1. Constraints and compromises

Tables 10.1–10.7 summarise some of the ways in which the conditions of working in an emergency situation affect the process of planning, monitoring, review and evaluation.

Shortage of time and rapidly changing situations

The essential difference between most development work and emergency situations is the need to make decisions and act quickly. The situation can also change very rapidly, especially where there is war or political instability. (See Table 10.1.)

Table 10.1 Coping with shortage of time and rapidly changing situations

Planning	Monitoring	Review/evaluation
• Must be done as fast and accurately as possible, to make decisions about the most appropriate response to the emergency. • Any approaches that take a long time are unsuitable, eg, there may be no time to organise workshops for in-depth participation, or to conduct large surveys early on. • Regular discussions with representatives of the affected population are essential to keep relief workers and the community up to date with changes in the situation and the programme. • Planning is an ongoing process when the situation is changing daily. • Information should be collected at any suitable opportunity, including relief distribution, registration, and so on. • The risk of the situation changing and the implications on possible strategies should be considered. • Standard procedures for needs assessment can be set up for countries that often experience emergencies.	• Monitoring is vital when a situation is changing quickly. • Systems for monitoring inputs: use of vehicles, food distribution, etc, need to be established quickly. It may be possible to set up standard procedures for countries that often experience emergencies. • The monitoring system needs to be able to identify the most important factors influencing the work, and make sure the people in charge of the relief programme have the information they need to respond to changes quickly. • 'Sitreps' (situation reports – a regular updating of the situation analysis) are the essential tool for regular internal reporting. They may be produced daily to begin with, and gradually become less frequent. • The monitoring system needs to be very flexible, to adapt to changes quickly. • Community participation in monitoring is essential, although a high degree of participation may be unrealistic for communities under stress.	• When a relief programme has been implemented very quickly, an early review of objectives, strategies and administrative systems may be needed to see how they should be developed. • Reviews may be needed periodically to see if the objectives are still relevant in a changing situation, or how they should be modified and how the work can be improved. • There is usually no time to collect baseline data specifically for use in evaluating impact, but any data collected in early planning or monitoring exercises can be used. For this reason it is vital to keep all data collected.

Short- and long-term objectives

The short-term objectives of an emergency intervention need to be defined, including specific objectives which can be monitored and evaluated. It is also important to consider the long-term objectives, since most emergency interventions develop into longer-term programmes. How will the work develop once people have adapted to the situation, or once it has returned to normal?

The long-term consequences of emergency interventions must also be considered. For example, while it may be appropriate to support health services in an emergency, who will be responsible for staff salaries once the emergency is over?

Table 10.2. Short- and long-term objectives

Planning	Monitoring	Review/evaluation
• Members of the affected population should be actively involved in *planning* to ensure that both short- and long-term objectives are appropriate. • Define short-term objectives: what do you intend to achieve? • Consider long-term results of interventions designed to meet immediate needs. • Identify longer-term objectives for involvement in an area. • Look at underlying causes of emergency, try to prevent situation becoming so bad again. • Will donors be willing to fund more long-term work in the area?	• Consider progress in terms of both short- and long-term objectives. • Monitor the side-effects of the intervention, so objectives and strategies can be modified if necessary. • Involvement of the affected population in monitoring will help keep the programme relevant, and will help strengthen local structures for longer-term development work.	• Periodic reviews may be needed to formulate long-term objectives in the light of experience of emergency work. • Evaluation should consider progress towards achieving both short and long-term objectives. • Self-evaluation and involvement of the community are important tools for strengthening local capacity to manage long-term development and future relief programmes.

Co-ordinating work with different organisations

In most emergency situations a large number and variety of agencies are involved. These could include different departments of the national government, a range of local and international agencies, major donors, and local groups which may have specific political and/or military aims.

Table 10.3 Co-ordinating work with different agencies

Planning	Monitoring	Review/evaluation
• One of the first steps in any relief operation is to establish a system for co-ordinating the different groups involved and to pool information about the situation. • It is important to find out in the initial assessment what other agencies are doing or intending to do to avoid duplication and coordinate efforts. • The agency needs to have clearly defined objectives to help decide how to respond to requests for support from different groups. • Key indicators for assessment need to be agreed between agencies so that different assessment teams working in different areas look at the same parameters.	• Relief managers need to know what other agencies are doing, in addition to their own activities, in order to make decisions. They will have to maintain an overview of the whole relief effort. • An effective and simple means of coordination at local/regional level is required to monitor the relief effort.	• Periodic reviews may be needed to help improve coordination between agencies. • Reviews may be useful to emphasise the need for resources in order to put pressure on donors. • The audience for an evaluation needs to be defined. For example, donors sometimes have very different expectations from an evaluation than the operational agency.

Managing large resources: budget, supplies and staff; and problems of communication and access

Emergency programmes often have large budgets; a large number of staff who have been recruited quickly; a fleet of vehicles; and food, medicines, shelter materials and other supplies which have to be delivered and distributed. Problems of managing the logistics of an emergency are often made worse by difficulties in communication and access between areas affected by the emergency and the administrative centre.

Table 10.4. Managing large resources

Planning	Monitoring	Review/evaluation
• Need to think about resource requirements in detail. • Need experienced specialists to help assess needs and identify resource requirements for specific interventions, such as health, nutrition, water or transport programmes. • Standard procedures can be developed and used, for example, for assessment of nutrition needs. • Where emergencies are common, supplies can be kept in store and staff kept on alert for rapid redeployment. • Information about the best means of communication and access must be collected in the initial assessment. • Information is needed about the local legal framework, especially insurance and employment laws.	• A clear management structure and division of tasks is needed to analyse who needs what information. • A good, simple system for monitoring the use of resources is essential and must be set up quickly, otherwise a situation can become chaotic. • Administration and information systems need to be monitored themselves, so that problems with the systems can be dealt with quickly. • The supplies 'pipeline' must be monitored to keep track of resources that are on their way and target them effectively.	• Periodic reviews are useful to look at the effectiveness of management and administration procedures so they can be improved. • Evaluation is necessary to be accountable for the large amounts of public money. Long- and short-term objectives must be recognised in the evaluation. • Evaluation of the impact on the recipients is also necessary. What do they think about the effectiveness of the relief effort? It is important to be accountable to them for the large amounts of resources spent in their name.

Cross-border operations: working in areas of disputed sovereignty

It is sometimes necessary to respond to an emergency by working from across the border in another country and through organisations who are opposed to the recognised national government. In these situations, it is often difficult for relief agencies to have continuous direct access to the relief work.

Table 10.5. Cross-border operations

Planning	Monitoring	Review/evaluation
• The agency's own objectives need to be clear when negotiating and planning support. • Planning must include a careful analysis of the group through which the agency will be working: their objectives, organisational capacity and communication channels.	• Systems for monitoring use of the agency's resources need to be decided from the beginning. • Monitoring may be through sporadic visits. • Where the local group is supported by several NGOs and donors, the agency should cooperate with the others to standardise reporting formats and combine visits. Otherwise the group may be overburdened by all the different monitoring requirements.	• Periodic in-depth reviews are important to develop knowledge of the different organisations and how they work.

Initial shortage of staff and resources

In the early stages of an emergency, it may not be possible to recruit staff with specific skills and there may be a shortage of vehicles and other resources (see table 10.6).

Serious consequences of poor decisions

In most emergency situations, a large number of people die or face the risk of death. An emergency operation aims to prevent as much suffering and death as possible. Any mistake or poor decision made by people involved in an emergency operation might result, directly or indirectly, in suffering and death that might otherwise have been avoided (see table 10.7).

Table 10.6. Initial shortage of staff and resources

Planning	Monitoring	Review/evaluation
• This may limit the sort of methods that can be used to conduct an assessment. For example, a nutrition survey can only be conducted by someone with appropriate skills. • The size of the area which can be assessed may be limited by the availability of transport. • It may be possible to team up with other NGOs to share transport and resources.	• The expertise/ experience needed to carefully analyse information needs in order to set up a good monitoring system may not be available initially. Nevertheless, a monitoring system is essential and should be set up as systematically as possible, to be modified later if necessary. • A monitoring system should provide information where it is needed, so that different staff know where to find it.	• A review of the objectives, strategies and procedures may be necessary as soon as staff and resources are available.

Table 10.7. Serious consequences of poor decisions

Planning	Monitoring	Review/evaluation
• Thorough planning is vital to make sure decisions are as good as possible in the circumstances.	• Monitoring is needed to rectify mistakes as soon as possible.	• Any analysis of the experience that identifies what mistakes were made and by whom will be highly sensitive.

2. Specific aim and objectives

As discussed in Chapter 5, it is vital to define the aim and objectives of planning, monitoring, review or evaluation in order to focus the exercise. This will help to decide what information is required. In an emergency, where there is very little time, it is particularly important to be selective in order to produce useful findings quickly. As in all development work, only information that is needed should be collected.

Emergency assessment

In an emergency assessment, information is needed initially by the people responsible for deciding what intervention, if any, is appropriate, and for planning and implementing a relief programme. Save the Children has two distinct steps in the initial planning process:

- The first is to confirm or refute whether the situation is an emergency to which Save the Children should respond (first-tier assessment). This has a triggering function.
- The second follows when it is agreed that Save the Children should respond. The second-tier assessment is to provide information in specific sectors and the general situation in sufficient detail to allow an initial intervention design. This is usually submitted as a project proposal which is used as a basis for discussion between senior managers, technical staff, and community leaders, and for requests for funding from donors.

The next stage is detailed intervention design and activity plans which in turn depend on more detailed information gathering, and can be carried out once the intervention has been approved.

Objective of an emergency assessment

The objective of an assessment is usually to clarify the following issues:

- What is the context of the emergency?
- What are the relevant political and social structures?
- What is the appropriate response to the situation?
- What are the constraints to the response and how can they be addressed?
- Who is affected by the emergency and how? At whom should the interventions be targeted to ensure they reach the people (especially children) most in need?
- What are other agencies doing (including local, formal and informal, governmental and international organisations)? How are they being co-ordinated?
- What should be the agency's role in any response? What should the long- and short-term objectives be?
- What is the most appropriate form of intervention to meet those objectives?
- Who will the agency work with and through, and how?
- What budget and resources are needed to carry out the proposed activities?
- What financial, logistical and administrative systems will be needed?
- How can the work be monitored and evaluated?

When making decisions about appropriate interventions, you also need to consider:

- the long-term effects of different interventions

- the likelihood of continuing donor interest after the emergency
- how to support people (the local and the displaced populations) and local structures as they adapt to the situation.

If these questions are not answered at an early stage, the intervention may not be appropriate and more serious problems may develop.

> A number of materials have been produced to help carry out an emergency assessment. For example, the *Emergency Assessment Toolkit* produced by Save the Children (2002) provides guidelines for emergency assessment including checklists of what information to gather.

A sample report format for assessment is given on page 172.

NOTE: Assessments are not neutral but are 'interventions' in themselves

An ethical approach to conducting assessments demands:

- a commitment to follow-up action, if required
- refraining from taking over if communities can cope, unless the community's response violates basic human rights
- foresight regarding any potentially negative impact of the exercise: avoid methodologies that risk stigmatising children, endangering them in any way, or increasing family separation. In extreme cases, assessments may even endanger the safety of these children, for example, by attracting the attention of groups that prey on defenceless children
- refraining from setting up false expectations.

Disaster preparedness and early warning

Disaster preparedness is an assessment of the likelihood of an emergency occurring, and the collection of information in advance that will help to plan a speedy and effective response. It is an essential part of country-level strategic planning for any agency that is prepared to work in emergency relief. It is needed:

- to anticipate possible sudden-onset emergencies and how people will react, so that any response can be fast and appropriate
- to monitor the progress of slow-onset emergencies, gather information to support requests for funding, and plan appropriate work to try to prevent and respond to the emergency.

Save the Children now requires all country programmes to produce disaster preparedness plans as part of their strategic planning process.

Where emergencies of a particular type are common, as in the following example of floods in Bangladesh, answers to many of the questions asked in an assessment may already be known. In this case, an assessment can be more specific, finding out how to implement the disaster response as quickly and effectively as possible.

> **For example:** In Bangladesh, Save the Children has developed disaster preparedness guidelines based on previous disaster relief experience (particularly floods). When a cyclone struck in April 1992, these guidelines provided a detailed outline for relief operations to fit the organisational structure of Save the Children in Bangladesh. For instance, staff filling designated 'reaction' positions were ready to travel to Dhaka and onwards immediately on request, as soon as they knew that a severe cyclone had struck. One of the most helpful parts of the guidelines were the supplies and equipment lists. It was a simple matter to calculate total needs from the supplies and usage equations, and the list of suppliers was invaluable (for instance plastic sheeting was obtained from about five different wholesalers until the manufacturer was working at full capacity). Budgeting was made relatively simple as unit costs were already available.

Defining relief programme aims and objectives

The overall aims of a relief programme are usually concerned with mitigating the effect of an emergency and minimising the suffering caused. The aims should also be determined by the particular focus, values and principles of the agency concerned.

> The Code of Conduct for the International Red Cross and Red Crescent Movement and NGOs in Disaster Relief [1] sets out ten principles, which a large number of relief agencies have signed up to. This Code may be useful in setting out aims. The ten principles are:
> 1. The humanitarian imperative comes first.
> 2. Aid is given regardless of race, creed or nationality of the recipients.
> 3. Aid will not be used to further a particular political or religious standpoint.
> 4. We shall endeavour not to act as instruments of government foreign policy.
> 5. We shall respect culture and custom.
> 6. We shall attempt to build disaster response on local capacities.
> 7. Ways shall be found to involve programme beneficiaries in the management of relief aid.

---

[1] For text see www.ifrc.org/publications

8. Relief aid must strive to reduce future vulnerabilities to disaster as well as meeting basic needs.
9. We hold ourselves accountable to both those we seek to assist and those from whom we accept resources.
10. In our information publicity and advertising activities we shall recognise disaster victims as dignified humans, not hopeless objects.

SMART objectives (see Chapters 5 and 6) are also required. There are a number of different tools that can be used to define SMART objectives against which an emergency response programme can be planned, monitored and evaluated. For example, the SPHERE project's Humanitarian Charter and Set of Minimum Standards in Disaster Response[2] can be used to specify the minimum standards to be attained in each of the following areas of disaster response:

- water supply and sanitation
- nutrition
- food aid
- shelter and site planning
- health services.

For each of the minimum standards there is a set of key indicators which show whether the standard has been attained.

For example: The Khovd Emergency Project in Mongolia aimed to alleviate the immediate and longer-term impact of the severe winter on the most vulnerable children and families by:

- reducing animal losses by providing animal feed to vulnerable herders
- preventing malnutrition by providing food aid to vulnerable families
- improving the diet of herder children by providing food to school dormitories
- improving the overall welfare of children in school dormitories by providing bedding sets
- contributing to the fuel supply for schools, dormitories, kindergartens and hospitals
- improving the emergency preparedness of major stakeholders (emergency committees, herders, etc) through the enhancement of capacity in planning and managing local resources in order to cope with future emergencies.

Save the Children has also produced guidelines for good practice for education and child protection in emergencies. These can be used to help set objectives in child protection and education.

---

[2] Sphere Project (2000) *Humanitarian Charter and Minimum Standards in Disaster Response*

Monitoring

Monitoring is essential in a rapidly changing situation. The purpose of monitoring is to find out whether the relief programme is effective, and how strategies should be modified to make sure that it is. To do this, it is necessary to monitor:

- **the programme**, including the process (how it is carried out) and the impact it is having
- **changes in the situation**, including population movements, political changes, and changes in factors affecting health, nutrition, and socio-economic activities (see also 'Information systems' on page 168).

A monitoring system can only work in the following conditions:

- For process monitoring there must be a clear management structure with a clear division of tasks (for example, movement of supplies within the country, shipping from outside, donor liaison and programme management at different levels). Each task has different information requirements, and the information must be collected, analysed, disseminated and stored in a way that is relevant to those tasks. Clear systems are particularly important where there is a high turnover of staff.
- For impact monitoring clear objectives must be set at an early stage.
- All staff, including managers and technicians, should be involved in planning a monitoring system to make sure they understand the purpose of the information as a tool for predicting future conditions and building institutional knowledge.
- The importance of monitoring must be recognised and the cost included in the budget.

(See Chapter 7 for more detail about monitoring systems.)

Review

The purpose of a review will depend on the problems that have arisen and any particular issues that need to be studied in more detail. For example:

- a review of the effectiveness of management systems and administrative procedures
- if the situation has changed, a review of the original objectives to see how they should be modified
- a review to see what effect the relief work is having on other factors that influence the problem (food production, etc)
- a review of the way in which different agencies cooperate, to see how this can be improved.

Evaluation

Evaluation in emergencies is often carried out for the following purposes and objectives:

- to demonstrate accountability to the affected population: what was their experience of the impact of the programme and of the various inputs?
- to demonstrate accountability to donors for the large amounts of money spent in relief
- to provide lessons for future emergency work. For this to be useful, general points must be extracted from the evaluation of specific experiences, the conclusions must be disseminated and the lessons learnt incorporated in future responses
- self-evaluation is necessary to help build up local capacity to respond effectively to emergencies. This is particularly important in countries which often experience emergencies.

It is often difficult to measure the impact of an emergency intervention and to produce useful evaluation findings for the reasons outlined in section 1 of this chapter (pages 147–153).

3. Key questions and indicators relevant in emergencies

The questions that need to be answered in planning, monitoring, review and evaluation of emergency response will depend on the particular situation, who requires the information and what for. The checklist of questions for an emergency assessment given in Save the Children's Emergency Assessment Toolkit[3] provide an insight into key questions that may need to be monitored in different situations.

Indicators

The following headings point to the major areas that emergency interventions will hope to affect, and which should therefore be included in planning, monitoring and evaluation. Each is discussed briefly below.

Mortality

Mortality rates are a basic impact indicator for all emergencies. This includes: the overall mortality rate (crude mortality rate – CMR); the under-five mortality rate; and cause-specific mortality rates.

---

[3] Save the Children UK (2002) *Emergency Assessment Toolkit*

Centre for Disease Control (CDC) defines an emergency with a crude mortality rate of one death per 10,000 population per day, or an under-five mortality rate of two deaths per 10,000 per day.

Mortality data is often required by donors, but data is hard to obtain and the information is sensitive. Surveys would need to be very large to be meaningful and are not practicable. Mortality can be recorded as part of a healthcare system. It may be possible to look at the causes of death over a specified period to see how they differ from the norm for that time of year. Where mortality data is not available, rates of malnutrition are a useful indicator.

Morbidity

Morbidity data is another basic impact indicator that is always relevant in emergencies.

This includes age- and sex-specific incidence rates of major health problems and diseases that have public health importance, including sexual violence/rape.

Clinic data only reflects the diseases for which people come to the clinic for treatment. This depends on how well staffed, stocked and run the clinic is, and different perceptions of disease. Surveys are unnecessary. Reliable reporting of actual cases and the presence of health risk factors which would contribute to transmission of diseases are sufficient to require action.

Water supply and sanitation

People affected by disasters are more likely to become ill and to die from diseases related to inadequate sanitation and water supplies than from any other major cause.

The SPHERE handbook sets out minimum standards and indicators for analysis, water supply, excreta disposal, vector control, solid waste management, drainage, hygiene promotion, and human resource capacity and training (see Tool 14 for a summary).

Nutrition

Access to food and maintenance of adequate nutritional status is a critical determinant of people's survival in the initial stages of an emergency. Malnutrition can be the most serious public health problem and may be a leading cause of death, directly or indirectly. Those most commonly affected are children between six months and five years old.

Malnutrition is a key indicator, particularly in food emergencies. The prevalence of acute malnutrition in children under five years is a proxy indicator for the health and well-being of a community. If the prevalence of acute malnutrition (classified as a ratio of weight to height which is less than 80 per cent of the average) is greater than 10 per cent, the situation should be investigated further. If it is over 15 per cent, the situation is very serious.

A nutrition survey is the best way to obtain information about malnutrition, and can provide a quantitative measure which can be compared with later surveys (if they use the same methodology). Details of how to carry out nutrition surveys are given in the Médécins Sans Frontières nutrition handbook.[4]

SPHERE sets out minimum standards and indicators in nutrition under the headings: analysis, general nutritional support to the population, nutritional support to those suffering from malnutrition, and human resource capacity and training.

Food aid
All people need to consume adequate quantities of food of sufficient quality for their health and well-being. If a community's normal means of accessing food is compromised by disaster, a food aid intervention may be required. When they do not have enough food they may engage in short term survival strategies such as disposal of household assets, which can lead to destitution, ill health and other long-term negative consequences.

SPHERE sets out minimum standards and indicators for Food Aid under the headings: analysis, requirements, targeting, resource management, logistics, distribution, human resource capacity and training.

Shelter and site planning
Shelter is a critical determinant of survival in the initial stage of an emergency. Beyond survival, shelter is necessary to enhance resistance to disease and provides protection from the environment. It is also important for human dignity and to sustain family and community life in difficult circumstances.

SPHERE sets out minimum standards and indicators in: analysis, housing (shelter) clothing, household items, site selection and planning, and human resource capacity and training.

Health services
In emergencies, major loss of lives due to increased incidence of disease and injuries is common. Natural disasters, warfare and conflicts, and technological disasters tend to result in excess mortality and morbidity. Diseases responsible for such increases have also been identified: measles, diarrhoeas (including dysentery and cholera) acute respiratory infections, malnutrition and malaria.

SPHERE sets out minimum standards and indicators in: analysis, measles control, control of communicable diseases, health care services, and human resource capacity and training.

---

[4] Médécins Sans Frontières (1997) *Refugee Health: An approach to emergency situations.* Macmillan, London

Livelihood

The impact of an emergency on people's capacity to support themselves is also a vital consideration when assessing the severity of an emergency. Important factors include: food production (cereals and livestock); water availability; food storage; access to markets; terms of trade; security issues and the effect of the emergency on local structures and organisations.

Save the Children has developed the Household Economy Analysis and the Intra-Household Model to help assess these effects.

Psychosocial well-being

This term reflects the relationship between psychological and social factors. It is as important as physical health, particularly for children, since they are still in the early stages of development. Factors that affect psychosocial well-being include: the strength of family and community structures; daily routines, including play and school for children; protection from violence and fear. Save the Children has identified child protection and education as key factors that affect the well-being of children in emergencies. Frameworks to help monitor and evaluate these are given in Tool 14.

Child protection

Child protection is a complicated and socially sensitive area, and because of this it is difficult to assess in detail without trained specialists. Very careful and discrete enquiries with communities may be required to find out about the most taboo issues, such as sexual abuse. However, it is essential to monitor these issues in emergencies, where children are more vulnerable than ever, in order to protect the rights of children to survival, development, protection and participation.

The situation with regard to child protection can be examined by looking at the following: children's access to basic entitlements; the risks to child development, including work, sexual exploitation, malnutrition, recruitment into armed forces, separation; the risks of abduction or trafficking; the family's and community's capacity to provide security and protection for children; children's roles in the household both before and after the emergency; and support available to infants and small children left alone with fathers. The availability of safe areas for play and recreation, and the care of children who have had traumatic experiences are also essential.

Children under 18 who have been separated from their primary caregivers – usually parents – are termed 'separated children'. They are among the most vulnerable groups in emergency situations and require special attention. There may also be children in institutions who may be abandoned, or have their food and water supplies cut off, or find themselves in a conflict zone.

A framework to help monitor and evaluate child protection issues in emergencies has been developed by Save the Children and is given in Tool 14.

Education

Re-establishing a sense of normality after a disaster is essential for children's mental well-being. Education and play are both essential components of normality. A 'Basic Education Framework' (see Tool 14) has been developed by Save the Children for use in emergencies which emphasises the need for a holistic view in educating the child. The package is based on the UN Convention on the Rights of the Child, with its call for universal basic education, and emphasises the participation of children. This outlines the areas of curriculum that should be covered in education in emergencies, and can be used to develop objectives and indicators for both process and impact of emergency education programmes.

Assessing the underlying causes of a problem

It is important to identify the factors that combine to cause the problem and that influence its severity.

Information about the underlying causes of a problem can be used:

- to show how different interventions can affect the underlying causes of the emergency in the long and short term
- to see how the long-term effects of an intervention could make the situation worse, for example, depressing local food production by providing free food
- to identify indicators for monitoring changes in the situation
- to show how future events, such as rains, harvest, peace agreements, etc may influence the situation.

Who is affected, where and how?

Different groups of people will be affected by and will cope with the emergency in different ways. Information about these differences is needed to determine which interventions are most appropriate and how they could affect each of the groups. This is crucial in ensuring that certain groups are not discriminated against. It is also essential to help target interventions towards the most vulnerable people, particularly children.

- How are different communities and groups within communities affected (including different socio-economic groups, people with disabilities, women, children, religious and ethnic groups)? How has their livelihood been affected (for example, food production, access to markets, terms of trade, and access to and control over resources)? Which groups are threatened by loss of livelihood and destitution (eg, using the HEA described above)?
- How has the psychosocial well-being of different groups, particularly children, been affected (for example, disruption of families and communities, children separated from their families, fear, anxiety, neglect or abuse)? Which factors are causing distress?

Figure 10.1. Conceptual model of the causes of malnutrition in emergencies

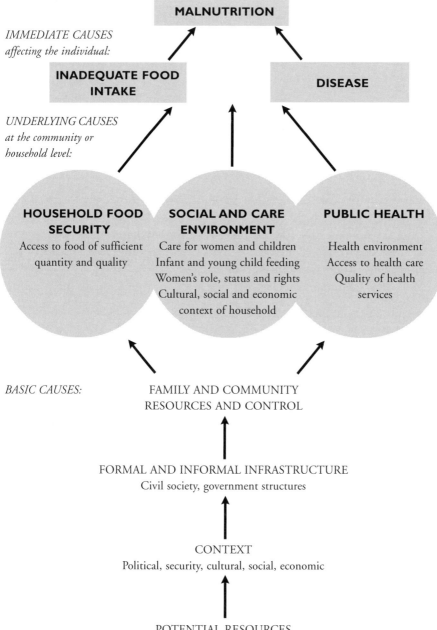

From *The Sphere Project: Humanitarian charter and minimum standards in disaster response* (2000)

- How are communities coping? What support do they need? Which individuals need specialist care?
- How are different people coping with the situation? What resources do they have, what do they need? How are they organised?
- How are children affected? How are they coping? What are their needs?
- How will different groups adapt after the crisis? (For example, nomads who have lost their stock as a result of drought will not be able to resume their former activities.)
- How have people been affected by this situation in the past, and which strategies were most successful?
- Where are the worst affected areas? How can they be reached?
- How can targeting best be done, and who should do it? (community based targeting can be a good way of ensuring transparency by setting criteria for targeting at public meetings, checking names, and so on).

Information about these questions can also be used to help make a case to governments and donors for continuing assistance after the crisis.

What is the performance and effectiveness of the disaster response?

Emergency activities are usually planned and implemented quickly, and administrative systems have to be established quickly to support them. It is important to keep monitoring both the activities and the administrative systems to see whether they should be modified or how they can be improved. To do this, it is important to answer the following key questions:

- What are the specific objectives of each activity and administrative system? (eg, see SPHERE minimum standards)
- What are the expected results of the activities?
- What indicators will show that the work is efficient and effective?
- Can targets be set (if relevant)?
- How can the work be managed? What are the logistical, administrative and financial requirements? What systems are needed to manage the programme?

(An evaluation of the administrative systems after the emergency is only useful if more general points can be extracted which could be applied elsewhere.)

The answers to these questions are essential for decision-making about the future of the programmes, and for learning effectively from experience. In order to answer them, it will be necessary to clarify specific objectives for the different activities and identify indicators to show how effective they are. This highlights the need to set objectives and indicators early in the programme.

The performance and effectiveness of the disaster response should be monitored and evaluated. Indicators for making sure this is done are given in SPHERE, Analysis standard 3 under all the sectors:

- Information collected should be timely and useful, accurate, logical, consistent and transparent.
- Systems should be in place to assess the impact – positive and negative.
- There should be regular analytical reporting.
- Systems should be in place for information flow between programme, sectors, affected population, etc.
- Information should be gathered on effectiveness at meeting the needs of different groups.
- Women, men and children from affected population should be regularly consulted and involved in monitoring.
- The programme should be evaluated with reference to stated objectives and minimum standards.

Is the work carried out according to widely accepted values?

The accepted values and principles of disaster relief are expressed in several instruments. These include international humanitarian law, international human rights law, refugee law, and the Code of Conduct for the International Red Cross and Red Crescent Movement and NGOs in Disaster Relief. The SPHERE Humanitarian Charter draws on all of these. These instruments can be used to monitor and evaluate disaster response.

For example: The Disaster Emergencies Committee (DEC) carried out an evaluation of the response to the Gujarat[5] earthquake of January 2001 using the Red Cross Code. The evaluation had to assess the disaster responses of a number of different DEC agencies, and the evaluators wanted to be as objective as possible. To do this they needed a set of values agreed by the participating agencies; and a method of analysing in a systematic manner the views of those affected.

A public opinion survey was used to gather views on the responses according to the principles in the Code which are set out briefly above. There were some difficulties with using the Code for evaluation, but on the whole it was felt that it was useful and fair. It enabled evaluators to assess the relief effort according to the principles upheld by the agencies, and compare them with the response of other agencies, including an Indian NGO. The DEC is now planning to develop indicators of compliance with the Code.

---

[5] Disaster Mitigation Institute, Humanitarian Initiatives, Mango (2001) *Independent Evaluation: The DEC response to the earthquake in Gujarat*, Disasters Emergency Committee.

4. Methods of collecting and analysing information

In an emergency it is important to collect essential information only, quickly and accurately.

The four main methods for collecting information discussed here are:
1. a review of existing information and knowledge
2. rapid appraisal methods: for qualitative information
3. surveys: for quantitative information
4. information systems.

These are followed by a brief discussion of how to decide which combination of methods to use and analysing and interpreting the results.

The first three methods listed above are useful for planning, monitoring, review and evaluation. Information systems may be useful for monitoring. Qualitative information is often the most accurate, but quantitative data may be required as evidence for donors that a problem exists. A combination of methods should be used. Cross-checking is always essential. (See also Chapter 4 and Tools 1 and 2 for methods of data collection and analysis.)

A review of existing information and knowledge

This includes the following steps:
•   Find out about any local information systems and contingency relief plans of government and UN.
•   Find out what happened last time there was an emergency, to identify useful precedents and to avoid previous mistakes.
•   Find out who was there last time, especially local employees of relief agencies, and learn from their experience.
•   Read relevant documents and publications and talk with the key people in your own and other organisations and in relevant government departments.
•   Summarise findings in the form of brief notes and tables to use for future reference. A set of questions should emerge, which may form the basis of the next stage of an assessment.
•   Analyse existing information critically for possible bias and inaccuracies.
•   Find out the names of local people in the area who may help during an assessment.

Rapid appraisals

Rapid appraisal techniques can give a preliminary understanding of an emergency situation after a short visit. The emphasis is on making the best possible use of local knowledge, and making contact with the communities who will be involved in the work. The approach can be used to find out how different people have been affected at household level. These details help ensure that interventions are relevant. For example, in food-related emergencies, insights into how people are eating and sharing and how they are supplementing their diet have allowed planners to introduce more appropriate rations.

Many of the rapid appraisal techniques are the same as those used in PLA (see Tool 1 for more detail), but in emergency situations the information is required more quickly than in most development work. The use of PLA techniques in emergencies is also constrained to some extent by the pressures on the affected population, including war or civil conflict, physical suffering, fear, grief and desperation. It is important to remember that in some situations interviewers and observers may pose a threat to the people, interpreters and authorities concerned. Rapid assessment teams can compromise these groups by asking the wrong questions, quoting their answers to the wrong person, or being seen to notice the wrong thing.

Surveys

Surveys are the best way to obtain objective measurements of, for example, the rate of malnutrition and quantitative household statistics. Nutrition surveys are the most common type of survey carried out in emergencies. (See Tool 2 for procedures, strengths and weaknesses of surveys.)

Information systems

Impact and process monitoring are both important in managing emergency relief programmes. In addition, in situations which regularly experience emergencies it is sometimes useful to establish an information system to monitor changes in the factors that can combine to cause an emergency. (The examples given below are all of long-term monitoring systems.)

For example: There has been an in-depth Nutritional Surveillance Programme (NSP) in Ethiopia that has delivered consistent high quality data for North Wollo/ Wag Hamra, Tigray, North Shewa and Wolayita since 1974. (It used to cover Oromia Zone, South Wollo and Hararghe as well.) The NSP reports are produced four times a year, and full 'Focus' reports are produced twice a year. The NSP has been a valuable tool in triggering relief responses, as it is widely seen as credible and accurate.

In addition to the NSP, the programme set up Nutritional Monitoring Teams (NMT) during 1998, as concern increased about the deteriorating situation. These teams were conducting nutritional assessments on a monthly basis to allow for more efficient and effective food aid targeting.

There have also been an increasing number of Household Food Economy reports produced, both 'baseline' and highlighting the deteriorating situation. This gives a clearer picture of what is actually happening in the different 'food economy groups' in these areas.

Strengths of information systems in emergencies
- They provide information on a regular basis to people who need it.
- They help to identify long-term trends from year to year.
- They establish communication networks between communities, field workers and relief managers.
- The continuous contact with communities and individuals can help build up an in-depth understanding of how people are affected and can be used as a basis for more long-term development work.
- They can provide a mechanism to identify flashpoints or 'critical thresholds' in communities.
- They can be used to record social stress indicators including local food supply and access to food, and individual stress indicators, including weight loss, disease, mortality and migration.
- The information can be used to support requests for relief supplies and to target relief to the most vulnerable.
- Donors do not have to send their own consultants to monitor the relief programme.

Weaknesses of information systems
- A full information system is expensive and labour intensive.
- It is difficult to make a system sustainable or to hand it over to the government because of the cost and possible difficulties in deciding which government department is most relevant.
- It is difficult to analyse information needs and select only useful information to collect.
- It is difficult to produce the findings in a form that will be useful for all the intended audience: that is sufficiently brief to be read, but detailed enough to be useful.
- Donors often do not respond quickly to information from the field: there are many political and institutional constraints.
- When information is always collected from the same individuals they may find this an imposition and become less cooperative.
- It raises expectations in the communities monitored. It is difficult to collect information for early warning when there is no relief programme providing goods.

- Nutritional status data is meaningless (unless it shows acute starvation) when taken out of context and without good background information to help interpret it.
- A system can become inflexible.

Prerequisites for the success of an information system
- A detailed understanding of local socio-economic relationships, including seasonal trends.
- Selection of essential and useful information, based on this understanding.
- Support and training of people collecting and analysing information.
- Data collection methods that can be easily standardised to make it possible to compare results over time.
- An established link between information and decision-making, to gain access to resources at local, regional, national and international levels.
- Precise objectives that define how the information is to be used, and what the system is trying to achieve.
- Any local intervention needs to be put in the context of donor policy and the national economic situation.
- Active involvement of people responsible for the work, including relevant government departments. Extensive community involvement may be unrealistic in communities under stress.
- Production of information in a form that is useful to a range of people.

Deciding which methods to use

A combination of methods should be used for collecting information. In order to decide which methods to use and in which combination, consider the following:
- What information is required given the feasible response?
- How will the information be used? (Is quantitative data required by donors?)
- Do you need information about the immediate and short-term situation ('snapshot') or long-term trends?
- What are the gaps in existing information and how can they be filled?
- How much time is available?
- Who is available and what are their skills and experience?
- What other resources are available (people, vehicles, fuel, money, computers, etc)?

See also Chapter 4 and Chapter 5 for a sequence of questions to ask in order to help decide which approach and methods would be most suitable.

For example: Save the Children arguably helped prevent a large scale crisis happening in Amhara, Ethiopia in 1999/2000. Save the Children participated in the crucial May 1999 helicopter survey that galvanised donors into action, and used a lot of the information from programmes on the ground and the variety of surveillance tools that Save the Children was running to great effect. The subsequent food aid prevented mass movement and may also have prevented mass starvation.

Analysing and interpreting findings

See Chapter 5 for questions relating to analysis.

It is important to analyse the findings as quickly as possible, in order to make decisions and act quickly. For both planning and monitoring it is important to concentrate on only the essential information, but also to pick up any unexpected information that could be relevant. When interpreting the findings it is vital to check that the interpretation is as correct as possible. Although lengthy consultation processes are not possible, it is important to seek the judgement of experienced staff and of people affected by the emergency.

For example: Community involvement in targeting the distribution of food aid has been used successfully in Mongolia. Community groups helped to establish criteria for targeting animal feed and food aid, and presented the criteria in public meetings. This made the process transparent and understood, which was confirmed by an evaluation. It also made it possible to highlight problems: one of the criteria was that recipients of animal feed should have a minimum of four children in a family. This inadvertently meant that younger families were excluded. This was identified by community respondants in an evaluation and will be incorporated into future relief programmes.

- Quantitative and qualitative findings should be interpreted together.
- Analysis of quantitative data should be carried out in the field if possible. This is easier with portable computers and programs like Epi-info.
- Learn as you go. Record important points in a notebook as soon as possible. Include observations, ideas and hunches, record reasons behind them. Label notes with date, location and names of people.
- Discuss findings regularly with other members of the research team, staff from different agencies and community members.
- Analyse nutrition survey results and discuss with community leaders:
  - What is their response to the findings?
  - Are the findings important to them?
  - Are they concerned about the malnourished and destitute in the community? What are their priorities?
  - What is their analysis of the situation?

5. Presenting findings

In an emergency it is important to present the findings clearly and unambiguously to all the people involved in the relief programme. For an assessment of an emergency, the first presentation of findings may be in the form of a quick communication to head office. There is a range of technologies that can be used for this, most importantly email which can be sent by land phones, satellite phones, mobile telephones, and radio. Fax and verbal messages from radio and telephone are also used.

Information and communication

Information management is vital to prevent the amount of available data overwhelming an organisation's ability to act.

1. The first step is to produce a preliminary assessment, as fast as possible, giving a broad picture, along the lines of the sample format below.

> **Sample format**
> I.   Summary
> II.   Quick-reference box of figures and statistics
> III.   Describe the sectors (parts of checklists) assessed and the methods used
> IV.   Background to current situation
> V.   General situation (following Section 10.1 in Emergency Assessment Toolkit)
> VI.   Report by sector, highlighting key problems (inadequacy re standards plus insufficient coping capability), and citing cross-checked evidence/ info for each key problem
> VII. Recommended course of action:
> •   Aim or problem
> •   Objective of action
> •   Recommendations for implementation strategies
> •   Activities
> •   Resources needed (financial, management, technical capacity)
> •   Recommendations for medium- to long-term solutions
> •   Constraints and assumptions
> VIII. Appendices, including at least:
> •   Agencies on the ground and their activities: NGOs, UN, governmental
> •   Map
> •   Contact list
> •   Other materials and details, organised.

2. Produce regular updates, or sitreps (situation reports). These will initially be required every two days, and may go down to every two weeks.

The following headings are recommended in Save the Children's format for internal sitreps:

1. Security/movements
2. Situation information:
   • political developments
   • relationships with government
   • other issues (eg, early onset of winter)
3. General humanitarian situation
4. Ongoing Save the Children programme activity, by sector
5. Ongoing advocacy/lobbying activity
6. New Save the Children programme initiatives/planning/assessments
7. Alliance
8. Human resources
9. Communications/media
10. Finance/funding
11. Planned initiatives for forthcoming few days.

Communities

When discussing findings with communities who have been involved in planning, monitoring, review or evaluation, it is important to be clear about possible results of the exercise in order to avoid raising unrealistic expectations. Describe the next stage of the work. It is also important to thank people for their help, information and time.

Oral briefings

This may be the best way to present findings to many audiences, including other agencies, donors and partners. Briefings should be well prepared, based on factual information, and if possible supported by diagrams and maps. The following example shows the importance of presenting accurate and detailed facts.

For example: When managing the cyclone relief distribution in Bangladesh, some information proved to be wrong in small but vital respects. For instance, near the end of one hour-long planning session it was discovered that bamboo poles were to be delivered in 20-foot rather than 12-foot lengths. For the number of poles per lorry this meant that they would be arriving on three tonne, rather than one and a half tonne trucks which could not reach the planned off-loading sites. So plans had to be remade and a lot of time was wasted. Thereafter all planning sessions were preceded with a request for accuracy and for clarification to be immediately requested when necessary. Everyone was reminded to differentiate properly between facts and assumptions.

Report writing

Advice on writing reports is given in *Emergency Assessment Toolkit* (Save the Children, 2002). Advice on writing up evaluations and reviews is given in Chapter 8.

Summary

- It is important to recognise the many constraints and compromises imposed on planning, monitoring and evaluation in emergency situations, and to work round them.
- The SPHERE project provides principles, minimum standards and indicators that can be used for planning, monitoring, review and evaluation in emergency situations.
- Programme aims can be based on accepted principles set out in codes of conduct for disaster relief. Objectives and indicators can be based on SPHERE minimum standards.
- Emergency assessment is undertaken in two tiers. First, to confirm or refute whether the situation is an emergency to which the agency should respond and second, to provide information on the general situation and specific sectors to allow intervention design.
- Key questions and indicators relevant in emergencies include mortality, morbidity, water supply and sanitation, nutrition, food aid, shelter, health services, livelihood, child protection, and education. The underlying causes of the problem need to be understood and monitored.
- Details of who is affected, where and how are required to ensure appropriate support is targeted to different groups.
- Disaster preparedness should be part of country level strategic planning. It involves collecting relevant information in advance to enable a speedy disaster response.
- Information systems – to gather this information on a continuous basis – have an important role in situations that regularly experience emergencies to make sure relief is effectively targeted.
- Analysing and interpreting findings must be fast and transparent. Community involvement is vital.
- Findings must be presented clearly and concisely in reports, regular sitreps, and oral briefings.

Chapter 11
Planning, monitoring and evaluating advocacy

Why should there be a special chapter on planning, monitoring and evaluating advocacy?

Advocacy has been carried out by NGOs for many years and is an increasingly important strategy in development. It is an essential component of rights-based programming, focusing on building constituencies around different issues, and working to change the broader context in which an agency works.

As with any other development activity, good planning, monitoring, evaluation and impact assessment are essential for good management of advocacy, for accountability, and to make sure lessons are learned to improve practice in the short and long term. To do this it is essential to define what you are trying to achieve through advocacy, and how you will know whether or not you are succeeding. The findings from monitoring and evaluation can also be used for further advocacy purposes.

For example: Targets were set for international action against child poverty at a major conference in 2001. Campaigners against child poverty, including Save the Children, produced a report a year later to remind the different conference participants of what they had promised to do, to acknowledge the action that has been taken, and to re-state what remains to be done. This report is a useful advocacy tool, and its launch was an important advocacy event in its own right.

Budget monitoring is a means of monitoring policy implementation, and so can help establish the impact of advocacy on the ground. It is a well known monitoring technique, with tools developed around it. The information can also be used later to facilitate further advocacy. For example, the Save the Children programme in Brazil is involved in supporting a national civil society coalition that advocates around the national education budget. This has been going on for a few years and the coalition is now very adept at defending the national education budget and making sure key priorities are included. New efforts are now underway to include budget monitoring activities to monitor the impact of their policy influence on children.

Section 1 of this chapter offers a general definition of advocacy and a description of some of the main styles of advocacy adopted by NGOs. Section 2 emphasises the importance of setting clear aims and objectives for advocacy activities. The rest of the chapter then focuses on monitoring and evaluating advocacy. Section 3 stresses the importance of looking at both the process and the impact of advocacy work. It considers ways of deciding what to monitor and evaluate by creating a 'model of change' as a means of understanding the advocacy process you are following. Each element of the process can then be assessed.

Section 4 goes on to consider how advocacy can be monitored and evaluated: how to use your model of change to develop a framework that can help to identify useful indicators (more frameworks are presented in Tool 13); who should be involved; a brief overview of some of the methods that can be used; and approaches to assessing the impact of advocacy.

Finally, Section 5 looks at some of the challenges involved in monitoring and evaluating advocacy activities and some ways of addressing them.

1. What is advocacy?

Save the Children defines advocacy as follows:

"Advocacy is acting with and on behalf of children to influence the policies and actions of others to improve the fulfilment of children's rights."

"Save the Children UK exists to fight for children's rights to survival, development, protection and participation. We can never fulfil these rights alone. To do so, those with power over children must be persuaded to behave more justly. This is advocacy".[1]

Different pathways are adopted by NGOs in advocacy strategies. These can be grouped broadly under two headings: a) direct policy influence; and b) developing capacity for advocacy.

Direct policy influence:

This is when NGOs influence governments, multilateral institutions and multinational companies. The aim is to change policy, legislation, or procedures, and to make sure those changes are implemented in practice.

This is done through a combination of:

- lobbying – influencing through direct, private communication with decision-makers
- campaigning – speaking publicly on an issue with a view to generating a response from the wider public, which in turn puts pressure on decision-makers
- education, raising awareness – using the press, marketing and education to

---

[1] Save the Children UK *Organisational Advocacy Plan*, Draft, October 2001

build an understanding of issues to provide a more receptive context for change
- shareholder, consumer and investor activism – using this to put pressure on companies to change particular policies and practices
- practical problem-solving – advising on ways in which policies can be improved and implemented.

> **For example:** Save the Children has been advocating on child labour in several ways:
> - Engaging with companies who have been targets of bad press in relation to child labour, developing programmes on the ground that aim to promote the best interests of child labourers.
> - Persuading companies not to fire children, but instead to work with Save the Children to provide safety nets for child workers and their families and to access quality education.
> - Working with the media to put across a more sophisticated understanding of reasons why children work.
> - Campaigning – using *Right Angle*, the Save the Children magazine for young people, to show young supporters of Save the Children what they as consumers can do to promote responsible approaches to child labour.
> - Lobbying the UK Government and others to ensure that children and civil society are consulted when government draws up national plans of action to respond to the relevant ILO convention.

Developing capacity for advocacy

This is when NGOs work to develop the capacity of other groups and organisations to influence policy themselves. These may include NGOs, community based organisations, civil society organisations (CSOs), field offices from the same organisation, youth groups, representative organisations (such as trades unions), groups, and individuals. Different organisations take different approaches. For example, this can be done through the following:
- Supporting and strengthening networks, movements, civil society groups and grassroots organisations.
- Supporting people to analyse their own situations, identify their rights, make their views heard, share their experience and hold decision-makers accountable. This is a process of empowerment, whereby previously marginalised groups become able to participate in shaping policy.
- Supporting children to participate in shaping policy – this is an essential role for promoting child rights.
- Drawing other civil society organisations into the debate.
- Facilitating debates between policy-makers and citizens or interest groups.

> **For example:** A three-day Children's Forum was organised immediately prior to the UN General Assembly Special Session on Children, in May 2002. This was an opportunity for children to voice their concerns directly to the leaders and policy-makers of the world, and to work on how they could influence decision-making in programmes that affect them. The outputs from the Children's Forum were reported back to the plenary session.

Advocacy can work at different levels and use different approaches simultaneously.

The weight given to each level will depend on the situation and how each partner wants to bring about change.

How is advocacy done?

Advocacy tactics depend on what approach is taken, and the approach to planning, monitoring and evaluation needs to be useful, realistic and responsive to those tactics.

> **For example:** Some advocacy strategies that aim at changing policy and practice are becoming very flexible and 'light-footed'. Governments and companies use sophisticated public relations techniques to deflect criticism, so you have to act very quickly, flexibly and opportunistically to keep exerting influence to bring about meaningful change, not just a change in rhetoric. The basic advocacy plan often consists of:
> - **A goal**: why are we saying this, and why now?
> - **Simple specific objectives**: long and short term.
> - **An agreement of what you will or will not do**: for example, talk in public, attack a particular organisation, talk on others' behalf, and produce a report.
> - **Then be really flexible**, and be prepared to 'piggy-back' on different events and actors.

The flexible nature of campaigning work makes good monitoring and evaluation particularly important. Ongoing evaluation can help adapt influencing strategies to changes in the political climate.

The rest of this chapter looks at approaches to planning, monitoring and evaluating advocacy activities, which need to be tailored to the particular style of advocacy being used.

2. Setting advocacy aims and objectives

Long-term aims

All the organisations involved must be clear about long-term aims, their vision, and political understanding of advocacy. It is also essential to be clear about each organisation's role and legitimacy in conducting advocacy work, who they represent, and why. This affects the approaches that should be taken and what is looked for in assessing impact.

Objectives

It is important to have objectives for advocacy work, which can be changed when necessary. However, setting clear objectives for development activities is often difficult and there are additional challenges associated with advocacy work. Analysing the advocacy process can help set objectives. This is described below (under 'what to monitor and evaluate'). Some of the challenges are listed briefly here:

- There are often a large number of stakeholders involved: this can make the development of agreed advocacy objectives a long and difficult process.
- Specific short- and long-term objectives are needed: for example, to achieve a policy change, followed by a change in practice as the policy is implemented, which should in turn result in actual change in people's lives.
- Advocacy objectives should incorporate a vision of social change which requires a long-term timeframe to be achieved.
- Making objectives realistic can be a problem; on the other hand it is good to aim high. (Ask for the earth and you might get it.)
- Changing objectives at strategic and tactical level is common. It is vital to be flexible and opportunistic, for example to take advantage of new political opportunities. Document the reasons for changes.
- Plurality of objectives: this allows a range of stakeholders to take part, and some flexibility of response. However, there is a danger in having too many objectives as it makes the campaign less focused.
- Objectives need to be simple and also provide oppositional contrasts.
- Objectives must be backed by good policy analysis and reliable evidence.
- Time limits on objectives are useful for motivation. They need to be reviewed frequently.

3. Deciding what to monitor and evaluate

Process and impact

As has already been stressed in earlier chapters of this book, it is important to assess both the process and the impact of any activity. Both are essential to allow us to modify and adapt our advocacy strategy during implementation.

Process monitoring of advocacy activities is needed in order to judge:
- are the techniques working?
- are people being reached and is the message understood by targets?
- are the most appropriate targets and channels being used?
- are you involving and collaborating with the relevant people, organisations and bodies?

Impact monitoring, evaluation and impact assessment are needed to know:
- are the objectives likely to be achieved, ie, will there be/have there been changes on the ground?
- what more needs to be done to sustain changes?
- what unintended impacts – positive and negative – have occurred?
- have promises of policy changes really been implemented (or are they still only rhetoric)?
- what can be learnt for future advocacy activities?

> **For example:** The UN General Assembly Special Session (UNGASS) for children was held in May 2002 to produce a global agenda for children for the next ten years. Children and young people were involved in the processes leading up to the special session itself to ensure they had a say in the agenda. Save the Children evaluated the process and tried to assess the impact of the children's participation.
>
> For example, there were regional meetings leading up to UNGASS. One of these was the Regional Consultation with children and young people, corporate leaders and governments of South Asia. In order to assess the process, children who attended were asked:
> - What did you like most?
> - Any suggestions for improvement?
> - Suggestions for future steps?
> - What did you not like?
>
> To assess the impact, children and adult participants were also asked to say "yes", "maybe", or "no" to the following statements:
> "We convinced government to invest more in children."
> "Got information about problems facing children in South Asia."
> "Children convinced corporations to invest more in children."
> "Made new friends."
> "Children were listened to by government and corporate leaders."
>
> Similar evaluations were carried out after the three preparatory committee meetings held in New York, which were attended by hundreds of children from many different countries.

Constant impact monitoring is particularly important in advocacy. It enables you to look for evidence of change as you go, to assess progress in bringing about the change, and to test whether your assumptions about the process of change are correct. Some methods for assessing the impact of advocacy are described below.

Developing a model of change

To monitor and evaluate the process and impact of your project, you need to be clear about the process or model you are trying to follow and then decide on what information is available to enable you to assess each part of the process. In other words, you need to develop a 'model of change'. (See also Chapter 9 on impact assessment.)

For example, the process of advocacy can be seen as an impact chain:[2]

build awareness > change policy > impact on people's lives

(This can continue and repeat itself: as a result of the impact on their lives, people feel empowered to ask for further change.)

The different pathways mentioned at the beginning of this chapter will have different types of impact chain, and different dimensions of success. For example, this is a model formulated by Oxfam for raising awareness and changing attitudes:

heightened awareness about an issue > contribution to debate > changed opinions > changed policy > policy change implemented > positive change in people's lives

An impact chain for developing capacity for advocacy could be:

group formation > group activities > group federation beyond village level > movement launched that takes on vested interests > groups of poor are involved in framing legislation and have control over resources

This sort of chain is useful as a first step to developing a model of change, but you have to be careful, and not assume that one change will automatically lead to the next. The impact chain does not assume a linear causal relationship between different steps. Rather it identifies the conditions (ie, what needs to happen) and how change is supposed to happen over time.

---

[2] New Economics Foundation, www.neweconomics.org

The purpose of the chain is to make it explicit what are the expected steps leading to change, so that they can be monitored over time and reviewed as necessary. Policy change does not always lead to change in practice and analysing the policy process in stages helps to expose the obstacles which might prevent positive outcomes for people's lives. These may include the following:

- Policies are enacted but not implemented because there is a lack of capacity within government departments or some vested interests that prevent it. This can manifest itself through the absence of procedures and regulations being instituted.
- Policy and regulations are enacted but budget is not allocated.
- Budget is allocated but not translated into positive outcomes in practice due to inappropriate expenditure, the diversion of funds through corruption or a lack of cost-effectiveness.

As policy and implementation processes can be long and complex, mapping out these stages can be helpful in deciding exactly what to monitor. For example, budget monitoring can be an effective and practical tool for civil society organisations to monitor policy implementation.

Organisational values

The values of your organisation should also determine what to look for in monitoring and evaluation and these can be incorporated into the model of change. For example:

- You could focus specifically on human and child rights and increased accountability for rights.
- Commitment to equity and non-discrimination means considering changes in gender and family relations. To monitor this, look at women's, men's and children's roles and responsibilities.
- Changes at individual level could look beyond material benefits to include psychological and attitudinal changes, especially in relation to political awareness, analysis and personal self-worth.
- Organisational changes can be tracked to show how vision and mandate change over time, often due to a change in the political view of leaders.

These values also determine who participates and who does not. For example, in the monitoring and evaluation of Save the Children advocacy it is important that, where possible, children and young people are involved.

4. How can advocacy be monitored and evaluated?

Developing indicators

When you have analysed the model of change for advocacy, it is possible to go on and develop indicators for both process and impact, and approaches to monitoring, evaluation and impact assessment. This is a relatively new area of work and is therefore still being developed. Some frameworks have been developed to help expand the models of change suggested above, and to identify useful indicators to show intermediate outcomes and longer-term impact. One is shown below and some more are presented in Tool 13. Frameworks should not be straitjackets. They are useful for giving an overview of areas to look at but should be seen as tools for facilitating creative thinking. The challenge is to remain open to unintended outcomes and respond to them if necessary, even when they fall outside the framework that may have been adopted.

For example the dimensions of policy change and developing advocacy capacity are drawn together in table 11.1, adapted from one by Ros David of ActionAid.

Table 11.1. Framework for understanding possible outcomes and impact of advocacy and campaigning work[3]

Dimension of work	Indicators of progress – good and bad	Indicators of change and longer-term impact
1. Policy change • National (executive, ministries, legislature, parliament, military, police, courts, etc.) • Provincial and local government • International bodies (UN, IMF, WB etc). • Private sector	• Increased dialogue on an issue • Raised profile of issue • Changed opinion (whose?) • Changed rhetoric (in public/private) • Change in written publications • Changes in key personnel • Offers of funding by corporations • Undermining activities from target or allies	• Changed policy • Change in legislation • Policy/legislation change implemented • High quality personnel in charge of implementing policy • (and in the very long term) positive change in people's lives as a result of the policy/legislation change
2. Developing capacity for advocacy by working with . . . • NGOs • Movements/networks • Trades Unions • Community-based organisations	• Change in individual members' skills, capacity, knowledge and effectiveness • Change in individual civil groups' capacity, organisational skills, effectiveness	• Increased effectiveness of civil society work • Civil groups active in influencing decision-makers in ways that will benefit poor people • More responsive policy-making structures set up

[3] Adapted from an approach by the Institute of Development Research, (IDR)

Dimension of Work	Indicators of progress – good and bad	Indicators of change and longer-term impact
• Popular organisations • Partner organisations • Local journalists • Academic organisations • Human rights lawyers • and so on	• Greater synergy of aims/activities in networks/movements . . . • . . . or alliances/networks break down • Change in collaboration, trust or unity of civil society groups • Greater freedom of expression • Greater acceptance/ recognition of civil groups • Existence of fora for civil groups to input into a wider range of decisions • Increased legitimacy of civil society groups • Increased number of civil society groups • People's monitoring committees on service delivery • Stakeholder consultation groups by companies	• Increased participation of civil society groups in influencing decisions • Change in accountability and transparency of public institutions • Change in accountability of civil society groups • Companies respond to stakeholder consultation groups
3. Supporting people to advocate eg, children's groups to advocate for themselves	• Greater awareness of individual rights and the power systems that withhold rights • Change in citizens' skills, capacity and knowledge to mobilise and advocate on their own behalf • Recognition of rights by decision-makers • Willingness to listen to children's view	• Improved access to basic rights such as health, housing, water, and food • Action on the ground reflects real needs of people

Who defines success? Who should be involved in monitoring and evaluating advocacy?

The same principles apply as for other types of exercise (see Chapters 2 and 3).

In advocacy it is important to have multi-stakeholder involvement in planning, monitoring, evaluation and impact assessment. It is important not to gloss over key differences and some stakeholder views should not hold more weight than others.

For example: An overall evaluation of the impact of children's participation in UNGASS was carried out. Questionnaires were sent to children/young people involved at the local, or national level; to children/young people involved at the regional and international level; and to adults involved in the participation of children/young people. Phone interviews were also conducted with key people, including UNICEF staff, participants from government delegates, and NGO partners. In addition, young evaluators in four countries developed their own evaluation process, determining, together with the adults, what their purpose was in becoming involved in the first place, translating this into some objectives, and finding out whether some or any of these objectives were realised.

Different stakeholders will have different views on what success is, depending on where they are within the impact chain. To get an overview of how successful you were, you need to solicit the views of a range of stakeholders: for example, ultimate beneficiaries, local people and their organisations, staff involved, advocacy targets, journalists and outsiders. Not all stakeholders have the same interest in telling you how effective the campaign is. Some may deliberately misinform. For example, companies may flatter campaigners to discourage them from continuing a campaign. There may also be a danger of campaigners exaggerating their success. It is therefore vital to ensure a rigorous analysis takes place, and that evidence is properly triangulated. This makes advocacy impact assessment more credible, even though based on a subjective approach.

Methods for monitoring and evaluating advocacy

A variety of methods can be used. For example:
- Surveys can provide an overview of what was achieved. Anonymous surveys can be useful where an organisation cannot be open about why change is happening.
- Interviews.
- PLA techniques such as ranking are useful for assessing the success of developing advocacy capacity among grassroots activities.
- Video can be an effective way of conveying emotion in evaluations, without which spirited campaigns turn into dry reports.
- Case studies that draw on a range of techniques and that are cross-referenced to avoid bias are a helpful way to provide useful lessons and to present complex material. These can be done for specific projects or institutions or groups of beneficiaries.

Where emphasis is on development of civil society and ability to hold decision-makers accountable, methods for monitoring, review and evaluation need to:

- be culturally appropriate
- encourage participation by children and young people
- be gender sensitive
- be developed in consultation with southern-based organisations
- emphasise values that organisations consider important in their work.

Methodologies need to reinforce transparent and co-operative ways of working, and strengthen the role of external agencies in helping to create space for marginal groups to have a voice. It is important to use a range of methods to get the information you need, and to cross-check the information. The methods also need to be suited to the nature of the advocacy work and provide information that is timely and useful.

See Chapters 2, 3 and 4 and Tools 1, 2 and 3 for more on who should be involved and possible methods to use.

Assessing the impact of advocacy

(See also Chapter 9 on impact assessment.)

There are a number of possible approaches to assessing the impact of advocacy. The choice of approach will depend on the particular advocacy strategy being used, what model of change is being used, and what resources are available. Although it would be useful, in many cases relevant baseline data is not available to help assess impact. There is often more emphasis on the systematic recording of evidence that comes up in the course of the work.

Two examples of different approaches are described below.

a) Focus on a particular policy change

This is dependent on a clear definition of the policy change required:

- Compare views of decision-makers at different levels, politicians or journalists targeted by advocacy work with those of their peers who were not targeted. Are their views expressed in private and/or in public? (This may indicate the level of their commitment.)
- Compare opinions of members of the general public targeted by campaigning work with those of people who were not targeted.
- Compare the positions of individuals in countries where specific policy change has occurred with those where it has not.
- Consider the position of those who oppose the advocated change.
- Does current and new policy incorporate the message?

b) Monitoring policy implementation

Even if a policy is changed or a new policy is developed, policies are enacted but not implemented because there is a lack of capacity within government departments or some vested interests that prevent it. So monitoring policy implementation can be as, if not more, important.

Budget monitoring provides a quantitative approach to impact assessment. It recognises that policy change is not always implemented, and so does not always achieve real change in people's lives. Analysing public expenditure allows us to investigate the detailed steps in the implementation process. These include:

- whether the budget is allocated
- whether the budget leaves the Ministry of Finance and is received by the relevant Ministry which will be involved in implementation. (It should never be assumed that allocations directly translate into expenditure.)
- whether the resources are received by the relevant local government agencies
- whether this translates into resources available to service users and citizens.

Budget monitoring is very useful for rights-based approaches as issues such as equity and inclusion can be situated in the forefront of expenditure discussions. Budget monitoring is also an interesting way to link micro level outcomes to discussions of national and international economic policy, for example, by analysing the budget implications of debt servicing.

There is some experience in carrying out budget monitoring particularly for children. This involves looking at resources allocated for children across a range of ministries such as the ministries of health, education, welfare, justice and policing. It can be difficult as data is not often made widely available by the relevant institution.[4]

5. Challenges

There are a number of specific difficulties in attempting to monitor and evaluate advocacy activities, and these need to be taken into account:

- **Attribution:** It is difficult to attribute responsibility for observed changes in policy. It may be better to acknowledge the collective nature of advocacy work and focus less on questions of attribution. Advocacy is increasingly being carried out in networks or coalitions. It is important to look at how organisations are working together for a common purpose and monitor and evaluate each organisation's most appropriate role in this.

For example: Oxfam Anti-AIDS drugs
Oxfam came in after many others had been working on the issue of patent rights for a long time – Oxfam's campaign was well targeted and timed

---

[4] For more information on the techniques and tools to use for budget monitoring, see the Save the Children UK publication on public expenditure analysis: *Holding Governments to Account: Public expenditure analysis for advocacy*, Magnus Lindelow, 2002

impeccably. Oxfam's campaign would not have had the same impact if others had not done a lot of groundwork before. On the other hand, without Oxfam's high-profile campaign, all the lower level work may not have had much impact – even in the longer run.

- **Co-option:** advocacy targets (for example companies) use sophisticated PR techniques to persuade the public of their good intentions, but may have no intention of making real changes in practice. It is important to keep referring to the long-term objective, and not be distracted by the appearance of short-term success.

For example: Save the Children is part of an alliance campaigning against child poverty. A major conference was held in London in February 2001 by the Grow Up Free from Poverty Coalition, at which UK government ministers, international financial institutions, UN agencies, governments and representatives of civil society committed themselves to renewed action to eradicate child poverty. Six areas for action were identified. After one year a report was published to show how the conference participants had begun to take action. For each of the six areas the report lays out: what is the problem? what measures did we call for? what promises did people make at the Conference? what progress has been made (by whom)? and what remains to be done? The report was presented at a meeting, has been distributed to participants at the Conference, and is available on the Save the Children website.

- **Lack of self-criticism, talking up success:** The nature of campaigning organisations, often driven by strongly motivated individuals, can make it difficult to accept criticism. Success may also be exaggerated to attract resources and keep up the fighting spirit.

- **Speed and flexibility:** Any monitoring and evaluation has to be useful in the context of fast and flexible decision-making.

Summary

- Advocacy is an essential component of rights-based programming.
- Different strategies can be adopted in advocacy. These fall into two broad categories: attempting to influence policy directly; and developing the capacity of others for advocacy.
- The approach to planning, monitoring, evaluation and impact assessment of advocacy must be suited to the particular strategy and tactics adopted.

- The findings from monitoring and evaluating advocacy can themselves be used as evidence to support advocacy.
- A 'model of change' can help to clarify how you expect the advocacy process to bring about change in people's lives.
- The impact of advocacy can be assessed in different ways, including budget monitoring to analyse the implementation of policy change.

Summary of process

1. Define aims and objectives of campaign or advocacy process.
2. Use and adapt some kind of framework to clarify the advocacy process in terms of intermediate and long-term objectives, and how you will know if you are getting there.
3. Identify some key indicators of process and impact.
4. Decide how these will be collected, communicated and documented at different stages of the advocacy process.
5. Review regularly to adapt to changing circumstances.

Tool 13 looks at frameworks that can be used and adapted to help develop to monitor and evaluate indicators and advocacy.

Part 3
Tools

Tool 1
Participatory learning and action (PLA)

Description

Background

Participatory Learning and Action (PLA) is a particular form of qualitative research used to gain an in-depth understanding of a community or a situation. It is based on the participation of a range of different people, including people from the community affected by the work The aim is for people to analyse their own situation, rather than to have it analysed by outsiders, and for the learning to be translated into action. This makes it a particularly useful tool for planning, monitoring, review or evaluation of any kind of community development. It used to be called PRA, participatory 'rapid' appraisal or participatory rural appraisal, and was initially used mainly for needs assessment in rural communities. But it has now been used in many different situations and for different purposes, and so has been re-labelled: Participatory Learning and Action.

PLA draws on the techniques and traditions of applied anthropology, participatory research, farming systems research and agro-ecosystems analysis. These are forms of research that look at the complex and inter-linked relationships and activities which exist within all types of communities. It has grown out of rapid assessment methods such as rural appraisal (RRA) and rapid appraisal procedures (RAP) (see below).

Many of the techniques have been adapted for work with children and young people, to help increase their participation in development activities that affect them.

What it is

PLA is both a philosophy (that outsiders need to learn about situations from the insiders, and that insiders can analyse their own problems), and a series of methods for carrying out participatory and qualitative research.

RRA and RAP are approaches that can be used by outsiders who need to find out in-depth information about communities. The information is extracted by the outsiders who then take it away and use it as a basis for their decisions. PLA, on the other hand, is a process in which communities analyse their own situation, make decisions themselves about how best to tackle their problems, and as a result feel empowered to take action. This is an important distinction, because the term PLA (or PRA) is often used wrongly for studies which use PLA methods but in which community members have no influence on how the information is used.

The overall aim of the PLA process is to give more power to the community, and to reverse power relations and hierarchies between communities and those perceived as being development experts and planners from outside. This is known as 'handing over the stick'. In other words, development programmes should be designed and controlled by the communities affected by the work, rather than by outside agencies.

This means that PLA as an approach should, wherever possible, be part of a long-term partnership in which those with direct experience of a programme and outside specialists work together, using the techniques of PLA at different points along the way.

When the PLA approach should be used

- Working with children's rights, to make sure children's perceptions are taken properly into account in a programme promoting their best interests.
- PLA is most suitable when participation by all concerned is essential for the success of the work being proposed, for example, in a community health programme.
- PLA techniques can also be suitable if 'community' is defined more loosely to include a professional community, such as health workers in a district, all government officials concerned with a particular problem, or staff in a particular team or office.
- When planning, monitoring or evaluating a programme concerned with social change.
- When you need a thorough understanding of a topic in a particular context.
- When you need to know what people think about their situation or a problem, and what their priorities are.
- When you need to find meaningful indicators for qualitative change.
- For a rapid assessment of a situation.

PLA or RRA can be used for:

- assessing the development needs of a community
- identifying priorities for further research into those development needs
- assessing the feasibility (on both social and technical criteria) of planned interventions and activities
- identifying priorities for development activities
- implementing development activities

- monitoring and evaluating development activities
- assessing the impact of a programme on different members of a community.

The most important considerations when deciding whether or not to use PLA are:
- the type and level of accuracy of information that is required
- the extent to which the community is going to be involved in the work
- the priorities of the community: food or participation?
- the availability of appropriate people to conduct the study
- the degree to which project structure and decision-making are sufficiently flexible to make use of new information gathered in this way (organisations are often unwilling to base project plans on information gathered in this way)
- the intended use of the findings.

Features of PLA

The following are the essential features of PLA:

Triangulation

This is a method of cross-checking qualitative information. Information about the same thing can be collected in different ways and from at least three sources to make sure it is reliable and to see whether it is biased. This is done by using a multi-disciplinary team to collect the information – in other words, one that is made up of people with different skills, experience and viewpoints (see below); by using different tools and techniques for collecting and analysing information; and by collecting information about the same problem or issue from different sources (from people, from places, and from events and processes).

Multi-disciplinary team

The principle behind the multi-disciplinary team is that people with different skills, experience and points of view will look for and find different things, so that the team as a whole will be able to obtain new and deeper insights. All members of the team are involved in research design, data collection, and analysis. Women should always be included in the team and, wherever possible, so should members of the community in question.

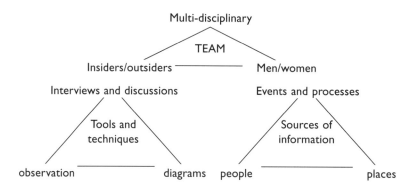

Mixing techniques

Using different techniques gives greater depth to the information collected. For example, direct observation may pick up different information from that gathered in interviews. The process of drawing maps may highlight points which were missed in observation.

Flexibility and informality

Plans and research methods are semi-structured and revised as the fieldwork proceeds. This allows the team to follow up any unexpected findings. Methods can be adapted as needed.

In the community

Most activities are performed jointly with community members, or by them on their own. This brings to the planning the benefits of participation discussed in Chapter 2.

Optimal ignorance and appropriate imprecision

PLA should avoid unnecessary detail or accuracy, and collecting data which is not needed. The team should ask itself what kind of information is required, for what purpose, and how precise it has to be.

On the spot analysis

The team constantly reviews and analyses its findings to decide how to continue. It builds on the increasing understanding it is gaining, and can focus on those aspects that emerge as being the most important.

Offsetting biases and being self-critical

The team has to analyse its own biases in order to prevent the PLA becoming too impressionistic, or simply a collection of rumours. It should try to identify possible sources of error and see how they influence the way information is interpreted. For example, what is said and what is not said, what is seen and what is not seen. They must try to avoid using value judgements about others. They should also obtain views of a cross-section of society, and so should actively try to seek out the least assertive members of the community, including the poorest, people with disabilities, women, children, ethnic minorities, the uneducated, and those living in the most remote areas. They should not rely entirely on information from the most educated and articulate (usually male) members of the community.

Experience has shown that it is essential for all team members to be sensitive to issues concerning less powerful groups (see Chapter 3). It will probably be necessary to have training in gender awareness, communicating with children, and other similar skills, otherwise it will not be possible for the team to make sure these groups really participate at all stages of the PLA.

Brief introduction to methods

PLA should be planned in the following stages:
1. Clarify goals and objectives of the study.
2. Choose main topics.
3. Prepare a list of subtopics, indicators and key questions.
4. Identify sources of information for each subtopic.
5. Select tools to gather and analyse information.
6. Design research tools.

PLA in its pure form is usually carried out as a workshop followed by fieldwork to gather information. The information is analysed throughout the study and in a group session at the end, when different ways of addressing the problems can be analysed and compared. The results can be presented to the community by the community.

A PLA trainer is needed to conduct the workshop in which members of the research team are introduced to the approach, philosophy and methods of PLA. The workshop clarifies the objectives of the PLA and the topics that are to be investigated. Participants can then decide which tools for collecting and analysing information would be the most useful and receive training in how to use them.

The fieldwork should be done in several rounds. Between each round of information gathering, the team should meet to analyse the results and to plan the next piece of information-gathering in the light of what they have learned.

The final analysis is done immediately after the fieldwork by the whole team.

The results can be presented in different ways for different audiences – to the community, to project staff, to programme managers, etc.

Tools and techniques for gathering and analysing information

Some of the tools below are always relevant. The others can be used if appropriate, and adapted as necessary.

Secondary sources (always relevant)

Project reports, records, baseline data and any other documentation about the place, people or problems should first be gathered and examined. This will help formulate questions and identify subtopics for the PRA to look at, and will help avoid duplicating previous studies.

Direct observation (always relevant)

Direct observation means observing objects, events, processes, relationships or people's behaviour systematically and recording these observations. Direct observation is a good way to cross-check people's answers to questions. Checklists can be used to help ensure certain factors are noted.

To draw up the checklist:
• Think about the objectives and broad topics of the PLA.
• Identify indicators that you can assess through direct observation.
• These indicators make up the checklist.

It is also important to note the unexpected and anything else that might be relevant to the programme.

Another way of using direct observation is for the team member to participate in activities. For example, if the PLA is concentrating on agricultural develop-ment, the team member can take part in harvesting, ploughing or sowing, and so understand the viewpoint of the farmers better.

If observation of the same thing is to be carried out by different people, it is important to standardise techniques, since different people perceive things differently. This can be done by carrying out a simple exercise where several people observe the same event together and record what they see. They can compare notes afterwards to see what differences there are. People supervising or coordinating the data collection can also monitor any differences.

Semi-structured interviewing (always relevant)

Interviewers do not use a formal questionnaire. Instead they use a checklist of questions related to each topic of interest.

For example:

Topic: How do people in this area cope with inflation?

Key issues and questions:

- What are the problems caused by inflation (economic, social, etc)?
- What are the overall coping strategies?
- What are the coping strategies for each problem?

Questions can be added or omitted as appropriate.

This is a flexible tool which must be used systematically in order to produce valid results. The following brief guidelines are suggested in the PRA training manual.[1] The manual also gives more detailed guidelines.

- The interviewing team should consist of between two and four people of different disciplines.
- Begin with the traditional greeting and state that the interview team is here to learn.
- Begin the questioning by referring to someone or something visible.
- Conduct the interview informally and mix the questions with discussion.
- Be open-minded and objective.
- Let each team member finish their line of questioning (do not interrupt).
- Carefully lead up to sensitive questions.
- Assign one note-taker (but rotate).
- Be aware of non-verbal signals.
- Avoid leading questions and value judgements.
- Avoid questions that can be answered with 'yes' or 'no'.
- Individual interviews should last no longer than 45 minutes.
- Group interviews should last no longer than two hours.
- Each interviewer should have a list of topics and key questions written down in his or her notebook.

Common mistakes include: failing to listen closely; repeating questions; helping the interviewee give an answer; asking vague or insensitive questions; failing to cross-check a topic; failing to judge answers (believing everything); asking leading questions; allowing the interview to go on too long; over-generalising findings; relying too much on the information from the well-off, the educated and men; ignoring anything

---

[1] Theis, J and Grady, H (1991) *Participatory Rapid Rural Appraisal for Community Development: A training manual based on experiences in the Middle East and North Africa*, International Institute for Environment and Development and Save the Children. See also McCracken, J, Pretty, J and Conway G (1998) *An Introduction to Rapid Rural Appraisal for Agricultural Development*, International Institue for Environment and Development.

that does not fit the ideas and preconceptions of the interviewer; giving too much weight to answers that contain quantitative data; incomplete note-taking.

Analysing findings from semi-structured interviews

The analysis of responses from unstructured or semi-structured interviews can be more difficult than analysing responses to a fixed questionnaire, since there will be a wide variety of answers, different people will raise different points and some of the answers might be long.

One way to analyse the responses is to summarise each interview into the main points that were raised. It may then be possible to create a limited number of categories of response which will help to see how many people agree or disagree with different views. It is also useful to report any particularly interesting views word for word.

Different types of interview include:

Individual interviews

A cross-section of people can be interviewed on the same topic to reveal a range of attitudes, opinions and behaviour. People to be interviewed must be selected to give a good cross-section and to avoid bias only to the most educated and articulate. Answers may be more personal than in group interviews and more likely to reveal conflicts.

Key informant interviews

Interviews with specialists in the topics you are interested in, or with outsiders who have moved into a community, such as teachers, who can sometimes give a more objective view. Key informants should be able to answer questions about the knowledge and behaviour of others, and give a good overall view of the way things work in the community.

Group interviews and discussions

Interviewing a group of people together provides access to the knowledge of several people at once. There is also cross-checking from others in the groups. Groups should not be larger than between 20 and 25 people. Group interviews are not good for revealing sensitive information, and responses may be misleading if the group thinks the questioner has the power to give or withhold financial support. The interviewers should encourage alternative views and opinions. Informal conversations afterwards can be useful for getting information from people who did not express their views during the group interview.

Group interviews need more planning and preparation than individual interviews.

Group interviews need well prepared facilitators who can encourage each person to speak, keep the discussion to the point, bring out important issues and summarise the information gathered.

Focus group discussions

A small group of people (6–12) with specialist knowledge or interest in a particular topic are invited to discuss specific topics in detail. A facilitator is chosen to keep the discussion on or around the original topic, and to stop individuals dominating the discussion. It can bring together people who have a particular problem, those who cannot speak up at large meetings (such as women or minority groups), or those who are peripherally involved in a community, such as nomadic herders.

Focus groups can also be used to clarify specific topics which can then be discussed by a larger group, or can be used as working groups to help design and run the study itself.

Successful focus group discussions need: to be held in a comfortable place, with no interruptions; an informal atmosphere; equality and trust between group participants and facilitators; understanding and agreement within the group about the purpose of the discussion; respect for the right of all participants to speak and be listened to; an agreed and open method of recording the discussion, such as flip charts.

Oral history

People can be asked to talk about the history of a place or a particular situation, or of their own lives, and the results used to build up a picture of what has happened over time.

Listening surveys

A survey can be carried out by listening to what people say in different situations (in the fields, drawing water, on the bus, etc), and the answers recorded by theme, topic or group.

Ranking and scoring

Ranking or scoring means placing something in order, and reveals differences within a population. It helps to identify the main problems or preferences of people, and the criteria they use when deciding in what order to place things. It enables the priorities of different people to be compared. Ranking exercises can be used in interviews or on their own and they can lead to more direct and revealing questions (for example, Why is . . . a more serious problem than . . . ?)

There are different sorts of ranking:

Preference ranking
Where people vote to select priorities.

Pairwise ranking
A matrix is drawn to compare which is the preferred of two options.

Direct matrix ranking or scoring
This is a way of identifying criteria for choosing certain objects. It can be used as a means of understanding the reasons for local preferences for such things as tree species or crop varieties. The criteria are likely to change from group to group. Women and men may use different criteria.

Example of pairwise matrix
Given the choice of reading or watching TV, this person prefers TV; given the choice of music and TV he/she prefers music, etc.

Table 1a.1. Favourite pastimes

	TV	Reading	Sleep	Music	Sport
TV		TV	TV	Music	TV
Reading			Reading	Music	Reading
Sleep				Music	Sport
Music					Music
Sport					

From this example:

Music was preferred four times	Rank A
TV was chosen three times	Rank B
Reading was chosen twice	Rank C
Sport was chosen once	Rank D
Sleep was never chosen	Rank E

Example of direct matrix scoring
Table 1a.2. Tree species

Criteria	Eucalyptus	Palm	Acacia	Pine
Fuelwood	4	1	2	3
Building	4	1	2	3
Fruit	1	4	2	3
Medicine	4	1	3	2
Fodder	3	–	1	2
Shade	4	3	1	2
Charcoal	2	–	3	4
TOTAL SCORE	22	10	14	19
RANK	A	D	C	B

If you could choose only one species which tree would you choose? Eucalyptus
4 = best   1 = worst
Repeat for a number of interviewees

Wealth (or well-being) ranking

This can be used to investigate perceptions of wealth differences and inequalities in a community, to discover local indicators and criteria of wealth and well-being, and to establish the relative wealth of households in the community. This can be useful if, for example, a project is trying to target the poorest people. It is done by making a list of all households and asking different people to sort them into categories according to their own criteria of 'wealth'. The term 'well-being' is often used, since perceptions of wealth usually include non-economic criteria. Often only three categories are needed: the poorest, middle and richest.

Construction of diagrams and maps

A diagram is a model that presents information in an easily understandable form. It is a simplified model of reality. Diagrams are useful because:
- they simplify complex information
- the act of constructing a diagram encourages people to analyse the data they are using
- they facilitate communication
- they stimulate discussion
- they increase consensus among team members
- they are an excellent way of involving community members and discovering their views.

Different types of diagrams include:

Maps

It is useful to draw maps in groups. They are useful for finding out about an area, and about how different groups use the area. For example, a map drawn by a group of women will show different features from one of the same area drawn by a group of men, or one drawn by a group of children.

Social maps

These are maps of a village or area which show where groups of people live. They can be combined with wealth ranking exercises to identify which are the poorest households, landless, female-headed households, different ethnic groups, number of children in a household, etc.

Mobility maps

These record, compare and analyse the movements of different groups in a community, and are a useful indicator of a person's contact with the outside world.

Transects

These are diagrams of the main land use zones in the target area. They compare the main features, resources, uses and problems of different zones. Transects can be constructed by walking in a line through an area with a key informant, using direct observation to note specific factors, and talking to people you meet on the way.

Seasonal calendars

These are ways of representing seasonal variations in climate, crop sequences, agricultural and income-generating activities, nutrition, health and diseases, debt, etc. They can help identify times of shortage – of food, money or time – and the best time of the year for particular kinds of development work.

Time trends

These are graphs to show how things have changed over time. Time trends can be used for many variables including: crop yields, area under cultivation, livestock population, prices, interest rates, migration, population size, birth and death rates, malnutrition rates, rainfall.

Time lines

These are flow charts showing the sequence of different events. For example, they may be used to show the daily activities of different people or how a programme has developed. Several time lines can be shown together to see how events influence each other, for example, how political events may influence decisions made in a programme.

Historical profiles

These can be simple lists, giving a summary overview of the key historical events in a community and their importance for the present.

Daily routine diagrams

These help compare the daily routines of different groups of people, and seasonal changes in the routines. They can help identify suitable times for meetings, training courses, visits, etc. They can also be useful for assessing changes in household roles over time. This may be useful for assessing the impact of a programme over time (see Chapter 9).

Livelihood analysis diagrams

These can help interpret the behaviour, decisions, and coping strategies of households with different socio-economic characteristics. Variables for livelihood analysis may include:
- household size and composition
- number of labour migrants in the household

- livestock and land ownership
- proportion of income by source
- expenditures
- seasonality
- relative income
- credit and debt.

Flow diagrams
A flow diagram shows causes, effects and relationships between key variables. For example:
- relationships between economic, political, cultural and climatic factors causing environmental degradation
- flow of commodities and cash in a marketing system
- effects of major changes or innovations (impact diagrams)
- organisation chart.

Causality diagrams
People can draw linkages between different events or findings and offer their own explanations of how they are related.

Venn diagrams
These can be used to show the key institutions and individuals in a community and their relationships and importance for decision-making. Different circles indicate the institutions and individuals. When the circles are separate there is no contact between them. When they touch, information passes between them. If they overlap a little there is some cooperation in decision-making. If they overlap a lot there is considerable cooperation in decision-making.

Techniques for working with children

PLA can be used to find out from children about their lives, perceptions and expectations. Implementing the UN Convention of the Rights of the Child in a child-centred way must include the perspectives of the children and young people whose 'best interests' are to be promoted. Successful PLA with children depends on a good rapport between children and team members. Experience has shown that training in communicating with children, child development, and awareness about age and gender issues are essential for the techniques to be used successfully.

It is important to obtain informed consent from children and their parents or guardians when working with children. (See Chapter 3 for more on working with children, and Chapter 2 for ethics in participation.)

Some techniques that can be used with children include:

Participant observation

Insights into the daily activities of children can be gained by accompanying them on their tasks, or by watching them at places where they gather at certain times of day.

Group interviews

Children, particularly girls, are often shy with adults but may be more talkative in groups. Group interviews or focus group discussions can work well with children.

Child-to-child interviews.

Children interview other children. This can work well, particularly in discussing sensitive issues. It has been used successfully in evaluations carried out by children. But it is important to train the children properly in interview techniques. It should not be assumed that children will naturally empathise with each other.

Drawing and mapping

Drawings of various aspects of life can be useful tools when working with children. But children who have not had much exposure to pictures may find it difficult to draw (for example, children from remote areas who do not go to school).

Drawings can be used in different ways. For example:

- to illustrate something they are trying to explain (eg, what has changed as result of a project)
- to provide insights into areas of their lives, (eg, 'homelife', 'running away' or' hopes and dreams')
- to illustrate ideas and identify criteria for preference, (eg, what is a 'good thing', a 'bad thing', a good or a bad person)
- Maps can be used to look at children's daily routines, contacts, and mobility.

Songs

In some cultures the songs sung by children and women can give an insight into their concerns and priorities. Children who are shy may find it easier to sing their own songs than talk.

Theatre for Development (TFD)

This approach has been used to help explore difficult issues and has been used to carry out evaluations.

It consists of the following stages:

- Work with a group of children to explore issues which are important to them.
- Select issues to concentrate on.
- Develop a drama based on the issues.
- Perform the drama to an audience.

- Discuss the issues raised with the audience.
  This technique is described in more detail in Tool 10.

Games and role play
These can be used to explore issues in children's lives.

For example: *The Children's Perspectives Protocol* was constructed as part of the Radda Barnen study: *Children's Perspectives On Their Working Lives*. It provided a common framework for local investigators in four countries to find out about the perspectives of working children in diverse occupations.

The approach comprises semi-structured activities and games focusing on key themes in children's lives. They are used as resources for group work. Many are based around locally produced picture-cards which participants are asked to compare, sort and range, yielding a combination of individual and group responses. In brief, the activities are:

1. 'My day' invites young people to describe their daily lives, orally and using drawings and mapping techniques.
2. 'My work' explores the circumstances of children's work and the detail of the activities they undertake.
3. 'Who matters?' asks about young people's social networks, the quality of key relationships, as well as their own self-evaluation.
4. 'Work and school' asks participants what they consider are the bad as well as the good things about their work, and repeats the activity for school, before establishing which is their preference.
5. 'Which work is best?' asks participants to rank children's occupations (including their own) in terms of relative desirability/undesirability, and explores the criteria on which young people base these judgements.
6. 'What is a child?' examines young people's own views on child development. They are asked to chart a wide range of work activities in terms of age-appropriateness.
7. 'What if?' presents young people with common dilemmas facing working children and invites them to comment about what is likely to happen next and what could be done to help.
8. 'Life stories' provides investigators with an opportunity to explore the issues in Activities 1–7 with a particular child, in order to enrich the level of detail provided from group work.

For further reading on participatory approaches with children, see References and further reading.

Analysis of the findings of qualitative research

Analysis is often the most difficult part of qualitative research. It can be done in different ways. For example:

- Some qualitative research is presented as a detailed description from which people are free to draw their own conclusions.
- Alternatively, a framework can be developed to look at different aspects of the problem and how they relate to and influence each other, for example:
  - **setting** or context
  - **events**: What do people do in specific situations, and what happens to them? From this it is possible to find out about their attitudes, relationship to power, etc
  - **processes**: how and why things change over time, and what factors influence these changes
  - **actors**: who is involved, why and how.
- As more information is collected, it can be entered into the relevant part of the framework to help clarify how different factors affect each other, and how they affect the main question that is being investigated.

Group discussion to analyse findings of a PLA

- This is an intensive semi-structured session in which information gathered in the field is analysed and recommendations for further action are made. It is important for members of the community to be involved in this, as it is part of the decision-making process. The whole team should be involved.
- The results of the fieldwork should be summarised and prepared for presentation before this session. Diagrams can be constructed during the session to interpret the findings and to encourage discussion.

The following guidelines for group analysis may be useful:

- Community involvement is essential.
- Analysis is the process of making sense of the information that has been collected. It should not be left until all the data has been collected.
- Prepare a list of key issues and arrange the findings according to this list. Rearrange the lists, sort through the information and look for patterns, differences, variations and contradictions. Weigh the relative importance of the information. Be self-critical.
- Formulate a series of questions based on the research topic (including new ones which came up during the fieldwork). Try to answer them with the help of the information collected.
- Discuss each subtopic in turn, summarise the results, and draw conclusions based on the information gathered.

- Use diagrams, matrices, ranking methods and other analytical tools.
- For further clarification, tabulate the information to help compare differences between individual interviews and observations.
- Check your findings and conclusions by presenting them to key informants or a group of community members.
- Findings have to be consistent and must not contradict each other. If the findings contradict other sources of information, you must be able to explain why.
- If it is not possible for different people to agree on the interpretation of certain findings it may be better to record the different views, rather than to attempt to reach a consensus.

Activity assessment

This is the final stage of the analysis group discussion which helps assess and prioritise possible options for development activities according to:
- amount of benefit for the community
- degree of community participation
- sustainability of the project
- equitableness of distribution of benefits
- technical feasibility

A sheet can be drawn up for each proposed activity with the headings:
- what:
- why:
- where:
- when:
- who implements:
- who benefits:
- how:
- cost:

Analysis of objectives

This is the key exercise for future monitoring and evaluation of the activities, in which the group has to define the objectives and indicators for each activity. A sheet can be drawn up for each proposed activity with the headings:
- Activity:
- Goals:
- Objectives:
- Output indicators (for activities):
- Impact indicators (for objectives):
- Strengths (what we do well):

- Weaknesses (where we have problems):
- What should we continue doing:
- What should we start doing:
- What should we stop doing:

Presentation of the findings

The findings of the PLA may be written up as a proposal for submission to a funding agency. They should also be presented to and by members of the community, and by and to other people who will be involved in the work, for example local and national government. The form of presentation will depend on the audience. It may be more suitable to give a presentation than to present a written report.

Written reports often do not represent the range of information, the variety and contradictions which came up in the PLA process. It may be useful to supplement a report with diagrams, video or role play to help present the more complex and contentious issues. (See Tool 10.)

Variants of PLA

Rapid Rural Appraisal (RRA)

The essential principle of RRA is for a multi-disciplinary team (for example, an economist, an agriculturalist and a community development worker) to carry out research together on a community. The combination of their skills and experience should throw light on the community workings as a whole. It is called 'rapid' because it aims to get an in-depth view of a community, but rather than spending perhaps a year carrying out fieldwork, as an anthropologist might do, the information is collected in a few weeks.

It uses a similar approach and techniques to those described for PLA. But while community members may be included in the research team and in the analysis of information, this is not always the case. The purpose of RRA is for outsiders to learn as much as possible about a community, whereas the purpose of PLA is for the community to analyse itself in a way that helps it to have more influence over development activities.

Rapid Assessment Procedures (RAP)

These were developed as a methodological aid for research into nutrition and primary healthcare. The approach has been modified through fieldwork and various workshops. RAP uses qualitative research techniques to investigate those concepts related to health-seeking behaviour which vary from culture to culture. It is not necessarily carried out by a multi-disciplinary team, and does not necessarily involve the community.

RAP is used to investigate concepts, including patterns of resort (who people go to first), healthcare decision-making, outsider/insider relationships (perception and contact), the community, the household, the nuclear/extended family, health, disease, the role of the sick person, and the medical system.

The methods used are: interview (formal and informal), conversation, observation (of behaviour and events), and focus group discussion. Information is collected by the researcher and fieldworkers in a diary, and in brief field notes which are then written up into expanded field notes and filed by theme.[2]

Table 1a.3. Comparison of conventional and RRA approaches

Techniques employed	Conventional	RRA
Statistical analysis0	Often a major part	Little or none, use of triangulation
Formal questionnaire	Often included	Avoided
Interviews with local people and key informants	Through formal questionnaire if at all	A major component using semi-structured interviewing
Qualitative descriptions and diagrams	Not as important as "hard data"	Considered at least equally as important
Sampling	Statistically acceptable sample sized regarded as necessary. Often random sampling	Often small sample size, selecting key areas, or farms, households, etc. Statistical requirements not always adhered to
Consulting secondary data sources	Yes	Yes
Measurements	Detailed, accurate	Qualitative or indicators used
Group discussion	Informal unstructured sessions	Via semi-structured workshops and brainstorming
Analysis and conclusions	Often carried out away from the field. Results not always accessible to community	Produced by team immediately after fieldwork. Results accessible to community

(from: *An introduction to RRA for agricultural development* by J. McCracken, J. N. Pretty and G. R. Conway – modified by L. Gosling.)

---

[2] Guides on what questions to ask and suitable methods for investigating the above are given in the publication: *Rapid assessment procedures for nutrition and PHC anthropological approaches to improving programme effectiveness* by Susan Scrimshaw and Elena Hurtado, UNICEF, 1987 (order from the United Nations University, Tokyo, Japan).

Table 1a.4. Reversals and shifts required in PLA³

	Normal tendencies	Needed reversals
Professionalism	Things first	People first
	Men before women	Women before men
	Professionals set priorities	Poor people set priorities
	Transfer of technology	Choice of technology
	Simplify	Complicate
Bureaucracy	Centralise	Decentralise
	Standardise	Diversity
	Control	Enable
Careers and behaviour	Tying down (family)	Also releasing
	Inwards (urban) `	Also outwards
	Upwards (hierarchy)	Also downwards
Modes of learning	From above	From below
	Rural development	Rapid, relaxed and
	Tourism	participatory appraisal
	Questionnaire surveys	Ranking scoring
	Measurements	Self critical judgement
	Statistics	Empowering
	Extractive	
Analysis more by	Us	Them

Strengths and weaknesses of the PLA approach

Strengths of the PLA approach

- It gives a good understanding of a community and its capacities and problems to all the people involved in the assessment, including community members. People involved in the assessment can include community members, local government officials, NGO staff.
- It gives community members more influence over development work that affects them. This is essential for rights-based programming.
- It ensures that community members understand the project objectives and activities and so are more committed to the project.
- You find out what local people think. It ensures that local priorities and perceptions of different problems, opportunities and constraints are taken into account.
- Results are produced rapidly and in a form available to the local community.
- It is useful for identifying indicators for qualitative change which are locally relevant.
- You learn as you go, rather than waiting to analyse the data at the end.

---

³ From: *Rural Appraisal: Rapid, relaxed and participatory* by Robert Chambers

- Qualitative research can be quicker and cheaper than a more formal quantitative survey of the same scale (although this is not always true).
- PLA and related methods often produce unexpected information.
- They can be less intrusive than formal interviews using questionnaires.
- There is no need for accurate population estimates.

Weaknesses of the PLA approach

- The results only apply to the communities visited and do not allow you to make generalisations about a whole population in the same way that a large survey may do.
- It can be time consuming for all concerned, including members of the community.
- Bias may creep into the results and so give a false picture of the situation. For example, if the team is not aware of gender issues they may never find out about women's concerns.
- It is difficult for people outside the team to verify the results because statistical methods are not used.
- Direct observation limits you to what you see before you – there may be things you are not seeing.
- If not done systematically, the results can be impressionistic.
- The findings may not carry the same weight with decision-makers as quantitative data.

The following list of difficulties and possible dangers show how a PLA can be weakened. (NB: some of these can apply to other approaches too.)

- Using a participatory approach when it is not necessary or appropriate.
- Difficulties in finding the right team.
- Going too quickly might lead to superficiality.
- Not seeing what goes on 'behind the scenes', such as hidden power relations.
- The desire for the security of a fixed questionnaire.
- Difficulties in finding the right questions to ask.
- Difficulties in finding the poorest and least educated community members, especially women and disabled people.
- Failure to involve community members properly and fully.
- Lack of rapport with the community.
- Failure to listen and lack of respect.
- Seeing only part of a situation or problem and not getting the full picture.
- Making value judgements about others.
- Being misled by myth or gossip.
- Generalising based on too little information or too few informants.
- Overlooking the invisible.

- Lecturing instead of listening and learning.
- Raising expectations in the community where the PLA is carried out.
- Unconsciously imposing ideas, categories and values.
- Male teams and neglect of women.
- Language: what people say and the way they say it can be lost in translating from one language to another.

The fact that there are more potential weaknesses than strengths in these lists does *not* mean that PLA is a doubtful approach to assessment! In the right circumstances it can be the most effective approach of all.

Prerequisites for success

Positive attitudes
- A self-critical awareness by members of the team, a readiness to recognise, discuss and challenge preconceptions and bias and to change behaviour. Also a willingness to admit mistakes.
- A readiness to deal with conflicts that may arise when sensitive issues are discussed in the open.
- It is essential to be open about the different agendas of agencies and groups involved, to develop trust and avoid raising unrealistic expectations.

The right team
- A research coordinator to bring together the work of each team member and give direction.
- Team effort. All members must work together contributing their skills, knowledge and understanding. It may be best to assign different members of the team to tasks they do best. For example, some people may be better at interviewing, others may be better at recording results.

Skills
- The availability of people with appropriate skills and the right approach to conduct the study. If the approach is wrong PLA will not work. The right attitudes and behaviour are the key to the success of a PLA.
- Interviewing skills are vital. It takes time to learn how to look, listen and encourage others to speak, especially when people come from a variety of backgrounds.

Good preparation
- Training and thorough preparation are essential. Training should concentrate on the importance of PLA as a process which gives more power to community members. Training methods should strengthen the skills and attitudes

required to promote this reversal of power relations between outsiders and community members. It should not just teach the assessment team how to use the different techniques.

- Training should also be given in gender awareness, working with children, awareness of issues concerning disability and less powerful minority groups, and community development.
- All those involved, including senior managers, need to understand and support the principles and methods of participatory assessment. If possible they should be involved in planning the PLA.
- A long-term relationship with the communities is essential for participatory assessment to lead on to greater community participation in programme implementation: to develop sufficient trust between the different stakeholders involved, to deal with conflicts, and to provide continuous support for institutional development within local groups and communities.

Appropriate methods

- The methods used need to be appropriate to the participants in terms of culture, experience, educational level, etc. It is important to be flexible, if a technique is causing problems or not being enjoyed it may be better to use another one.
- The techniques must be used in combination.
- Analysis must be continuous and involve community members. If it is left to the end the original information and the PLA experience itself may be lost through over-analysis, over-interpretation, or by being ignored.
- The organisational structure and decision-making must be sufficiently flexible to make use of new information gathered in this way.
- There needs to be enough time for the assessment to allow it to evolve and respond to findings as they emerge, including unexpected ones.

Example of participatory action research (similar to PLA) with vulnerable children and young people in migrant communities in South-East Asia

Save the Children carried out a Participatory Action Research project with migrant children and young people in cross-border areas of China, Myanmar and Thailand. The project was from April 1999 to March 2001.

PLA approaches were used to provide opportunities for migrant children and young people to identify their concerns, vulnerabilities, needs and interests. Project participants were also encouraged to develop pilot interventions to address their needs. Few (if any) interventions had previously been undertaken with migrant children and young people, so this approach provided a great deal of insight and interest among the community and national and regional partner organisations and advocates. The pilot interventions undertaken included a wide range of activities and a variety of implementation strategies for raising awareness and strengthening capacity building, life skill training and outreach services.

The PLA approach was found to be an effective way of involving children and young people. It is particularly helpful when working with vulnerable populations and a wide range of sensitive issues. The tentative situation in which many migrant children live requires a tremendous amount of flexibility and sensitivity, as well as open exchange with project participants. It was felt that this approach could be adapted for use in other border areas in South-East Asia, as well as other migrant populations in the region.

There were also many challenges in undertaking this research. For example:

- The diversity of ethnic populations with their various languages, cultures and circumstances is an essential component of working with migrants. The numerous languages and dialects involved made communication very difficult, and the need for several translations slowed the research documentation process. Ethnic and cultural differences, religious prejudices, feelings of discrimination all affected the participation of different groups.

- It was difficult to reach young people. Some were in remote areas, some were constrained by employers. Many people in communities, including children and young people had very little free time for participating in the research.

- There were limited partners in the field sites with whom to work. It often took months to get to know them, to develop the community's trust and collaboration, and to assess potential partners, their relationship with the community and other allegiances.

- Many of the field reasearchers from within the migrant communities had limited literacy skills in the national language of the country where they were working. They also had limited qualitative research experience. Frequent feedback and follow-up training was required.

- Coordination was difficult due to the distances of field sites and lack of communication channels, and the confidential nature of much of the information.

For more detail about this research see: *Small Dreams Beyond Reach: The lives of migrant children and youth along the borders of China, Myanmar and Thailand*, by Therese M. Caouette, a participatory Action Research Project of Save the Children.

Tool 2
Surveys

Description

Surveys are used to collect a broad range of information (quantitative and qualitative) about a population. The emphasis is usually on quantitative data which can be analysed using statistical methods to give precise estimates. The qualitative information is used to help interpret the quantitative findings.

Carrying out a survey

The basic steps in carrying out a survey are:

Survey design

- Formulate the question(s) you want the survey to answer. This should be in the form of a hypothesis which the survey should prove or disprove (for example, that a woman's level of education affects the health of her children). Alternatively, the purpose of the survey may be to measure the scale of a specific problem.
- Select variables that will enable you to answer the question. A variable is any characteristic that can vary (for example, the height of a child, the number of years a mother spent in school, or the preferred source of advice about health care).
- Design methods of collecting information about the variables. This can be done by physical measurement or by asking people questions using a questionnaire. In a questionnaire everyone is asked the same questions in the same way, so that results can be compared and analysed numerically. For example, 90% of people responding to one questionnaire said they would go to a traditional healer before going to the government health centre. Questionnaires must be carefully designed, since the number, order and wording of questions can all have a significant effect on the way they are answered.
- If necessary, translate questionnaires and guidelines into the local language(s). This may be time-consuming and requires considerable expertise.
- It is usually not possible to collect data from a whole population, so a sample of the population is selected. This should be representative of the whole population and has to be selected randomly to avoid bias. The precise method of selecting a sample varies according to the type and purpose of the survey.

(See Chapter 4 for a summary of types of sampling.)

- Plan the data collection according to the population sample selected. It will be necessary to organise transport and accommodation, and to devise a timetable to take into account travelling, public holidays, and when would be the best time of day to find the people in the sample. For example, it may be best to ask questions in the evenings after the day's work and the evening meal.

Data collection

- Train people to collect data (enumerators). It is important that data collection methods are used consistently, to avoid bias (see Chapter 4). It may be necessary to produce guidelines on how to ask questions, how to make physical measurements, how the variables are defined, and so on. Supervisors will also be needed to ensure data collection methods are used correctly.
- Carry out a pilot survey. The data collection methods, including questionnaires, must be tested on a small group and then amended if necessary. This will expose any problems (for example, in the wording or translation of questions, in gaining access to respondents, in the training of enumerators, or in the length of the questionnaire) that should be addressed before starting to collect data from the whole sample.
- Data is collected and collated from the sample by enumerators and supervisors.

Data analysis

- After the information has been collected, collated and checked, it is analysed. Data collected using quantitative methods can be analysed statistically. This can give:
  - **averages** (eg, the average number of children per family)
  - **ratios** (eg, the proportion of a population suffering from malnutrition)
  - **range between minimum and maximum levels** (eg, the largest land-holding in a village and the smallest)
  - It can demonstrate whether or not an apparent difference is a **statistically significant difference** and not just the result of chance (eg, whether health workers who have attended a training course really do know more than those who have not)
  - It can also demonstrate whether or not an apparent **relationship** between two separate variables is meaningful statistically (eg, whether malnutrition of a child is related to household income). A statistical relationship between variables does not, however, imply that one variable causes the other
  - It can estimate the extent of the likely **standard error** in the results caused by taking data from a sample rather than the whole population.

- The results from statistical analysis can be very precise, and quantitative data produced from surveys and then analysed statistically is called 'hard data'. This implies that the results are objective and accurate; in other words, that they reflect the reality of the situation. However, it should be noted that:
  - Sample survey results provide estimates, and the precision of the estimates can be quantified by calculating standard error. In the right circumstances, it is possible for a survey to obtain very precise estimates. However, for something to be accurate it must be both precise and unbiased (see Chapter 4).
  - Statistical tests are only valid if the data on which they are based are valid. For example, if the samples used in a survey are not selected properly, the statistical tests will be meaningless. If data collection techniques are not used correctly or consistently, the results will not be valid.
  - Different statistical tests can be used on different sorts of data and to demonstrate different things. If unsuitable tests are used, the conclusions will also be meaningless.
  - The statistical results can be presented as graphs and tables and can be interpreted with the help of qualitative findings.

For example: A survey was carried out in the Ogaden region of Ethiopia to assess the needs of the population which had been under great stress from drought and from the return of people who had previously been refugees in Somalia. Sampling techniques were used to select 78 pastoral, agro-pastoral and settled farmer sites as representative of the whole population. It was important to gather information quickly, so helicopters were used to get to the widely scattered sites. Teams stayed overnight at each site and measured the weight and height of all the children aged under ten to assess their nutritional status. An economic and social questionnaire was filled in, to obtain information on livestock and grain production, consumption sale and exchange, and the prospects of the food economy. This provided a large amount of quantitative information. Discussions were also held with elders, government officers, Peace and Stability Committee members, traders and returnees in the main towns to gain qualitative information to add deeper insights to the survey, and to find out how different people saw their situation.

Strengths of surveys

- Surveys provide precise, statistical answers to carefully defined questions.
- The accuracy of results can be verified by checking the methods and statistics that were used.

- A sample usually includes people from several different locations. This means that the people carrying out the survey have contact with a large number of people in different places.
- The techniques of data collection and analysis are widely known and understood (although not necessarily correctly).
- The methods of analysis are clear and relatively quick, especially when carried out in the field using portable computers.
- The findings can give support to an argument by demonstrating the size and severity of a problem.
- Surveys allow comparisons to be made between different groups in the survey or with other surveys which used similar methods.

Weaknesses of surveys

- Considerable resources are usually needed (personnel, vehicles, fuel, computers) to carry them out.
- They may take several weeks to complete.
- Collecting data from the selected sample can be intrusive and inconvenient. Non-cooperation may be a problem and could lead to unreliable results.
- Surveys are often planned and results analysed far from the survey sites with little or no involvement of people from the community.
- Working with an inflexible questionnaire hinders a relaxed discussion with the person being interviewed.
- Surveys only look at certain pre-defined variables and the possible answers to questions on a questionnaire are limited. Important details or variations may be missed if they do not come into the preconceived model.
- The numerical analysis of large amounts of data is time-consuming and needs expertise. If a survey is not carefully designed, so much information may be generated that it proves impossible to analyse or use effectively.
- When data collection and analysis methods are used incorrectly the results may be invalid.
- Surveys are often designed to prove what the researcher believes, so it is important to look at the methods and conclusions critically.

Prerequisites for success

- Knowledge and experience in survey design, sampling and statistics.
- People to collect data who are literate, numerate and accurate.
- Experience of field conditions to ensure sampling methods are practical.
- Proper preparation, planning and execution which includes a pilot survey to test the questionnaires.
- Proper training and supervision of enumerators.

When they can be used

- To provide accurate, precise data.
- When you need to have a broad view of a whole population.
- To identify major differences and relationships in the characteristics of a population, and find out which sectors of the population are worst affected.
- To produce 'hard data' to prove that certain problems exist, or to justify a particular strategy to donors, government and other decision-makers.
- To establish clear baseline information which can be used for evaluating impact later on.
- Repeated surveys can be used to measure changes in a population over time. This may be useful for monitoring the impact of a programme, or for detecting significant changes in selected populations; for example, increased levels of malnutrition in a population which is constantly at risk from food shortages.

Tool 3
Logical framework analysis (LFA)

Much of this section has been based on *The project framework approach to population project planning and management* by Neil Price (see section on references and further reading for more details). It has been revised in the light of comments from John Sartain. Any errors or misinterpretations arising from adapting the above document are the responsibility of the author.

Description

Logical framework analysis (LFA), also known as the project framework approach (PFA), was originally developed for the United States Agency for International Development (USAID) in 1969. Since then it has been adopted by many bilateral and multilateral agencies such as the International Planned Parenthood Federation (IPPF) and the Department for International Development (DfID). NGOs have also found it a useful tool for project planning in certain situations.

It is a way of testing the *logic* of a plan of action by analysing it in terms of means and ends. This helps to:
- clarify how the planned activities will help to achieve the objectives
- be explicit about the implications of carrying out the planned activities in terms of resources, assumptions and risks.

The analysis can be carried out by the project planners, a consultant, or by using participatory techniques to involve staff, managers, partners and communities affected by the work. The process of analysing a proposed project in this way can be a particularly useful exercise for managers.

LFA is: "a set of interlocking concepts which must be used together in a dynamic fashion to permit the elaboration of a well designed, objectively described, and valuable project" (Gilroy Coleman, *The Logical Framework Approach*, University of East Anglia, 1987).

"The Logical Framework is simply a tool which provides a structure for specifying the components of [a project] and the logical linkages between a set of means and ends..." (International Service for National Agricultural Research, quoted by Neil Price, parenthesis added by the author).

"It is *not* a set of project planning procedures, nor a set of monitoring and evaluation guidelines. It is a means by which a project may be *structured* and *described* in a logical fashion" (Neil Price).

Brief outline of methods

The objectives and plans of action for the work should first be established using an appropriate method. This may be done by programme managers and staff, by participatory methods involving project beneficiaries, or by a consultant. Stakeholder analysis (Tool 12) and Objectives trees (Tool 6) are often used at this stage. Once the programme has been designed, the LFA approach can be used to analyse the logic of the relationship between its aim and the proposed activities. This is done by presenting it in a table, or matrix, with the following rows and columns:

The 4 X 4 matrix of the project framework

	Project structure	Indicators and values	Means of verification	Assumptions and critical factors
Aim, or wider objectives				
Project objectives				
Outputs				
Activities (inputs)				

Column 1: the project structure

First describe the project as a series of hypotheses. For example: *If* we carry out all the activities necessary to support the family planning clinic, *then* they will provide family planning services to the community. *If* people have access to family planning services *then* they will use family planning methods effectively. *If* the use of family planning methods in the community increases, *then* the population growth rate will fall. From this, you can construct the 'logical hierarchy', or the project structure, in terms of cause and effect.

Wider objective, or aim

/

Project objective

/

Outputs

/

Activities

N.B. Different donor organisations use different terminology, for example, "A Narrative Summary of Activities, Outputs, Purpose and Goal". The important thing is to recognise the layout of the logical framework, whatever the terms used.

The four levels in the framework represent the following steps:

- We undertake certain *activities*, using specified *inputs*. If the logic is right then these activities will result in specific *outputs*.
- It is assumed that these outputs will have an effect on the project beneficiaries, and this effect is known as the *project objective*.
- Furthermore, the project is expected to contribute to the *wider objective*, or the overall *aim*.

In carrying out the project we 'do' the activities and procedures using the inputs; and if all the 'ifs' stand up, we achieve the outputs, project objective, and the wider objective.

These steps are now explained in more detail.

Wider objective or aim

This refers to the aim or purpose of the work as defined in Chapter 5 and should be accompanied by a statement describing the way in which the proposed work is expected to contribute to achieving the aim. For example, to reduce the national population growth rate through lowering the total fertility rate from 6.0 to 5.6.

Project objective

This is the intended effect, or impact, of the project on the target population, including how long it will take to achieve this change, and who will be affected. For example, to increase the effective use of modern contraception by eligible couples in Village X from 10 per cent to 30 per cent over the project period.

Outputs

These are the results of completed project activities, which are within the control of project management, and which use the inputs provided. The results of these activities should lead to the achievement of the project objectives.

For example: clients attend clinic; clients receive family planning counselling; clients accept contraception; primary health care clinic renovated; fully equipped and functioning; road to primary health care clinic upgraded; paramedics trained in family planning counselling and service provision; project support staff trained in vehicle and equipment maintenance and record-keeping.

Activities

These are what we actually do. We obtain the necessary inputs – money, materials, personnel and certain types of activity such as training – needed to start the project and then carry out the activities. For example: we help train staff; organise the regular supply of equipment and funding for recurrent and capital costs; and use these to develop, implement and support a good community-based family planning service.

We only **do** the activities. The rest will follow, provided the logic is right.

Column 2: indicators and values

For each level of the project structure (activities, outputs, project objective, and aim) there must be one or more ways of measuring performance. Indicators enable project managers both to see whether the project has achieved what it set out to achieve at each level and to have a measure of this achievement.

Activities indicators

Carrying out the activities should achieve the outputs, so the success of the activities will be measured by the indicators for outputs. There is therefore no need to put any indicators in the matrix at the activities level. This means the inputs required to carry out the activities can be listed there. (This is common in logical frameworks used by several donor organisations.) The inputs should include capital and current expenditure on the purchase of equipment and a schedule for any staff training, or other activities that need to be completed before the project can start. For example, if the inputs are contraceptive supplies, equipment, etc, the amount needed and the cost should be entered in this column. Some donors ask for a budget to be put in the next box (in the Means of verification column).

Output indicators

For outputs, indicators are often numerical and can usually be measured using existing records (see Chapter 5). The output indicators can be used as targets for monitoring and evaluation purposes, but it is important not to be too rigid about targets. They may need to be revised as the project evolves. Indicators for the sample outputs would include the number of patients attending the clinic, receiving family planning counselling, etc.

Indicators for project objectives

These are often more difficult to identify than output indicators (see Chapter 6). They may be quantitative or qualitative, depending on the nature of the objective. When the objective is to achieve qualitative change, it is sometimes better to use quantitative proxy indicators; sometimes qualitative indicators are more appropriate. The key indicator for the sample project objective would be the increase in the effective use of contraceptives.

Indicators for wider objective or aim

The key indicator for the sample wider objective or aim of the work would be the reduction in the population growth rate.

Indicators as targets

If the indicators are to be used as targets, it is better to use indicators that are quantitative. It is important that targets are regularly adjusted and revised during the project in response to internal and external developments. They are only useful if they are feasible and realistic.

Column 3: means of verification

There must be a way of measuring or collecting information about each of the indicators. This is called the 'means of verification'. It is important to identify the sources from which information to verify indicators can be gathered. If it is difficult, expensive or time-consuming to verify the indicators, it may be done badly if it is done at all. The resources needed for collecting information should be considered at the project planning stage.

For example, when will the inputs needed for the activities be available? How will the patient numbers be recorded: through regular record keeping or periodic surveys? How can the effective use of contraceptives be measured? How will the population growth rate be measured?

Column 4: assumptions and critical factors

The assumptions underlying a project, and the critical factors necessary for its success, need to be acknowledged and thought through at the planning stage in order to be realistic about what is feasible. They are, in effect, the uncertainties that will be faced during implementation of the work. They are generally external to the project and those responsible for the project have little or no control over them.

Factors affecting implementation: assumptions and critical factors relating to activities

Planning at the implementation stage of a project usually involves the least uncertainty. For example, an architect will be able to estimate reasonably accurately the resources necessary for renovating a clinic. The availability of materials may not be quite so predictable, and hence progress from implementation to outputs may be less certain than the accuracy of the level of resources required.

Factors that need to be considered include:
- Are personnel of the required standard likely to be available at the salaries being offered?
- If not, are trainers available to bring staff up to the required standard?
- If resources are to be supplied by other agencies, or government, when will they be available? Timing of the project may depend on when essential supplies or funding are available.

Factors affecting outputs

Factors to take into consideration which will affect the timing of activities and the way they turn inputs into outputs include:

- seasonal climatic variations (for example, will the rainy season prevent people coming for training?)
- management capacity
- retention of key staff
- relations with partners, formal and informal.

Factors affecting objectives

Generally, the significance of assumptions and the degree of uncertainty increases as you go up the framework. There are fewer uncertainties about whether the inputs will lead to the outputs than there are about whether outputs will result in achieving the objectives.

For example, the successful completion of a clinic and the availability of trained staff does not necessarily mean that people will demand family planning services. Such demand will require changes of attitude, the acquisition of knowledge and awareness, and/or improved accessibility. If the maintenance of the clinic is to be the responsibility of the community, this assumes that the community is willing to do it and has the necessary organisational capacity. At the planning stage, therefore, an assessment of likely community support should be made.

Factors affecting aims

Since the aims are usually so broad, there will be many uncertainties which could influence whether or not achieving the objectives will contribute to achieving the aims. Since many other factors outside the control of the project management affect the link between objectives and aims, it is not generally worth analysing these in much detail. But it is useful to acknowledge from the start the existence of major constraints (such as political uncertainty or war).

The use of the LFA for monitoring and evaluation

By identifying indicators for outputs and objectives at the planning stage, monitoring and evaluation should be relatively straightforward. Where targets have also been set, these can be used to assess progress quantitatively. As stated above, it is important to revise targets continuously during the project.

Process of producing LFA

A team approach to project planning is now generally emphasised by users of the LFA. There is also a recognition of the importance of the pre-planning research and survey work required to ensure that problems are properly identified and that their causes and effects are related to the real experiences and needs of individuals and groups of people. These problems can then become the basis for agreeing objectives and hence programme design.

For example, Objective Oriented Intervention Planning (OOIP) is a specific approach. OOIP workshops, led by an external facilitator, are organised at different stages of the project cycle with different levels of detail. In general terms, the steps of an OOIP workshop can be described as follows:

1. **Preparatory steps**: definition of the subject that will be analysed during the workshop; identification of the parties concerned by the subject; identification of representatives of these parties (see stakeholder analysis, Tool 12); practical preparation of the workshop.
2. **The analytical phase**: analysis of the position of all parties involved using stakeholder analysis (see Tool 12), problem analysis (construction of a 'problem tree' to show how different problems are related and combine to cause other problems); objectives analysis (transformation of the problem tree into an objectives tree – see Tool 6); analysis of the alternatives (consideration of alternative ways of achieving the objectives, and agreeing on priorities for action).
3. **The planning phase**: definition of the four columns of the logical framework matrix.

These stages are carried out in workshops, using presentation aids such as flip charts and cards on which people write their points and which are then arranged in groups and 'trees' during group discussion (see Tool 12).

OOIP has also been used as a participatory planning tool. The workshops can involve people from communities and partner organisations in analysing problems and priorities, and in planning a programme according to the logical framework matrix. When used as a tool for community participation, the method needs to be adapted to make it locally relevant. For example, the different stages may be spread out over a longer period. This allows more time to consult with different members of the community, and to make sure the analysis of problems and objectives genuinely reflects the different views in the community before constructing the matrix.

Example of a logical framework

HIV prevention amongst school-going adolescents in Vietnam
This example is not an actual project document but is based on an actual project. It is a peer education project in Vietnam, involving school children. Educators will assist in the development of Information, Education and Communication materials (IEC), and the groups will be trained in peer education methods.

The goal of reducing HIV infection cannot be directly attributable to the project, but the national surveillance figures will represent the impact of the bigger national effort to which the project contributes. The key indicators for objectives and outputs (see table 3a.1) were generated with the project staff. These can be measured. All the data should be disaggregated by age and gender of the respondent, to identify the differential impact of the project on girls and boys.

Table 3a.1. HIV prevention among school-going adolescents in Vietnam[1]

Narrative summary	Objectively verifiable indicators	Means of verification	Assumptions
Aim: To reduce HIV infection in children in Vietnam	Sentinel surveillance		
Purpose: Increase levels of knowledge regarding HIV/AIDS and reduce levels of risk behaviour in school-going children in Ho Chi Minh City and Hai Phong provinces	Key indicators: 1. % of children able to name three transmission routes of HIV 2. % of children knowing three means of STD/HIV prevention 3. % of children willing to talk to a person living with HIV/AIDS 4. % of sexually active children who have ever used condoms 5. % of children who are virgins 6. % of children intending to use condoms in the future	• Pre- and post-knowledge, attitudes and practices (KAP) questionnaire. • Focus group discussions • In-depth interviews.	• No other major disruptions to school affecting attendance • Raising awareness results in changed behaviour • Peer educators continue for period of project • Stigma/discrimination towards people with HIV is not too great • HIV/AIDS recognised as problem that people want to address
Outputs: 1. 16 peer educator groups established for school children (8 in Ho Chi Minh City, 8 in Hai Phong) 2. Information, education and communication materials produced for three age groups	1. 16 peer educators groups (10–12 educators) trained and active in 16 schools by month 7, working with 3 age groups 2. Drop-out rates of educators 3. Number of children involved in education sessions	Monthly reports and supervisory visits	• Children have time to participate in programme along with other school pressures and commitments • Staff and parental support for children to take part in programme

---

[1] Example taken from *Learning to Live: Monitoring and evaluating HIV/AIDS programmes for young people*, Douglas Webb and Lyn Elliott, Save the Children, 2000

1.4 % of all children
receiving education
1.5 % of all children
exposed to IEC
materials.
2.1 manual produced and
distributed to 16
groups
2.2 240 posters produced
(80 per age group) and
distributed to 16
schools by end of
month 9.

Activities: Inputs:
1.1 Develop criteria for   • Training materials,
    school identification   condoms
1.2 Identify 16 schools   • Material for IEC
1.3 Meet with school   development
    administration, raise   • Transportation
    awareness of   • audio-visual equipment.
    project
1.4 Develop criteria for
    educator
    recruitment
1.5 Recruit peer
    educators
1.6 Initial training of
    220 educators
2.1 Hold IEC
    development
    workshops
    etc

Strengths of the LFA

- It is a good way to check the internal logic of a project plan and to ensure that strategies, objectives and aims are linked.
- It makes planners think about how they will monitor and evaluate the programme by identifying indicators at the beginning.
- It makes planners state the assumptions they are making, and identify the critical factors for success. This is useful for stimulating discussion about the feasibility of activities.
- It brings together key information on one document and ensures that project objectives are clearly spelt out.
- It encourages people to consider what their expectations are and how these can be achieved.

Weaknesses of the LFA

Process

- The construction of a project framework is time-consuming and requires considerable training in the concepts and logic of the approach.
- The use of the project framework is relatively complicated.
- People are obliged to summarise complex ideas and relationships into simple phrases which may be meaningless.
- The logic is very western. The rigid 'cause-effect' concept may be alien to many cultures.
- By focusing on 'problem analysis' the OOIP process can be rather negative. It has been suggested that 'capacity analysis' (ie, analysing the resources and skills that people have rather than what they lack) could be used instead to encourage a more positive approach. Alternatively, focus on 'objective analysis'.

Application

- There is a danger that project managers can become too rigidly focused on setting and meeting project-centred targets, or on measuring indicators. This means the project may become less flexible and less responsive to changes in the situation as the project progresses.
- If unrealistic targets are set, project staff may be disappointed when they cannot be met.
- The approach is really designed for large-scale projects where each level (input, output, purpose, goal) is monitored by a different level of management. This makes it less suitable for a project with a small management team, and may encourage a more hierarchical approach to project management.
- It stresses a quantitative assessment of progress, rather than a qualitative approach, through the use of quantitative indicators. This may affect the way managers think about development.

Prerequisites for success

- Targets and indicators must be continuously revised during the project in response to project development and changes in the external situation.
- It should be considered as a flexible tool to be adapted to specific needs and programmes.
- Trained facilitators are essential to ensure it is done properly.
- Indicators should be chosen to reflect quality as well as quantity of work.
- If OOIP is used for participatory planning it should be used within a well established relationship, and enough time should be taken to make sure the problem analysis reflects real priorities, and to set realistic objectives.

When it should be used

- The LFA is most useful as a way to structure and describe a project in a logical fashion. It is an aid to logical thinking and should not be seen as a set of project planning procedures or monitoring and evaluation procedures.
- As in the example from Uganda, it may be useful in the pre-planning phase to help develop management skills and to strengthen the partnership between the different people involved in programme planning.
- The analysis of the relationship between activities and objectives can be useful in an evaluation.

The Logic Model

A variation of the log frame is the Logic Model. If properly used it can help in the development of indicators for measuring process and impact. The model, recently adapted for use in evaluating HIV/AIDS programmes[2], in its simplest form specifies:
- the behaviours to be changed
- the determinants of each of those behaviours
- the particular programme/project activities designed to change each selected determinant.

There are four steps in generating the model:
1. **Identify the specific behaviour(s) to be changed.** These would be discreet behaviours such as 'increasing condom use', 'reducing the number of sexual partners' and 'delaying sexual debut'.
2. **Identify the specific risk and protective factors for each identified behaviour.** This can be a brainstorming exercise, such as in the development of a problem tree, or it can be based on empirical research. A risk factor would be anything that encourages a risk behaviour, increases vulnerability to a risk behaviour, or represents a greater opportunity to engage in a risk behaviour. A protective factor promotes positive behaviours, provides controls against risk behaviours, indicates commitment to society and moderates the impact of risk behaviours. Risk and protective factors can be related to the environment or the individual directly.
3. **Select specific determinants to be addressed by the project.** Projects should assess how easily a determinant can be influenced (for example, knowledge levels may be relatively simple to change, whereas poverty may be more difficult), as well as the influence of that determinant over the behaviour. For example, knowledge levels may be easy to influence but on their own may

---

[2] Kirby, D (2000) *Logic Models: A useful tool for designing, strengthening and evaluating programs to reduce adolescent STD/HIV and pregnancy*, ETR Associates, Draft paper

have little direct relationship with behavioural change. Projects should focus on determinants which are more likely to change as a result of a project, and which themselves have a big influence over a behaviour.

4. **Identify particular activities to address the selected determinants.** Some factors may need more than one activity to address them sufficiently.

An example is given in table 3a.2 regarding increasing condom use. Only selected determinants/factors are given. Note that the factors in the table are represented as objectives.

Table 3a.2. Logic model as applied to condom use[3]

Environmental factors	Individual factors	Behaviours	Goal
• make sure that adolescents are not denied condoms or birth control on account of their age (policy change) • expand media and folk messages promoting condom use • enhance social norms against unprotected sex • establish or expand community-based condom distribution • provide information on safe sex through health services • improve access to affordable condoms at clinics • develop adolescent-friendly health services • develop appropriate life-skills curricula for schools • increase teachers ability and willingness to teach effective sex/STD/HIV education programmes • implement effective alcohol prevention • increase family support and values for delaying sex • increase parent–child communication about sexuality and condoms.	• reduce belief that using condoms reduces sexual pleasure • increase belief that most sexually active adolescents are using condoms • reduce stigma attached to condoms • increase self-efficacy to say no to unprotected sex • increase self-efficacy to use a condom properly • increase beliefs that having unprotected sex is against personal standards • increase feelings of safety when using condoms • increase ability to seek help from a trusted person • increase ability to refuse alcohol or drugs	Increase protection by increasing the use of condoms	Reduction in HIV and STDs

---

[3] Example from *Learning to Live*, (op. cit)

Further reading on logical framework analysis

Information is usually available from the particular donor for which the logical framework is being prepared. This gets over the problem of variation in terminology, use of spaces, etc.

Tool 4
Cost-effectiveness analysis

Description

It is essential to think about the costs and benefits of a programme at the planning stage and the cost-effectiveness of different strategies.

A proper cost-benefit or cost-effectiveness analysis requires considerable economic expertise and is often not relevant to development work, where objectives are more social than financial. However, the consideration of costs and benefits and cost-effectiveness is always important, and formal techniques can be used in as much detail as necessary.

Cost-benefit analysis examines a project proposal in terms of its projected costs compared with its projected financial benefits, or other benefits converted to financial terms. While it may be relatively straightforward to measure financial benefits (for example, in an income-generating programme), it is difficult to quantify social benefits, except in an arbitrary way.

Measuring the financial costs may also be relatively straightforward, but it is also necessary to consider the non-financial costs involved. Some can be converted into approximately equivalent financial costs. (For example, if someone is offering their labour free of charge to a project, it can be converted into figures by finding out how much the person would be able to earn if they were not working on the project.) Others, such as environmental degradation, cannot easily be given financial equivalents.

A full cost-benefit analysis is most useful for a programme whose objective is to increase the wealth of a specific target group, such as micro-enterprise development. In this case, the assessment process will need to estimate whether or not the income, or the disposable income, of the target population is likely to be increased by the project. Where objectives are both economic and social, the financial and social benefits need to be considered together, and then compared with the costs.

The concept of cost-benefit can also be applied usefully in a less precise way by posing questions such as: could we achieve the same level of benefit at less cost by using a different approach? or could we make substantial savings with only a small loss of benefit?

Cost-effectiveness, on the other hand, can be defined as the ability to achieve objectives at a reasonable cost. It can be calculated as *the cost per unit of service given* (for example, the cost per dose of vaccine), or *the cost per beneficiary* (for example, the cost per child immunised). This is calculated by dividing the cost of an activity by the quantity of its output, or by the number of beneficiaries. This is useful when comparing different possible ways of achieving the same objectives.

A cost-effective project should yield benefits to the target population that are greater than the overall costs of running the project to the community, donor and implementing agency. One way of incorporating considerations of cost-effectiveness into project assessment is to include questions on costs and benefit in the project proposal.

For example: Several income-generation schemes are supported by Save the Children in Vietnam. When planning a project, in addition to the requirement for a situation analysis, clear objectives, a description of who will be responsible for what in carrying out the strategy, and details of how monitoring and evaluation will be carried out, the following questions must be answered:

Budget
- items of expenditure, with details of amounts, numbers, and underlying assumptions
- allocations of costs into: family contributions, local contributions, donor contributions
- when in the project cycle are different inputs needed? cashflow analysis.

Profitability schedule
Profitability
- how much input is needed per unit of time (as appropriate)?
- how much is the projected revenue per same unit?
- allow for depreciation of fixed assets (value of asset/productive lifetime)
- revenue minus input minus depreciation = profit per unit of time.

Repayments
- calculate repayment rates based on profitability (ie, quickest repayment which still leaves enough profit to make the activity attractive)
- systems for holding the real value of repayments, eg, linked to non-inflationary goods, like rice
- consider the case for interest rates and set realistic ones
- specify use of repayments: eg, that they must be used as principal for further loans, and the interest used to make up losses in the fund; if losses are low, the remainder can be used to recover some management costs.

Cost analysis

Cost analysis is an essential element in cost-effectiveness analysis. As in any tool for planning, monitoring, or evaluation, it requires planning to ensure that the right information can be collected and analysed. It can then be combined with different tools to look at benefits, or impact.

For example, the following simple spreadsheets have been set up to analyse project costs from materials and labour in a community water management project in Ethiopia:

Table 4a.1. Community/Save the Children contribution to projects:
Cost accumulation sheet for material inputs

Date	Name of contributors	Item/ material	Unit of measure	Quantity received	Cost/ M'st	Total cost in Birr	Remark
9/3/00– 30/5/00	Community	Sand	M3	33	20.00	660.00	Transport cost covered by Save the Children UK
9/3/00– 30/6/00	Community	Stone	M3	37	50.00	1,850.00	
25/3/00– 30/6/00	Save the Children UK	Cement	Quint	46.5	80	3,720	
25/3/00– 30/6/00	Save the Children UK	Pipes and fittings	Ls	–	–	3,137.19	66m pipe laying
25/3/00– 30/6/00	Save the Children UK	Other	Ls	–	–	3,341.79	Reinforce- ment bar, timber, hand tools, etc.
					Total	12,708.98	

Table 4a.2. Community/partner/government contribution to projects
Cost accumulation sheet for labour service

Date	Name of contributors	Avg no. days service	Type of service	Total man-day particip- ated	Rate/ day	Total cost in Birr	Remark
15/3/00– 15/4/00	Community	22	Unskilled labour on excavation	539	5.00	2695.00	
10/4/00– 10/ /00	Community	50	Unskilled labour on masonry work	451	5.00	2255.00	
25/3/00–	Save the Children UK	70	Semi-skilled labour on masonry work	298	40.00	11920.00	
					TOTAL	16870.00	

Table 4a.3. Project cost summary sheet
Project name: community water management
Zone: South Wollo
Woreda: Legeambo
Site. Jaro

Total no. beneficiaries: 420
Cost/beneficiary: 98.60 Birr (this will vary depending on site facilities and accessibility).

Month	Particular	SC/Grant	Communty	Govern-	Others	Total cost	Remark
March–June, 2000	Community	10,198.98	2,510.00	–	–	12,708.98	
March–June, 2000	Labour	11,920.00	4,950.00	–	–	16,870.00	
March–June, 2000	Overhead	70	11739.60			11831.59	
					TOTAL	41,410.57	

In planning for a cost analysis, the following questions need to be considered:
- How will you obtain cost information from partners or communities?
- How far will you go in analysing and allocating core administration costs borne in support of a range of programmes?
- How can you estimate the number of beneficiaries? In some projects it may be relevant to consider direct and indirect beneficiaries.

The Technoserve method for cost-effectiveness analysis

A full cost-benefit or cost-effectiveness analysis has to be performed by an economist, and the concepts involved will not be discussed here. However, the following is an outline of a method developed for use by programme managers who are not economists and which is suitable for development projects.[1]

Technoserve is a private non-profit-making organisation in the USA which assists economic enterprises in developing countries. It has developed a cost-effectiveness methodology to analyse its own programmes. It was developed after careful consideration of more complicated cost-benefit analyses used by organisations such as the World Bank, and after discussion with economic departments in US universities.

The Technoserve model has been used by development projects and found to be effective. It aims to assess the effect of donor assistance to economic enterprises in financial terms, and to assess its effects on the long-term economic and social well-being of the poor. Both are important, since some enterprises may make a profit, but not increase the social and economic well-being of the

---

[1] Bowman, Margaret et al., *Measuring our Impact: Determining cost-effectiveness of non-governmental organization development projects*, Technoserve, 1989; 148 East Avenue, Norwalk, CT 06851, tel: (203) 852 0377; fax: (203) 838 6717.

poorest people. It is also possible for a non-profit-making enterprise to bring considerable benefits to the poor.

The Technoserve method has two components:

1. Cost-effectiveness ratio =

$$\frac{\text{Net benefits attributable to Technoserve assistance} + \text{Financial benefits to group without Technoserve assistance}}{\text{Technoserve's cost}}$$

2. Non-quantifiable benefits rating = a weighted average of values ascribed to carefully defined:
   Social benefits
   Economic benefits
   Policy benefits

1. Cost-effectiveness ratio

This is calculated using a computer spreadsheet.

The **net benefits** are broken down into three parts:

- increased community-level incomes (farmers, suppliers, owners)
- increased enterprise profits (before dividend payments, mandated reserves, reinvestment or taxes)
- increased aggregate salaries, wages, and benefits to enterprise employees or directly contracted services.

Each is calculated as the difference between that which is attributable to the project, and that which would have occurred in the absence of the project. (Standard methods for estimating financial returns such as shadow-pricing, foreign exchange components and taxes are not included as they will probably not influence management decisions for small-scale enterprises. This is an example of sacrificing a certain amount of precision for the sake of making the process more simple.)

Projections over ten years are made for the two scenarios: with Technoserve assistance and without it. Standard methods for handling inflation and other discounting factors are used, to give the present value of net benefits.

Costs are composed of Technoserve project and administrative costs, less the fees paid by the enterprise for Technoserve services (which are usually minimal, but represent a certain amount of commitment from the enterprise).

A cost-effectiveness ratio of 1:1 is neutral. If it is more than 1:1, there has been net benefit, if it is less than 1:1, the cost has been greater than the benefits.

2. The non-quantifiable benefits rating (NQBR)

This is calculated by weighting specified aspects, or components, of social, economic and policy benefits for a particular project, and then assigning a value to each which indicates how much of an impact the project has had on that particular aspect.

The components (as defined by Technoserve in their model) are:

- Social benefits: improved managerial and technical skills; increased access to public services; increased control over quality of life; greater participation for marginalised groups (eg, women, ethnic minorities); increased community solidarity.
- Economic benefits: increased and sustainable productivity; enterprise replicability; increased enterprise sustainability; increased employment; improved linkages between different activities and parts of a process.
- Policy benefits: improved national policy environment for rural enterprises; regional/commodity sector policy impact; institutional policy impact.

A numerical value from 1–10 is assigned for each component independently by three different members of field staff, all of whom are familiar with the project and the impact it has had: the project advisor, the project manager, and the project director.

Strengths of cost-benefit and cost-effectiveness analysis

- The consideration of cost-effectiveness is always important in project planning.
- Analysis of the financial benefits of a project is relevant for projects aiming to increase incomes.
- It is a useful tool to help compare different strategies.
- It is useful for giving information to donors.

Weaknesses of cost-benefit and cost-effectiveness analysis

- Economic expertise is required to do a full analysis.
- Non-quantifiable benefits are difficult to value. The estimation of shadow prices and opportunity costs can be quite arbitrary.
- Cost-benefit analysis is often not relevant for social development projects.

When it should be used

- The cost per beneficiary can be used to compare a set of possible interventions at the planning stage.
- When it is necessary to reflect on the overall cost of a programme or field

office, and the number of people who are genuinely benefiting from the activities.

- It can be a helpful tool in identifying projects that do not generate sufficient benefits for the costs incurred, and so would not be appropriate interventions.
- When an agency is working with a partner who is trying to decide what kinds of project activities to do.
- If projects are to be replicated, agency staff should be able to document clearly cost per beneficiary.
- It can be used to help compare different projects which have similar impact, to see whether some projects are more expensive than others, and why this is so.

Tool 5
Strengths, weaknesses, opportunities and constraints (SWOC) analysis

This tool provides a framework for group analysis of a given situation. It encourages input from many people, helps people brainstorm potential solutions (opportunities) and constraints, and is a way of gathering information that can be useful in problem analysis, monitoring and evaluation.

The idea is simply to brainstorm under the following headings:

Categories	Description
Strengths	Those things that have worked. Things that one is proud to say about the project/situation/activities.
Weaknesses	Those things that have not worked so well. Times when things could have gone better.
Opportunities	Ideas on how to overcome weaknesses and build on strengths.
Constraints	The constraints that exist which reduce the range of opportunities for change.

A slight variation: Alternative descriptions of strengths and weaknesses can be as factors that are internal to an organisation, and so can be controlled by management; opportunities and constraints can be seen as external factors affecting the environment in which you are working.

Together these make up SWOC analysis. For each heading, the group defines, discusses, and records as many factors as possible. From this analysis, issues that need to be tackled emerge and objectives and strategies can be identified. It is also a way of reviewing progress in tackling these issues.

Tool 6
Setting objectives

Producing a problem tree and turning it into an objectives tree

What it is

A useful analytical method which allows participants to focus on a central problem, identify its causes and impacts, rank these factors, and define objectives for an intervention.

How to do it

1. Identify a 'core', 'central' or 'focal' problem. For example, in an HIV project in Zambia the central problem was identified as the non-use of clinic services for sexual and reproductive health by young people. (Focus on the specific age group concerned.)
2. Brainstorm to produce a list of causes and consequences of the focal problem. In the example the discussion focused on why young people do not go to clinics and what results this may have.
3. Rank them in terms of importance. The facilitators can discuss each topic as it is raised, and how it relates to the central problem.
4. Write 'core problem' in the centre of a piece of paper and arrange the causal factors below and the effects above. Discuss the links between the factors and draw arrows linking them where appropriate. Some causal links will be clear, and may go in one direction only, whereas others may be more complex, linking with other factors in a complex web of causal relations.

Turn the problem tree into an objectives tree by turning each causal factor into an issue to address. For example, if 'ignorance' is given as a cause, then the objective box would read 'reduced ignorance' or 'provide education'. Do the same with consequences, so an effect that says 'high rate of sexually transmitted diseases (STDs)' would read 'reduced number of STDs'. This helps identify key problems, objectives and indicators, though not all the objectives may be relevant to the project.

Figure 6a.1. Example of a problem tree, generated with young people in Lusaka, Zambia[1]

Problem tree showing the causes and effects of non-utilisation of clinics for sexual and reproductive health (SRH) problems in adolescents.

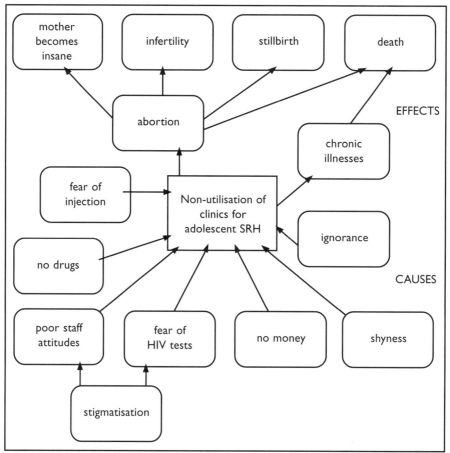

When it can be used

- **At the planning stage.** To analyse connected problems in terms of cause and effects. Problem trees can be conducted separately with boys and girls to determine gender elements of a specific problem. In this way project activities can recognise and respond to different needs. If many problem trees are used with different groups around a central problem, the aggregation of findings can give an overall picture of how young people see an issue.
- **To develop objectives and indicators within a programme.** Objectives trees are often used to start building a logical framework (see Tool 3). The central

[1] Taken from *Learning to Live: Monitoring and evaluating HIV/AIDS programmes for young people*, Save the Children, 2000

objective becomes the project purpose, and the objectives which feed into it can be the outputs for different activities. The effects can be used as indicators. For example, a reduced number of abortions would indicate a successful impact of the project.

It can show how different causes must all be addressed in order to make a difference to the central problem. For example, it is no use providing more drugs or reducing ignorance amongst young people if staff attitudes remain poor.

For example: Causes and consequences of risky sex
A focus group was conducted with young people and teachers at the Children First Project in Spanish Town, Jamaica. The focus group drew a problem tree around the issue of 'risky sex'. To begin with they were asked to identify what causes young people to have 'risky sex'. They were then asked to identify the results of 'risky sex'. They drew the tree below. The boxes in bold are issues that the project staff feel they can directly address.

Figure 6a.2. Causes and consequences of risky sex (Children First, Jamaica)[2]
(Boxes in bold are issues which the project staff feel they can directly address.)

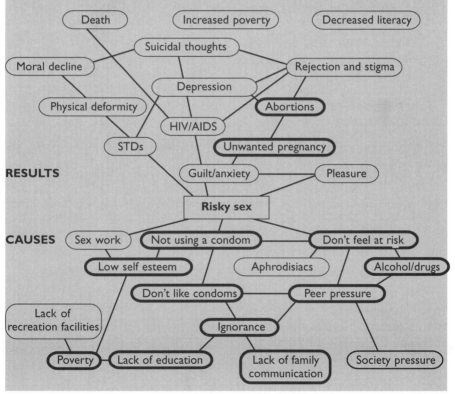

---

[2] Taken from *Learning to Live: Monitoring and evaluating HIV/AIDS programmes for young people*, Save the Children, 2000

Constructing objectives trees in existing work where objectives are not clear

Description

The following method of setting objectives has been developed for use by social work teams in the UK.[3] The method demonstrates the process and problems of clarifying objectives as a group. It is described in some detail here since the clarification of objectives is particularly important for assessment, monitoring, review and evaluation. It is possible to adapt the method for use outside the UK.

What it is

The method is based on four criteria:
- It should enable objectives to be set in such a way that they are intelligible to all interested parties.
- It should not be designed for use by a planning 'elite' who expect others to implement the results without question.
- It should help people set objectives in such a way that they can easily be linked to action.
- It should form part of a continuous process where objectives are regularly reviewed and reset when necessary.

Conflict resolution

The exercise can help programme staff and managers focus their energies more constructively if they all agree on the objectives. However, it is unlikely that everyone will agree completely and there will almost certainly be some unreconciled differences within the group. This means that the final statement of objectives is likely to be a negotiated agreement rather than a consensus. As a precondition for this approach to be successful, all participants must have equal power, otherwise the most powerful will have more influence. The method is designed to help ensure that all participants make an equal contribution.

How it works

There are three steps:
1. creating objectives

---

[3] Based on Miller, C and Scott, T, *Strategies and Tactics: Planning and decision making in social services fieldwork teams.* Paper no. 18, National Institute for Social Work 1984, ISBN 0 902789 32 5

2. classifying objectives, activities and inputs
3. building an objectives tree.

It is important to involve all the relevant people in this process, including, for example, staff, managers, partners and community representatives (see Chapter 2).

Step 1: Creating objectives

The purpose of this step is to elicit ideas from all group members. A danger is that the most confident members will contribute most ideas and hence set the tone of the whole exercise. This can be overcome by using the following technique:

Each person is given a set of blank cards (say three or five). All are asked to complete the following sentence on each card: 'This programme/project/piece of work ought to do the following...' Everyone should contribute one idea for each card, no more and no less. This means that everyone makes the same contribution.

Problems and remedies

The ideas contributed may not be sufficiently specific to be used as objectives. For example, they may be single phrases like 'health education', 'community participation', 'social worker training'. These are not useful as objectives without a verb (such as: 'extend', 'make more effective', and so on). Cards which are not specific enough should be given back to the person who wrote them, and they should add the verb they consider appropriate.

Step 2: Classifying objectives, activities and inputs

The group will now be faced with a pile of cards with statements about what the work should do. The problem is how to sort them out to discover the overall direction the group wishes to take. Some statements will be more concerned with the ends, or impact the work should attempt to achieve; others will be about the means, or process. Statements about impact will refer to the needs and conditions of the target group, and these are what are termed 'objectives' in this book. Statements about processes are more varied. They may concern action that might be taken to achieve a particular objective (termed 'activity outputs' in this book); or they may relate to the organisation, type and quantity of resources needed to back up a particular activity to achieve an objective (termed 'inputs'). If the group is to develop a viable plan of action, it must be able to distinguish between objectives, activities and inputs, and ensure that all three are linked together in a sensible way. In other words, the activities should be organised and resourced in the best way possible to help them achieve the objectives. There needs to be a clear distinction between means and ends.

This method of creating objectives uses the distinction between means and ends as the basis for the first stage of analysis of the statements on the cards. The group is asked to classify the statements concerned with ends as impact objectives, and those concerned with means into either activities or inputs. The distinction between these three types is as follows:

Impact objectives: The effects the group wishes the team to have on the target group and the wider community.

For example, the reduction of disabling conditions such as poverty, the improved ability of the target group to reach their potential, or a reduction in child mortality.

Activities: The action that the group considers would be the best way to achieve the impact objectives.

For example, working within a ministry to influence policy development, developing training programmes, providing services.

Inputs: The organisation and provision of resources to implement the activities.

For example, provision of secretarial services, specific training programmes for staff, agreed budgets, constructing infrastructure, buying and servicing vehicles, and an organisation structure which facilitates decision-making and maintains staff morale.

Problems and remedies

The distinction between the three types of statement may appear to be clear on paper but is often difficult to make in practice. One approach is for group members to attempt to classify their own cards into one of the three types. The group is then asked to sit in a circle and each person is asked in turn to read out one card and define the type of statement he or she believes it to be. The rest of the group is then asked whether they agree with the classification. Anyone who disagrees is then asked for an alternative classification and its reasoning. The group then debates the alternatives and agrees on a final classification.

It is not always possible to put a statement into only one category. Some statements may include a number of clauses, each of which may fall into a different category. In that case each clause should be classified separately.

For example:

- to improve the health of women (impact) through developing training programmes and policy for staff (activity)
- to provide better community health services (activity) by improving the recruitment of appropriate community health workers (inputs)
- to promote the welfare of the population in the area (impact) by assessing the needs of the population (inputs)
- to increase uptake and awareness of primary health services (impact) by

renovating buildings (inputs) required for clinic and training activities (activity).

A further classification problem arises from statements about the process of development; for example, 'to increase the community's self-help capability'. This could be classified either as impact objective or activity. Classification as an impact objective would be argued for by saying that it is a desirable state of being in the community, and this is an end in itself. Classification as an activity would be argued for by saying that it is a means of achieving more tangible improvements in well-being. This is really an ideological debate, and one way to resolve it is simply to ask the person who made the statement whether it was intended as a means or an end.

Classification triangle

The classification process can be carried out by marking a triangle on the floor within the group circle. The corners of the triangle are labelled 'impact objectives', 'activities', and 'inputs'. As each statement is classified, the card is placed in position on the triangle. If it is written exclusively in terms of impact objectives, activities or inputs then the card is placed at the appropriate corner of the triangle. If it is a mixture of any two of the types (eg, impact objectives and activities) then it is placed on the side of the triangle between the two appropriate corners. If it is a mixture of all three terms, it is placed in the middle of the triangle.

Step 3: Building an objectives tree

The classification of statements will leave the group with cards placed at various points on its triangle. Any multiple statements should now be split into their component parts and placed at the appropriate corner of the triangle. The group should then decide whether to concentrate first on building a tree of impact objectives, activities or inputs. It may be easiest to start with the type of statement of which the group has the most examples. Leave this card on the floor and store the rest for future analysis.

The group should now inspect the card left on the floor. Two features may be noticeable:

- some may contain statements that are abstract or general, others may be much more down to earth and specific
- some of the more specific statements may have similarities.

The building of an objectives tree is based on these two features: generality versus specificity; and groups of cards of similar content.

Objectives tree format

The size, shape and meaning of an objectives tree can vary enormously. The following three levels have been found useful in this method.

- At the top of the tree is a general statement of objectives. For any one type of objective, it sums up the overall values and intent of the work. This is the **overall objective**.
- At the bottom of the tree, and greatest in number, are the most **specific objectives**.
- In between are the objectives that express the various streams of thinking contained within the overall objective. They each, in turn, express the common theme that binds together the more specific objectives. These are the **intermediate objectives**.

Before embarking on the construction of a tree it is useful to place a few restrictions on its final size. A good objectives tree should be short. It should be constructed to be able to communicate a complex message in as few words as possible. If possible, restrict the number of intermediate objectives to three or four. Each of these should be similarly restricted to three or four more specific objectives. This will produce a tree with a maximum of 16 specific objectives. Any relaxation of the restrictions is bound to produce a broader and more complex tree. This will be more difficult to take in at one go and will be more difficult to communicate to others. However, when producing the first draft of a tree it may be helpful not to worry too much about its size and shape. It can be 'pruned' later.

Intermediate objectives

The group should begin constructing the tree at the intermediate level, by creating piles of cards representing similar objectives. Each person in turn picks up one card and places it next to another that is felt to be similar. Sometimes a group member may wish to indicate a totally different objective and place a card in a pile of its own. This process should be continued until all cards have been placed in their appropriate piles.

The group should remain silent throughout this initial sorting process. Discussion or casual remarks may deter a member from creating a pile that he or she feels is important. Also an outbreak of discussion at this stage can bring the whole process to a halt, a state from which it is difficult to help a group recover. Once a card has been placed in a pile it may not be reassigned. Although not perfect analytically, this process does allow all the members of the group to influence the analysis.

After the initial sorting it may be obvious to the group that some piles could be split into two and reassigned to others. Likewise, piles which are very similar could be integrated. Statements should only be regrouped when all the group members agree about the changes.

The different groupings of objectives are a matter of opinion. The debate about alternative groupings is part of the process of clarifying objectives. To stimulate the debate, it may be worth repeating the process of clustering objectives several times to see how many alternative sets of groups suggest themselves. Once piles have been agreed, a single statement of an objective needs to be found to summarise each pile. This should be written on a new card.

Overall objective

The creation of the overall objective can be as difficult as the intermediate objectives. It should summarise all the objectives and show the overall intended direction of movement, of which all the objectives form a part. It may be helpful to extract the most general statements of objectives from each pile. A successful overall objective will not only summarise these statements but extract and highlight the underlying ethos.

Specific objectives (outputs)

These are specific statements of objectives which provide the answer to the question 'how?' asked of the intermediate objectives. They are a contrast to the intermediate objectives which are more general and can be interpreted in different ways. Within each pile of objectives the group should cluster the statements that represent different aspects of the objective. A single statement should be written to represent each specific objective.

Problems and remedies

When forming the initial piles there may be some cards that could equally well be placed in any pile. These tend to contain statements of a fairly high level of generality. The best way to deal with them is to exclude them completely. These statements are then used as a basis for forming the final overall objective. Cards which are written in a very specific form may be treated as specific objectives and linked to existing intermediate objectives. If no relevant intermediate objective exists, it may be necessary to create a new one.

Using the results

The outcome of this exercise should be three 'trees': one each for impact objectives, activities and inputs, and an exhausted group! The process of debate and choice the exercise creates is a crucial part of any team's life, but only if it leads to some action.

First, the compatibility of the three sets of objectives should be checked by asking the following questions:

- Will the activities help to achieve the objectives?

The process of generating objectives may lead to activities being chosen on their own merit and appeal rather than for their direct contribution to the achievement of particular objectives. As a result of this check, it may be necessary to make alterations to the activities tree.

• Will the inputs support the activities?

For example, the impacts may require an activity for which the organisation does not have sufficient skill. Do the inputs include an assurance that a training goal will be included to help people acquire that skill?

Second, the group should consider the tasks and activities that are already being carried out, and how these relate to objectives.

Such an examination of tasks and activities could lead to quite dramatic changes in team policy and individual practice. For example, any fundamental conflict between members of the group may come to the surface when the purpose of the work is clarified.

Tool 7
Example of evaluating participation

This has been included as an example of:
- a method for monitoring what progress a programme has made, through continuous 'self-evaluation' by the people involved in the work
- a method of identifying and using qualitative indicators for measuring the progress of a programme towards achieving its objectives
- a selection of indicators to show progress in developing the capacity of groups to organise, manage and implement development activities.

(See Tool 10 for an example of a diagram representing the results.)

The following information is taken from: Norman Uphoff, *Participatory Self-evaluation of PPP Group and Inter-group Association Performance: A field methodology,* prepared for the People's Participation Programme of the UN Food and Agriculture Organisation by Norman Uphoff, Rural Development Committee, Cornell University, Ithaca, NY, USA, May 1989.

The people's participation programme

The People's Participation Programme (PPP) of the UN Food and Agriculture Organisation (FAO) aims to establish self-managed and self-reliant groups at the community level so that people can improve their own economic and social conditions through collective action. The capacity (skills and resources) of the group to design, manage and implement development activities should be developed in a participatory manner, through the ideas, action and initiative of group members themselves. 'Group promoters' act as facilitators and supporters of growing group capacity. The methodology for 'self-evaluation' presented in the above publication is intended to help group promoters assist PPP groups to develop the capacity to evaluate their progress in a participatory way.

Identifying the indicators

This method for self-evaluation is based on the identification of indicators that can be used to show what progress has been made in developing a group's capacity. A list of suggested indicators, or key questions, has been compiled by analysing the problems and successes of PPP groups in several different countries.

The basic steps in identifying indicators are:

1. Identify the common problems and successes of a programme.
2. State these as specific questions to be discussed in a group.
3. Define a range of answers on a scale of 0–3 to classify different situations.

These steps may be adapted for use in other situations where indicators are needed to monitor qualitative change.

> A similar approach has been taken in monitoring the success of a training programme in the Ministry of Health in Zanzibar. Training needs among health staff are assessed by first identifying problems and then deciding which of these can best be addressed by training. It was agreed that hospital orderlies needed to know more about medical procedures. One indicator to monitor the success of their training is to see whether or not they stop using hospital sterilising equipment to make coffee, as this was the problem that highlighted the training need in the first place.

Using the indicators for self-evaluation

The PPP self-evaluation methodology provides a structured way for a group to consider a relevant set of questions about its progress, in terms of what it is trying to achieve, and to arrive at a consensus on the group's current situation.

- The first stage is for a group to select the indicators concerning capacity and performance that are *relevant to the particular objectives of that group*. (A minimum number of relevant indicators should be selected.) A list of over 80 different questions from which to choose is provided in the publication which describes the methodology (examples are listed below). The process of reaching agreement within a group about the most appropriate set of questions helps to educate and strengthen the group.
- Once the questions have been agreed upon, the important thing is the amount and honesty of discussion that is devoted to each question, to arrive at a shared understanding of how well or how poorly the group is doing in that particular area.

The group has to agree which of four possible answers or statements best describes its own position. Each statement has a number, or 'score', to reflect progress. A score of 3 is very satisfactory, 2 describes a satisfactory situation but with room for improvement, 1 is unsatisfactory with definite room for improvement, and 0 presents a very unsatisfactory situation with a great deal of room for improvement.

For example: Let us assume that the group has agreed that it wants to have active participation from all group members in its meetings and activities. (This should contribute to both short- and long-term group survival and success.)

Whoever is leading the discussion will ask the group: 'Which of the following statements best describes members' participation in the group?'

3 = **All** members participate actively in meetings and group activities. Everyone feels free to speak up and play an active role.

2 = **Most** members participate actively in meetings and group activities. Most feel free to speak up and play an active role.

1 = **Some** members participate actively in meetings and group activities. Some feel free to speak up and play an active role.

0 = **Few** members participate actively in meetings and group activities. Few feel free to speak up and play an active role.

The group has to discuss this and come to some agreement as to which is the most appropriate description of their situation. If a consensus is not possible after discussion, it may be best to vote and take the majority view or to agree on an intermediate score (such as 1.5) to reflect a difference of opinion.

If the process of self-evaluation is carried out regularly and openly, with all group members participating, the answers they arrive at are in themselves not as important as what is learned from the discussions and from the process of reaching consensus.

Inventory of indicators

The indicators drawn up for the PPP come under six major headings, which are then broken down into subheadings (where necessary) and into specific areas which reflect the objectives of the PPP.

I.   Group operation and management

A. Management responsibilities

Style of management, sharing of responsibility (within group), supervision of officers (by members), rotation of officers, pool of leadership, specialised functions.

B. Meetings and participation

Frequency of meetings, decision-making method, speed and effectiveness of decision-making, members' participation, women's participation, productivity of meetings, attendance at meetings, records of meetings, progress reports, facilities for meetings.

C. Operation of group

Constitution and by-laws, communication, quality of discussion, inter-personal relations, discipline, assignment of tasks, conflict management, problem-solving.

D. Work of group

Work plan, assistance of group promoter, group goals, group achievement, group work, contributions.

2. Economic performance

Income generation, economic diversification, expansion, production, production credit, emergency loans, assets, savings, group purchases.

3. Technical operation and management

Improved technologies, local technologies, technical information, maintenance, quality control, technical responsibilities, technical diffusion.

4. Financial operation and management

Financial affairs, financial records, depreciation, profits, repayment of loans, security of resources, contributions of resources, inventories.

5. Group institutionalisation and self-reliance

A. Potential autonomy
Progress towards self-reliance, independence from group promoter, meetings without group promoter, legal status, resource mobilisation, broader benefits.

B. Membership base
Group solidarity, knowledge sharing, members' self-confidence, membership growth, reasons for group formation, ensuring effective leadership.

C. Knowledge base
Monitoring and evaluation, evaluation for self-management, experimental approach.

D. Broadening the base
Spreading the programme, linkages outside the programme, linkages within the programme, linkages with other local organisations, support of the programme at several levels, community support, ability to resist pressures, continuation of the group.

6. Other considerations

Access to assets, reducing inequality, improvements in nutrition, literacy, health improvements, socially undesirable activities, environmental protection, agricultural improvement, breaking impediments, balanced programme.

Each indicator is then phrased as a specific question. The questions given under heading 5 (above) are listed here as detailed examples. For details of questions under the other headings, the source document should be obtained.

Group institutionalisation and self-reliance

A. Potential autonomy
PROGRESS TOWARD SELF-RELIANCE: How *dependent* is the group upon the Group Promoter (GP)?

    3 = Group can now or very soon operate essentially on its own with only minimal assistance from GP and programme.

2 = Group can within 6–12 months operate on its own with minimal assistance from GP and programme.

1 = Group can within 12–24 months operate on its own with minimal assistance from GP and programme.

0 = Group cannot within foreseeable future operate on its own.

INDEPENDENCE FROM GROUP PROMOTER: How able is the group to operate without direction or intervention of GP?

3 = Group always tries to solve a problem itself before taking it up with the GP.

2 = Group often tries to solve a problem by itself before seeking the help of the GP.

1 = Group occasionally tries to solve a problem by itself.

0 = Group never tries to solve a problem by itself.

MEETINGS WITHOUT GROUP PROMOTER: How well does the group carry on its meetings without GP?

3 = Group is able to meet regularly and effectively without GP.

2 = Group can meet without GP, but GP's periodic attendance at meetings is necessary for regular and effective meetings.

1 = Group can from time to time meet effectively without GP.

0 = Group cannot meet successfully without GP present.

LEGAL STATUS: What is the legal status of the group?

3 = Group has all necessary recognition and approval to be able to get loans, hold property, etc.

2 = Group has some ability to get loans, hold property, etc.

1 = Group has plans for getting recognition and approval.

0 = Group has no legal status and no plans for getting this.

RESOURCE MOBILISATION: To what extent is the group able to mobilise resources from within group and/or externally to meet its needs?

3 = Group can always mobilise resources from savings, loans, sales or other means to meet its financial needs.

2 = Group can mobilise most of the resources it needs now from its own resources or from outside.

1 = Group can mobilise some resources internally or externally.

0 = Group is unable to mobilise resources to meet its needs.

BROADER BENEFITS: How able is the group to produce benefits beyond those to group members? Are benefits being generated also for individuals and for the community?

3 = Group has produced and is producing substantial benefits beyond its original economic activities, such as building a school or repairing roads.

2 = Group has created some benefits beyond its original economic activities.

1 = Group has considered producing benefits not in its plan.

0 = Group has undertaken and is concerned only with original activities.

B. Membership base

GROUP SOLIDARITY: Do members help each other apart from group activities?

3 = Group members frequently help each other with harvesting, loans, or other acts of service to others.

2 = Members sometimes help each other.

1 = Members once in a while help each other.

0 = Members never help each other.

KNOWLEDGE SHARING: Do members who get training share their new knowledge with others?

3 = Group actively provides for the sharing of members' new knowledge and skills with others, both other members and even persons outside the group.

2 = Group supports sharing of members' new knowledge.

1 = Sharing of new knowledge occurs only at individual initiative.

0 = There is no sharing of new knowledge.

MEMBERS' SELF-CONFIDENCE: Do members show increased self-confidence as result of participation in group activities?

3 = All members have gained much self-confidence from group.

2 = Most members have gained some self-confidence from group.

1 = Some members have gained some self-confidence from group.

0 = Members have not gained self-confidence from group.

MEMBERSHIP GROWTH: Has group membership grown? Or have new groups arisen alongside original group?

3 = Group has enjoyed substantial increase in membership, or to keep its size small, parallel group or groups have been started because others have been impressed with the group's accomplishments.

2 = Group has enjoyed some increase in membership.

1 = Group has enjoyed no increase in membership.

0 = Group has had a decline in membership.

REASONS FOR GROUP FORMATION: Why was the group formed?

3 = Because of shared conviction that collective self-help would improve position of all members.

2 = Because some members had conviction about collective self-help and others anticipated cheaper credit or other material inducements.

1 = Because members anticipated cheaper credit or other material inducements.

0 = Because GP got people together, not that they had any clear idea for purposes of group action.

ENSURING EFFECTIVE LEADERSHIP: Does the group have capability or experience in replacing ineffective leadership?

3 = Group has replaced ineffective leadership or is very confident that it could and would do so; it has specific procedures and provisions for this.

2 = Group agrees that it should and could replace ineffective leadership.

1 = Group willing to consider replacing ineffective leadership.

0 = Group afraid to take action to replace ineffective leadership.

C. Knowledge base

MONITORING AND EVALUATION: How does the group get and ensure feedback on its performance?

3 = Group has well established procedures and roles for monitoring and evaluating group performance.

2 = Group has periodic monitoring and evaluation of its performance.

1 = Group has occasional monitoring and evaluation of its performance.

0 = Group has no provision for monitoring and evaluating its performance.

EVALUATION FOR SELF-MANAGEMENT: Does group use participatory monitoring and evaluation for improving capacities of organisation?

3 = Group maintains good records and analyses them regularly.

2 = Group maintains records and analyses them periodically.

1 = Group maintains some records and considers them.

0 = Group maintains no records.

EXPERIMENTAL APPROACH: Do members adopt an empirical, trial and error method to experiment and test innovations?

3 = Members all very active in innovative experimentation.

2 = Some members very active in innovative experimentation.

1 = A few members active in innovative experimentation.

0 = No members active in innovative experimentation.

D. Broadening the base

SPREADING THE PROGRAMME: Does the group take initiative to spread the programme to other areas and other groups?

3 = Group has helped numerous other groups to get started or to become more successful.

2 = Group has helped some other groups to get started or to become more successful.

1 = Group has helped one other group to get started or become more successful.

0 = Group has not helped other groups.

LINKAGES OUTSIDE PROGRAMME: How does the group relate to government agencies?

3 = Group has excellent interaction with many relevant agencies that can help it achieve its goals.

2 = Group has some good interaction with some agencies.

1 = Group has a few interactions with some agencies.

0 = Group has no reliable interactions with any agencies.

LINKAGES WITHIN PROGRAMME: How does the group relate to other parts of PPP?

3 = Group has excellent linkages with other PPP groups through intergroup association (IGA) and with PPP staff and supporting NGOs.

2 = Group has some good linkages with IGA, PPP and NGOs.

1 = Group has a few linkages with IGA and NGOs or to PPP.

0 = Group has no reliable linkages with IGA or NGOs or even to PPP.

LINKAGES WITH OTHER LOCAL ORGANISATIONS: Does the group have linkages with other groups at the local level, like cooperatives, church associations, youth clubs, etc?

3 = Group has very active and good cooperation with other voluntary organisations at local level.

2 = Group has some very good cooperation with other voluntary organisations at local level.

1 = Group has at least one cooperative link with another voluntary organisation at local level.

0 = Group has no links with other voluntary organisations.

SUPPORT OF PROGRAMME AT SEVERAL LEVELS: Does inter-group association monitor and assist groups within programme?

3 = IGA actively and effectively oversees group activities and takes steps to help weaker groups, utilising the skills and experience of stronger groups.

2 = IGA undertakes some monitoring and assistance of groups.

1 = IGA has plans for monitoring and assisting groups.

0 = IGA does not exist or does nothing to help groups.

COMMUNITY SUPPORT: How much understanding and support has the group created within the community?

3 = Group enjoys strong and enthusiastic support from the community at large for its activities and continuation.

2 = Group has good understanding and support from some parts of the community, such as chief or local administrators.

1 = Group has a little understanding and support from the community.

0 = Group has no understanding and support from the community.

ABILITY TO RESIST PRESSURES: How able is the group to withstand economic or social pressure from opponents of collective self-reliance, such as merchants or shopkeepers who lose from group bulk purchase of consumer goods or officials who want to keep rural people dependent?

3 = Group fully united to resist hostile outside pressures.

2 = Group generally united in resisting pressures.

1 = Group somewhat united in resisting pressures.

0 = Group not at all united in resisting pressures.

CONTINUATION OF THE GROUP: How confident is the group that it can maintain itself after the FAO-assisted programme is withdrawn?

3 = Group is quite confident it can maintain itself on its own.

2 = Group is somewhat confident it can maintain itself on its own.

1 = Group thinks it might be able to maintain itself on its own.

0 = Group lacks confidence it can maintain itself on its own.

Strengths of the PPP method for participatory self-evaluation

- It is a method which groups can use to evaluate their own progress in terms that are relevant to them.
- It is a tangible mechanism for looking at progress, using qualitative indicators.

Weaknesses of the PPP method

- The indicators have been predetermined, and may not be entirely relevant for a particular situation unless they are adapted and others are developed.
- By selecting indicators from the existing list, other more important questions may be missed out.

Prerequisites for success

- The method should be used and adapted to make sure it is relevant. For example, the criteria for a 'successful group' can be developed by the group itself, analysing which key factors have contributed to the success or failure of other groups, and working out criteria from this.
- Be selective. Use the minimum number of criteria required for the exercise so it does not become overwhelming.

Tool 8
Using consultants

Written with extensive contributions from Belinda Duff, Human Resources Development Adviser, Save the Children Fund.

Description

The way in which a planning exercise, a monitoring system, a review, an evaluation or impact assessment is directed and managed should be determined by its main purpose and audience. Consultants may be required to help carry out all or part of any of these processes for the following reasons:
- to gain a wider view of a piece of work than insiders are likely to have
- specific expertise which staff do not have may be required
- a particular view may be required quickly
- a combination of the above.

Always consider what value the consultant can add – to the organisation and to the people in the organisation. When the consultant leaves, what will people be able to do that they could not do before?

Role of the consultant

Consultant(s) may play a number of roles and there are often competing demands placed upon them. Managing such demands is not only the task of the consultant, it is also the responsibility of the agency employing them. Different expectations can surface in the wide range of interpretations of the role amongst managers, staff, partner organisations and others who have an interest in the consultancy. The role the consultant is asked to play should be clearly set out and the communication (both oral and written) about the consultancy should define and explain the role in terms others can grasp. Many problems arising from consultancies are related to role ambiguity, role overload or in some cases, role underload.

A consultancy can be directed towards conducting a task that has to be done or providing more participative consulting which addresses a task or tasks using approaches that enhance the development of skills and knowledge on the part of those working with the consultant. This difference in emphasis has been described as 'task-focused consultancy' or 'process-focused consultancy'. They are not mutually exclusive since consultants are usually invited to perform a range of activities and produce specific outcomes related to both, but the emphasis on what has to be achieved will be critical in shaping how consultants work and the methods they employ. How a consultancy process is conducted is of vital importance and will leave a legacy of ways of working which will continue to exert influence long after any report has been produced.

Key questions that need to be considered when recruiting a consultant

Identifying the need for a consultant

- What aspect of monitoring, review, evaluation or impact assessment needs to be addressed, and who is involved in it? Who will be using the information?
- Who would most benefit from addressing it?
- Why use a consultant?
- Is the timing right?
- Are resources available to pay for a consultancy and to allocate the necessary staff and management time?

Drawing up a consultancy brief

- Define the **purpose of the consultancy**. This should be expressed in a document outlining the **terms of reference** for the consultancy and needs to be precise to ensure clarity.
- State the key outcomes expected and prioritise them. What is to be achieved in terms of **products** (reports etc) and **other outcomes** (eg, learning)? How will these be used (eg, improving programme management, strengthening advocacy messages, increasing donor awareness, greater accountability to the community)?
- There may be different expectations from different stakeholders. These should be clarified and negotiated to ensure the consultant(s) is not trying to meet too many demands. What are the main steps in the consultancy process, who else will be involved in them and at which stage? The tasks and responsibilities of different people who will be taking part should be defined at the beginning as far as possible (see Chapter 2).
- Key principles underlying the process should be defined: (eg, rights-based approach, focus on children) and expected ways of working which support the purpose, such as a high degree of participation and involvement with staff and local people. How will children and young people be involved in the exercise?
- What kind of consultancy is needed? What role should a consultant play? (See above.)
- Who will manage and implement the consultancy and its outcomes? What

sort of steering committee may be involved, and who has ultimate responsibility?

- What opportunities will there be to review the consultancy regularly and keep it on track or make changes if necessary?
- What may prevent the consultancy from achieving its purpose? It is useful to identify risks, dependencies and assumptions currently operating or likely to affect progress during the consultancy well in advance. Can sufficient time be allocated to deal with problems when they arise?

All of the people who will be affected by the findings of the exercise should be consulted when a consultancy brief is being drawn up and terms of reference are being decided. This is important for promoting ownership of the process and results. When the consultant is expected to make any kind of judgement about the work, it is particularly important that those who have a direct interest in the outcomes are consulted and are involved not only in gathering information but also in drawing conclusions.

Continuing the involvement of a wider group of people can be formally arranged by setting up a reference group or a steering committee. This could include the programme director or senior manager, project managers or staff, representatives from the community, representatives from partner organisations and, if appropriate, a senior manager from the agency headquarters. A realistic number of people should be agreed to enable the consultancy to complete tasks on time.

One person should be given ultimate responsibility for the consultancy to ensure accountability, management authority and direction, especially where there are many demands which can throw the consultancy off track and cause delays.

Preparation is key to defining any consultancy, but it is important to build in flexibility. The range of consultancy interventions is varied, and can include diagnosing problems as well as coming to a judgement about effectiveness. Important changes may need to be made to accommodate different demands and changing circumstances, so it is wise to demonstrate flexibility during negotiation and recruitment and to build in reviews of the consultant–agency agreement during the consultancy.

Identifying the right consultant

- What criteria can be used to choose a consultant? What are the key ways of working and technical skills required from the consultant?
- Where are reliable sources of information on consultants?
  Consider relevant institutes and any links they put on their internet sites, as well as consultants' networks, professional conferences, university faculties, etc.

- How can the consultant's suitability be assessed? Possibilities include inviting proposals, interviewing, requesting CVs, references, or a combination of these.
- What kind of written agreement should be prepared and finalised?

The consultant profile or description of the skills and experience of the person(s) looked for will depend on the purpose of the exercise. Their approach to children's rights and to development issues, their awareness of factors affecting women and children, and a general sympathy with the aims of the agency and the piece of work in question are vital. The background of the consultant(s) will inevitably have a considerable effect on the methodology, focus and findings of the consultancy.

Selecting the right consultant is a process in itself which should be managed by the person with ultimate responsibility for the consultancy. How this is conducted depends on the need and on who is available and interested in the brief. The process should be fair and be seen to be impartial by others, or the independence and credibility of the consultant may be called into question.

There is no 'one best way' to recruit a consultant, but two points are vital. First, the agency should produce a comprehensive document outlining a brief or **terms of reference** for a potential consultant or consultants (see below); and second, the engagement of one or more consultants is done on the basis of an explicitly negotiated agreement about what will be achieved and how, including terms of payment and other conditions which apply. It is binding on both parties: the consultant and the agency.

More than one consultant?

Sometimes pieces of work demand skill sets which cross more than one professional area. If a team of consultants is to be used, the following advantages may be gained:

- a balanced perspective on gender issues, by including women in the team
- a mix of relevant technical expertise and experience
- disabled people can be part of the team, especially when the exercise is concerned with work involving people with disabilities, but also for other work where people with disabilities will be affected by the programme
- cultural perspectives may be better understood where two or more people are gathering information and listening to people's experiences of the situation or piece of work, as different people tend to draw out different aspects of a problem and views of local people in discussions or interviews
- there should be a balance of people who know the agency and people who do not

- languages are a major asset and teams may include people who speak one or more languages used in the area.

Sometimes a combination of internal and external consultants is desirable, in which case enough time needs to be given to preparation and for consultation between those within and outside the agency before it begins. Negotiations between the agency and consultants should clarify the relationship, where and how they differ, and any particular roles each is expected to fulfil.

Preparing and managing the consultancy
Introductions and practical arrangements

- How will the consultant be introduced to colleagues with whom they will have contact? (This is essential for good relations with a staff team. For example, not knowing people's names can reinforce distance and the consultant's position as an outsider.)
- What logistical and practical arrangements are necessary (including adminis-trative support and facilities, computer, photocopying, transport, security)? An interpreter for the local language(s) may be needed.
- What background information and briefing does the consultant need to work effectively with the team? Who will ensure that the consultant will be aware of and be sensitive to the local situation (culture, politics, constraints, etc)?
- What information does the team need to work effectively with the consultant?

Efficient administration supports consultancies as much as it does any other programme activity. Getting the level of support needed is essential for good working relationships, problem-solving and delivering on time. Communication is also vital. This means not only passing on information to consultants, but consultants sharing information with others on progress, actions and decisions related to the consultancy.

Working with the team and with partners

Teams value consultants coming to work with them because this gives them many opportunities to discuss ideas, learn new concepts, talk about practice and try to imagine how theory and practice developed elsewhere can be used where they work. In many cases local staff and partners identify strongly with their clients or people they work with, and are keen to engage and learn on behalf of others and not just for their own benefit. However, they also bring something to the table and are not empty vessels waiting to be filled!

Local people possess skills and experience in working with their own social and political realities – the people, their lives and cultures and traditions which are the filter through which all knowledge acquired elsewhere must pass. This should be explicitly recognised in consultant briefs, terms of reference and other forms of agreement. Their ability to measure and test ideas using their experience far outweighs what an external consultant can do, and they are the ones who will be responsible for taking forward any recommended actions. A good consultant or manager of a consultancy needs to ensure that all this is treated as an asset and adds value to the consultancy.

Key questions that may help consultants to work more effectively with teams:

- In what ways is the consultant expected to enhance the performance of the team?
- How will consultancy activities be integrated into the day-to-day work patterns of team members? It is important that consultants understand people's roles and workloads and fit their timetable in as much as possible to other commitments.
- What kinds of meetings will the consultant be expected to attend and with whom? How often should the consultant(s) meet with the person who has been given responsibility for managing the consultancy?
- How will feedback from team members be incorporated into progress reviews with the consultant?
- How will problems be reported to and dealt with by the person managing the consultancy?
- How will the consultancy build on local knowledge and experience?
- How will the manager of the consultancy ensure that outcomes (learning and recommendations) are relevant and useful in the local context?

Carrying out the consultancy exercise

- What should be the limits to the consultant's independence? Ensuring that other people have the opportunity to influence the conclusions of the exercise must be balanced with not compromising the value of an external voice that is not tied to vested interests in coming to an overall judgement.
- Who is responsible for designing the methodology? Will the agency's interests and concerns be satisfied? Who will be involved in the proposed methodology? Should there be specific agreements, for example, about who will be interviewed and the questions to be asked? Again, a balance has to be struck between involvement and a critical eye, and the consultant will usually bring some experience in methods that is not available in the agency.
- It may be useful to identify a source of advice or support for the consultant, such as advisers within the agency or from a local institution.
- When are the results of the exercise required? What is the time frame for the consultancy covering the key stages and tasks? For example, when a draft

report is expected, and when the final report should be completed?

- How will the consultancy be reviewed on a regular basis to ensure that progress is monitored and any problems or delays are dealt with, responding to changing circumstances if necessary?

Outcomes of the consultancy

- Who uses the final report or other products (video, etc) and what use can be made of these outputs?
- What learning outcomes can be identified, both in the sense of lessons learnt and also knowledge and skills gained.

Learning should be high on the agenda for consultants, staff and partners alike. Staff and partners need to be actively engaged in gathering information and generating knowledge about the area under consideration, integrating that information into their working and life context, interpreting or making sense of the knowledge gained and then deciding on actions which they are empowered to take.

When this happens, the consultancy is far more likely to result in sustainable outcomes. Some models of consultancy enable this to happen and some do not. A model which uses local people as sources of information and then does not engage them with the next steps in the process leaves them stuck in the same place. In such situations the consultant is the subject of the learning process, taking knowledge acquired with them when they leave. This preserves a profitable situation for consultants, and a fragmented and passive one for the supposed beneficiaries of the consultancy.

What happens next? Reviewing the consultancy

- What are the main outcomes of the consultancy?
- Will the consultant be involved in any follow-up activities?
- Who learned from the consultancy and can apply this learning to the programme and more generally?
- What should be done differently the next time a consultant is recruited and deployed?
- Who will ensure that decisions and actions from the review are carried out?

Reviewing consultancies helps those who manage them and those who are intended to benefit from the experience to reflect and to identify what went well, what did not go so well, and what improvements can be made the next time a consultant is engaged. Using this learning will improve the competence and confidence of those working with consultants, and so increase their value to the programme.

Sample consultancy agreement

A sample agreement for services between a consultant and client is outlined here, to illustrate the kinds of areas that need to be covered. It is not a standard format and needs to be adapted for local use.

AGENCY NAME
CONSULTANCY TITLE, eg, Review of PAEC, Manila, 2000–2001
<u>AGREEMENT FOR SERVICES</u>

The following agreement sets out the respective responsibilities of xxx (the consultant) and Save the Children UK (the client).

1. The brief
1.1 The purpose
Define the purpose of the consultancy in one or two sentences.

1.2 Consultant tasks
List the main tasks the consultant is expected to perform in the course of the consultancy. It may be helpful to set these out in the sequence in which you expect them to happen, and to place ones that depend on previous task completion in that order. By the stage of drawing up the agreement these items should have been discussed in sufficient detail with the consultant.

1.3 Background
It is sometimes helpful to set out a few key factors which provide the background to the consultancy, or what has led up to this point. Keep these salient points brief and factual – long historical accounts are of limited use and tend to detract from the importance of other information contained in the agreement.

2. Liaison
Set out clearly your expectations of contact with the consultant and who is responsible for managing the consultancy. For example:
Liaison within Save the Children will include:
- direct contact with Unit trainers based in East and West Africa regarding trainer competence development (with reference to course structure and content, own development needs)
- ex-participants still working for Save the Children by phone, email or letter regarding trainer performance
- regular liaison with the Coordinator of the Unit regarding trainer recruitment, development and retention and implications of these for the organisation and delivery of courses
- **external contacts** (to be identified) re: trainer competence development, eg, previous consultant who conducted course review.

"The consultancy will be managed by the HRD Adviser. Regular contact will be maintained for support and reviewing progress with tasks".

3. Target dates
Again it is best to be explicit about dates and deadlines. This should cover key milestones or

points in time when tasks should be completed, eg, completion of field-based research or interviews, production of questionnaire, draft report submission.

4. Terms and conditions

This is the section that sets out payment and other matters regulating the relationship between agency and consultant. An example of the main items and text is given below; this should be adapted to reflect local requirements and situations.

It is agreed that the work will be carried out on the following basis:

4.1 Fees

This may be agreed as a daily rate or as a set fee.

"Remuneration has been agreed at the rate of . . . per day for . . . days/weeks commencing . . . The consultant will present an invoice upon completion of the consultancy.".

However, unless the number of days are clearly agreed in advance and it is known exactly how many days duration the work will cover, this is a risk for the agency as the amount payable can be increased. Increasingly agencies are negotiating a set fee for pieces of work.

"A fixed fee of . . . (note currency may vary), inclusive of VAT (again taxation varies) for completion of all tasks, divided into two equal parts:

> *first part payable on production of (here list key products or tasks you expect to be completed)*

> *second part payable on satisfactory production of the final report and completion of work according to the schedule and specification (see sections 1–4)."*

4.2 Administrative support and facilities

This depends on circumstances including the nature and duration of the consultancy and the capacity for providing admin support. For example:

"The consultant is expected to be self-servicing, eg, provide own computer, telephone, coming in to (agency) offices for meetings as and when required.

When conducting the consultancy, the agency will be responsible for providing any necessary admin and computer facilities."

4.3 Expenses

Again, this depends on the circumstances in which someone is recruited.

"Travel expenses will be paid, based on second or economy class travel, for which receipts will be required. Accommodation will be provided to a standard agreed by (the agency) in advance and there will in addition be a local subsistence allowance of (insert agreed rate) per day for meals, etc."

Other expenses which agencies can also pay include postage, stationery and reasonable incidental costs such as vaccinations. (In the case of longer-term consultancies, telephone expenses may be payable.)

It may be useful to state an upper limit for expenses.

4.4 Self-employed status
This has implications for taxation in the UK.

"The consultant is responsible for his/her own tax and national insurance contributions and providing any Schedule D number or a tax self assessment number in compliance with UK law."

4.5 Medical insurance
This differs according to the home base of the consultant and the policy of the agency.

Agencies should ensure that provision and policy on medical insurance for consultants working outside their country of domicile are clearly stated and understood by the consultant.

Consultants may be required to provide their own insurance or join the agency's insurance where the agency may be liable in case of accident or injury. An INGO recruiting overseas consultants for example might word this as:

All consultants working overseas for (agency) are required *either:*
To agree to go on to (agency) insurance for the period of their stay
or
to provide written evidence of their own insurance details, which satisfies (the agency's) criteria for adequate insurance cover.

Where consultants are working in their own country, different arrangements will apply.

4.6 Confidentiality
"All information about the agency and its partners or individuals with whom the consultant comes into contact while working for (the agency) shall be treated as confidential and not disclosed to any party outside (the agency).

If issues arise from liaison with others during the conduct of the consultancy that have an impact on the consultancy or the programme, the consultant will discuss with the project manager the most appropriate way to report back and/or progress an issue.

Partners and others interviewed will also have the right of access to information held about them. The agency will need to be clear about what this entails before the consultancy commences."

4.7 Copyright
Consider this carefully. An illustration of the choices is given below; these are not exhaustive and depend in part on copyright law and how it is applied in different countries and to different circumstances.

For the UK, for example, it is possible to insert a clause such as:
"The products expected shall be the property of … (client agency) and the consultant shall waive all rights under the Copyright Design and Patents Act 1988 in relation to these products absolutely, now and in perpetuity."

Another approach could be:
"The reports produced and interview data collected will be the property of the agency and will be published and disseminated as the agency sees fit, with the agreement of the consultant.

In the event of disagreement, the consultant will be given full details in writing of the agency's reasons and decision prior to either publication or withholding publication of all or part of the report."

4.8 Cancellation
It is pragmatic to think about this in advance. Consultancies can be delayed or not finished for many reasons, and having a clear understanding of what applies will help both parties to conclude the agreement on a positive note.

"In the event of Save the Children cancelling the agreement for services, the following will apply:

> *Before work commences, 25% of fees agreed for the consultancy.*
> *After work has commenced, pro rata payment for all work completed, on condition that the work is satisfactorily carried out as per the agreement.*

In the event of the consultant cancelling the agreement for services:

> *And a satisfactory arrangement for revised deadlines cannot be negotiated, or where sickness or accident covers more then 20 working days, pro rata payment will be made for all work completed on condition that the work is satisfactorily carried out as per the agreement.*

> *In the event of cancellation for any reason other than sickness or accident, Save the Children will pay a maximum of 25% of fees agreed based on proportion of work carried out."*

4.9 Equality and Diversity Practice
"People who experience discrimination include those defined by age, disability, gender, race or ethnicity, and sexual orientation. The consultant will demonstrate her/his commitment to working with people from different backgrounds through language used, appropriate challenging of oppressive and discriminatory behaviour and adaptation of any materials developed to specific requirements."

4.10 Child protection and / or other agency specific policies
Additional policies which are relevant to the work of the agency should also be inserted. Where child protection is concerned, this usually involves designing protection mechanisms into the recruitment process, for example in the UK seeking references which specifically refer to child protection and checks on the background of an individual through agencies holding relevant data such as the police force. If this applies, agencies are advised to ask for guidance and examples of best practice from reputable agencies that have developed specific policies and recruitment procedures.

Signature of Consultant   Signature for client agency

....

Date ....   Date ....

Please sign both copies of this agreement for services and return one copy to (here insert named representative of client agency) marked private and confidential.

Signing the document means it is binding on both parties, and in case of any dispute, provides a reference document.

Further reading

Milan Kubr, *How to Select and Use Consultants: A client's guide*, Management development series no. 31, ILO, 1993, ISBN 92-2-108517-1.

Tool 9
Programme or project visits

Description

Many programmes receive visits: from the agency's head office (if it has one); from advisers and managers; some also receive visits from staff from other country programmes, from other organisations and from donors. These visits may have several purposes, including:

- for the visitor to learn about the work of the agency in that country (to inform their own work)
- to discuss particular problems or issues with programme staff
- to offer advice and support in the visitor's specific area of expertise
- to share experience from other places visited
- to carry out a mini-review, or monitoring exercise: commenting on current activities, assessing progress, and feeding back the findings from the visit.

Regular project visits

Regular project visits are one of the most common monitoring activities.

> **For example:** In Sri Lanka, project visits are usually carried out by Save the Children staff and partners.
> Most project visits in Sri Lanka include the following activities:
> - individual conversations/interviews with beneficiaries and local stakeholders
> - group discussions and focus groups with children and other beneficiaries
> - observations of projects' activities.

In order to ensure consistency across the programme and focus on relevant information, it is possible to design:

- a common generic format for each of the visit activities (interviews, observation, discussion groups, etc) to be used across the programme
- a common report format to be used for each visit across the programme and by any staff or partner involved in monitoring.

Sample visit format
- Who did the visit
- Purpose of the visit
- Who was consulted during the visit

- In what way (ie, group or individual discussion)
- Issues emerging on the implementation of the project including achievements and constraints
- What has changed since last visit
- Any unexpected events or developments.

The findings from the visits can then be discussed in regular meetings.

Planning a one-off visit

It is important that all visits are properly planned. This will help ensure that everyone benefits from the visit, and that any reports that are produced provide useful feedback to field staff for use in future planning and programme development.

The following points should be considered when planning a visit:

- purpose of the visit
- preparation
- the timing of the visit
- terms of reference
- feedback and reporting
- language and interpreters
- evaluation of the visit.

These are discussed below.

Purpose of the visit

As in any monitoring or review exercise, the different people involved may hope to get different things out of a visit. It is useful to clarify the expectations of:

- the person visiting
- the office, department or section represented by the visitor
- the director of the programme being visited
- relevant staff at the country office
- partner agencies
- managers and staff of the programmes that will be visited
- people who are affected by the work.

Preparation

Time is often limited in a visit. The following pre-visit preparation may help to make best possible use of the time available.

Background information about the visitor

It would be useful for staff of the programme being visited to receive well in advance:

- a briefing note on the background, current work and interests of the visitor, for the information of field staff at different levels and for partner agencies
- any information on what the visitor has to offer (funding, advice, skills, etc) so that people being visited may be prepared
- what the visitor would like to see or achieve (in order of priority).

For example: When Save the Children's education adviser was first appointed at Headquarters, she sent a letter introducing herself to all field directors. She also outlined her intention to visit one country in each region, what she hoped to gain from the visit, and how this would then feed in to her future work as education adviser. In preparation for her visit to India, this letter was circulated to the different field offices. The India field staff were able to discuss the letter to plan a visit that could provide the adviser with a useful insight into the different types of education work carried out in India, and the policy and strategy issues being faced. They were also able to provide the adviser with opportunities to discuss her views with relevant staff and partners.

Background information about the country and programme to be visited

Before arriving, visitors should make sure they have a basic understanding of the culture, politics and economics of the country and area to be visited, and of the agency's country programme. They should also know something about any partners (when and how work started, the key players in the partner organisation, why and when the agency entered into partnership, activities carried out by the partner and the agency's experience of work with the partner). They can be briefed in more detail during their visit, but this will take less time if they already have a good basic understanding. Visitors should also be briefed on the cultural 'dos' and 'don'ts' in a country.

The timing of the visit

Timing of the visit should aim to make the most use of the visit for all the people concerned.

Cause the least disruption

Advance notice of the visit and flexibility about timing is essential. This will enable the field office to organise the visit so that it takes into account administrative matters, working days, holidays, availability of staff, 'breathing space' between visitors, etc.

Timing the visit to coincide with other events
It may be possible to time visits to coincide with other meetings, reviews or monitoring exercises which will help provide the visitor with an overview of a programme.

Opportunities for discussion with different people involved in the work
Visitors may need time to discuss their impressions and views with staff throughout the visit. Time for discussion should be scheduled into the visit to make sure all the relevant people can be involved. It may also be useful to meet people who are affected by the work, which could be done by attending meetings, accompanying staff on field visits and so on. Consultation with women may only be possible for visitors accompanied by female members of staff.

Terms of reference

Any visit to the field should have terms of reference which are agreed by the person visiting and the field office. If possible, the different programmes and projects to be visited should contribute to drawing up the terms of reference to ensure their interests are taken into account. The terms of reference should clearly describe the different objectives for the visit for all the different people involved. They should also provide a clear mandate about any relevant feedback and discussions required by different people.

While the terms of reference should be broadly agreed before the visitor arrives, it may be useful to have a meeting at the beginning of the visit to make sure the terms of reference are acceptable to everyone, and that the visit schedule is suitable.

Feedback and reporting

In order to fulfil its function as a monitoring exercise, it is important that programme and field staff have an opportunity to discuss the purpose of the visit at the beginning. This will help ensure that the issues they have identified will be addressed and that the feedback from the visit can be used to help make the work more effective.

Any feedback giving recommendations or advice to programme staff as a result of discussions held during the visit is usually best discussed first with the relevant managers. It can then be sent to programme staff through the appropriate line management structure and copied to any relevant advisers.

Different types of feedback

Different types of feedback may be needed to meet the different needs. For example:

- a discussion at the end of a visit with staff, managers, partners, and people affected by the work
- discussion papers that programme staff can use as the basis for further internal discussion
- discussion with relevant people at head office on return from the visit
- reports for programme managers, country directors, and senior managers and advisers.

Language and interpreters

When discussions are held between a visitor and local people (including field staff, partners or people affected by the work), it is important to consider what language the discussion should be in, since this will affect the ability of different people to participate, who will be at an advantage and who at a disadvantage. Where discussions are held with women, it may be necessary to have a female interpreter.

The style and language used in written feedback should be appropriate for its audience. If any of the likely users of the feedback do not speak good English, it is particularly important that the language used should be clear and easy to translate.

Evaluation of the visit

At the end of the visit it is useful to find out whether the visit did meet expectations, and if not, why not.

For example: The Save the Children South-East Asia and Pacific Regional Office have devised a visit evaluation form. The form is for use by anyone who makes or receives a visit within Save the Children. It is a channel for feedback and as such can be used by anyone involved with the visit. A copy may be sent to a visitor's line manager for information, but should always be sent to the person concerned first. This form can be used as a basis for discussion at the debriefing session at the end of the visit. It can be adapted and translated for local purposes. The questions asked are:

1. How well do you feel the visit objectives were achieved?
2. Were the objectives appropriate?
3. Was enough time allowed for the visit?
4. What were the good points of the visit?
5. How could the visit have been better?
6. Were your expectations of the visit met?
7. Any other comments.

Strengths and weaknesses of visits as a monitoring tool

Strengths

- A visitor from another part of the same agency has the advantage of being an outsider to the country programme but an insider to the agency. This means that while they may have a more objective view of the work, they will also have an insider's understanding of the organisation, its culture, underlying values and principles.
- Different visitors have different areas of expertise and interest, and so may address issues that have not been given a high profile before. They may also be able to bring with them lessons from the experience of similar work in other countries.
- If properly planned, the experience from the visit can feed back into the organisation at different levels. Different forms of feedback can be targeted at different audiences.
- Visits can be useful to all involved and help stimulate analysis of what the programme is doing. This is essential for monitoring.

Weaknesses

- Visits are usually expensive (air fares and use of programme resources, including drivers, vehicles, interpreters, staff time, etc).
- If a visit is poorly planned, the different people involved may not benefit as much as possible. There is also a danger that the visitor may gain only a superficial understanding of work.
- If programme staff are not properly briefed about the background and expectations of a visitor and if they do not have a chance to express what they want to get out of the visit, they often feel uninvolved in the visit and may even feel threatened by it.
- If there is only one report that is not targeted to meet the specific needs of people involved in the programme, it may be too general and not provide genuinely useful information to anyone.
- There is a danger of different visitors offering conflicting advice to field staff.

Prerequisites for success

- Proper preparation, including:
  - information about the visitor and their expectations to be sent in advance to the field and circulated to all the programmes to be visited
  - discussion in the country and programme offices about the visit and how to make best use of it

- briefing for the visitor about the country, programme, and partners.
- All programmes to be visited should have an opportunity to see how they can use the visit to provide useful and relevant feedback about their work.
- The visit should be timed to cause least possible disruption of the programme work, and to take advantage of events which can help to inform the visitor and provide a channel for feedback to the work.
- All those who will be affected by the visit should be involved in drafting terms of reference. The terms of reference should state what programme staff, field director and visitor hope to get out of the visit and should provide a clear mandate about relevant discussions and feedback. They can be discussed and amended if necessary at the beginning of the visit.
- Any recommendations or advice should be given with the approval of programme management through the line management structure, and with the knowledge of relevant advisers in the agency.
- There should be a debriefing in country at the end of the visit to enable the different people involved to get the feedback they require. This should be communicated to others involved in the visit.
- If a joint trip is made (for example, a regional adviser with someone from the head office), a joint trip report helps to save unnecessary duplication and conflicting advice.
- It can be useful to build in time at the end of the trip for report writing, before leaving the country.

Tool 10
Presenting and sharing information: meetings, diagrams, video and theatre

Description

Presenting and discussing the information emerging during a planning exercise, monitoring, review, evaluation or impact assessment exercise to any of the people involved in the work is vital, so that the findings are incorporated into discussions, plans and policy relating to the work.

The conventional form of presenting and sharing this information is a written report. This is only really useful as a means for communicating with literate people who are used to digesting and critically analysing written information. This excludes many of the people involved in development work, particularly when reports are written in English.

Alternative methods for presentation that do not depend on a high level of literacy include, meetings, diagrams, slide shows, puppet shows, theatre and video, and a combination of all of these. The use of meetings, diagrams, video and theatre in relation to planning, monitoring, review, evaluation and impact assessment is described below.

Meetings

Meetings can be used to present the findings of an exercise to participants. This gives people the opportunity to question findings they do not agree with, to raise issues which have been missed out and to clarify areas that are unclear. Slides, diagrams, photographs and other forms of visual presentation can be used to stimulate discussion.

For example: In a participatory planning exercise in Wollo, Ethiopia, different priorities for local small-scale development activities were discussed. The last day of the planning exercise was devoted to a meeting to which the whole village was invited. Representatives of each of the interest groups interviewed on the previous days also came. The groups were: Peasant Association leaders, older men, younger men, older women and younger women.

A number of major priorities for small-scale development had emerged. The team, including villagers who had been particularly involved in the exercise, presented back the findings (problems and opportunities) to the villagers, using diagrams produced by the villagers. Using the village map constructed by one of the peasant groups, the different development project options were discussed in turn. This provoked a great deal of debate. Everyone offered an opinion of the pros and cons of the proposed options. Finally it was decided that the villagers could go ahead themselves with a number of the options. Others would require external support which was supplied by Ethiopian Red Cross.

(from *A user's guide to participatory inquiry* (draft), International Institute for Environment and Development, 1993.)

Strengths of meetings

- Different people can comment on findings and different views come up.

Weaknesses of meetings

- Some people will not contribute to group discussions.
- Many people will only find the time to attend a meeting if they are certain to get some tangible benefit out of it.
- It is difficult to arrange a meeting that will be convenient for all the different groups who might be interested.

Prerequisites for success

- A facilitator who can make sure different people contribute and that the meeting is not dominated by a few individuals. Ensure that different groups have the opportunity to comment and indicate disagreements.
- Make sure all major differences are represented: do not try to reconstruct an 'average' or 'typical' position that represents nobody's reality.
- Imaginative use of visual presentation methods (slides, diagrams, video, etc), and smaller group discussions if necessary.

Diagrams

A diagram is any simple model that presents information in an easily understandable visual form. Diagrams offer a visual means – in which everyone can share – of representing participants' opinions. Diagrams and maps can be used to summarise data at all stages of planning, monitoring, review, evaluation or impact assessment and can also be used to present the findings to different audiences. Diagrams can be drawn on virtually anything: paper, overhead transparencies, blackboards, or in the sand.

Using diagrams, especially when using local materials on the ground, can help to depersonalise a discussion and create a neutral space. People concentrate on the diagram, not on each other, and there is less direct eye contact between individuals. It can break down barriers and facilitate communication between different groups (outsiders, government officials, villagers and so on). Some of these strengths are lost when pen and paper are used, since only one person can hold the pen at any given time. However, a diagram which is created on the ground and then copied onto paper for presentation may lose some of its meaning (like traces of mistakes and corrections).

The diagrams can be presented by the people who made them.

> **For example:** In one PLA exercise in Sri Lanka, each group had drawn diagrams that were then copied onto flip charts. These were shown to other members of the group. At the end of the PLA there was a final exhibition. The flip charts were stuck up on the walls and each group explained their own diagram. A public hearing was then held in which the diagrams were presented again. The woman who presented to the public group the diagram produced by a group of women gained respect from the rest of the community.

Examples of using diagrams for presentation are given below. (See Tool 1 for a brief description of the different kinds of diagram.)

Social mapping and resource mapping can be used to help present baseline data, to show who is affected by a programme, and to show how the lives of different households have changed in relation to the programme and other factors.

> **For example:** An evaluation of a rural development programme in India used social maps to show the proportion of time different households spent working on their own land and on outside labour before and after the programme.

Maps can also be used to show changes in the external environment, including resources, political changes, and conflict. These can be compared with changes in the programmes.

Time lines have also been used, with several columns to show how political events outside the area, inside the area, and in the region have coincided with changes in the programme. This helps to analyse how different decisions have been made.

Impact diagrams can be used to show what has changed as a result of a programme.

For example: An evaluation of a project for rural women in India (facilitated by OUTREACH – volunteers for rural development) used participatory methods to construct a diagram. This shows the situation before and after the programme, and what had been the most important cause of the change:

Figure 10a.1. Diagram of an evaluation of a project for rural women in India

Ladder exercise	BEFORE	AFTER	PROJECT	NON PROJECT	REASONS
AWARENESS			OOOOO		Mainly from agriculture training and from agricultural families
PRODUCTIVITY AND YIELD			OOO	OOOOOO O	Through agriculture training and technology implementation
CONFIDENCE			OOOOO	OOOOO	Through training and better economic status
DECISION MAKING			OOOO	OOOOOO	Increased ability and confidence

KEY — Range Level

'Spider' diagrams can be used to show how different organisations are progressing in relation to different aspects of institutional maturity. (See figure 10a.2 and also Tool 7, for indicators of institutional maturity.)

Strengths of diagrams

- They greatly simplify complex information.
- They can condense a large amount of information into a small space.
- People can develop maps and diagrams themselves, which is part of the process of analysing information.
- People not used to public speaking may be able to present their views more easily when describing and interpreting a diagram they have developed themselves.

Weaknesses of diagrams

- Diagrams have been used with variable success. They are very culturally specific. For example, pie charts are only understood in some cultures.

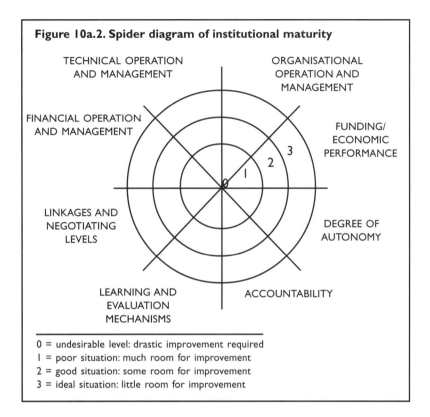

Figure 10a.2. Spider diagram of institutional maturity

TECHNICAL OPERATION AND MANAGEMENT

ORGANISATIONAL OPERATION AND MANAGEMENT

FINANCIAL OPERATION AND MANAGEMENT

FUNDING/ ECONOMIC PERFORMANCE

LINKAGES AND NEGOTIATING LEVELS

DEGREE OF AUTONOMY

LEARNING AND EVALUATION MECHANISMS

ACCOUNTABILITY

0 = undesirable level: drastic improvement required
1 = poor situation: much room for improvement
2 = good situation: some room for improvement
3 = ideal situation: little room for improvement

Drawing on the ground may be difficult in cultures where this disturbs the ancestors.

Prerequisites for success

- Diagrams should be simple, without too much information on one page.
- Any writing should be clear and large enough for people to read from a distance.
- They should have clear titles and should include the names of the authors, and place and date of preparation.
- They should be presented by the people who constructed them, to explain how they were constructed.
  (See below for suggestions of how video can be used to present diagrams.)

Video

Video has many potential uses at different levels in development projects. Ideas and information can be communicated from one community to another and from communities to managers, policy-makers and donor agencies. In planning, monitoring, review, evaluation and impact assessment, video can be used in two main ways: as part of a participatory process for analysing a situation; and, more simply, as a means for recording and presenting findings.

As a tool for participatory analysis

Video can be used directly as a PLA tool, for collecting, analysing and presenting information in a participatory way. This can be done by using the video camera as an observer which can be manipulated by the participants. The participants decide exactly what they want the camera to see, how the image is framed, what it focuses on, what is included and what is left out. They then record a commentary over the image to explain in their own terms what the camera sees.

For example, it can be used **to rank activities** or households in order of success or well-being. Participants may be asked to show the camera the things they think are successful. The recorded image can be shown to participants to check whether it is what they wanted to show, and how they see it. The image can then be explained and made into a commentary which is recorded onto the film by the participants, in their own language. In this way, rather than the camera 'capturing' something out of the participants' control, they are showing the camera what they want it to see. In the process, participants also learn how films are made and the way a message can be manipulated by combining a particular image with a particular sound.

The camera can also be used to **explore different options** in a programme.

The possible consequences of different situations can be explored using role play. For example, what would it be like if the proposed new water supply were to be situated in the middle of the village, or in the health centre compound? The role play can be recorded on video and the resulting film can be shown back. Since watching yourself or your friends on film is almost always funny, it can provoke discussion about different options in a non-threatening way.

With careful planning, it is possible to shoot the film in sequence so that it does not need to be edited afterwards. This means the message will not be reinterpreted by an outside editor.

This approach will only be participatory if it is initiated by a facilitator who uses a PLA approach. He or she must be able to hand over control of the process successfully to the participants.

Interactive video, whereby short video extracts are used to stimulate discussion, is another participatory technique whereby the audience are encouraged to exchange ideas.

For recording and presenting information about the work.

Video can be used simply to document different aspects of a project or programme.

For example: A review was carried out of a project to promote the use of smokeless stoves in the Tibetan refugee community in India. People who had smokeless stoves in their homes were interviewed on film by one of the field workers from the project, who then translated their replies. The people were able to explain why they were not using the smokeless stoves as much as had been expected. The film was shown to project workers in India to help them decide how they could address the problems, and to other communities using the stoves to promote discussion. Tapes were also sent to the programme director in Europe, to show him why the projects were not all working and to edit for use in fundraising and promotion.

Video can also be used for documenting work as it is carried out.

For example: In Lesotho, the Save the Children Integrated Education programme uses video extensively. The programme director videos discussions of the training committees, work on education materials, teaching sessions, follow-up discussions, buildings at different stages of completion, and so on. The videos can then be used for training teachers and parents of children with disabilities: for example, by showing them different teaching sessions, showing how different parents work with their disabled children and how training materials and equipment can be used. The videos can also be used to stimulate discussion about the programme aims and activities with parents and teachers. They can be used to show how individual children have improved over time, and how the programme itself has developed. This can be shown to government partners, Save the Children staff in the head office, other organisations, etc.

For recording the process of collecting and analysing information

The process of asking questions, conducting group discussions, drawing maps, etc can be filmed on a daily basis and then shown back to facilitators, field staff and other members of the community. This type of video can show, for example, how different people reacted to the exercises, who did not participate, how questions were asked and so on. This can be used to help modify the techniques and approaches to make sure they do involve all the relevant groups. It can also be used to promote further discussion among other members of the community who did not take part in the exercises.

Video can also be a good way of recording a mapping exercise, where maps and diagrams are constructed on the ground. The process can be filmed at different stages, and this can be used to present the maps at their different stages of completion, with a verbal explanation of what the different symbols represent.

This is an alternative to copying the maps onto paper, which involves reinterpreting the map and adding a written explanation of symbols.

Videos in presentations

The film recorded in all the activities described above can be used in presentations about an exercise. This is particularly useful when people involved in making the video are also involved in the presentation. This type of presentation can be useful to promote discussion at a local level. It can also be used to bring the insiders' perspective into discussions about the work in country, regional and head offices. This is useful for people from inside and outside the area concerned:

- Local people (including field staff and local government officials) who were not directly involved in making the video will benefit from being able to understand the language and concepts. It may show them familiar scenes with different interpretations and points of view that they did not appreciate before.
- Local people involved in making the video will know that it shows a situation from their own point of view. This can make them more confident in dealing with outsiders or powerful insiders.
- People from outside (including agency staff, government officials and donors) will learn about the work from an insider's point of view and gain more information about the context of the work.
- Agency staff can use the video to help communicate between different parts of the organisation.

Strengths of video

As a process
- The exercise of focusing the camera can help to focus ideas.
- Less confident people, including women, people with disabilities and children may find it easier to express their views through a camera than directly to outsiders.
- The process of presenting their own views can give local people more confidence in dealing with outsiders.
- Video can reveal something about the way different people react to each other, to field workers, and to others.
- It can show changes over time.
- It can be edited to convey different messages, as required.
- Video is widely used for entertainment, so playback facilities (television and video cassette recorders) are increasingly available even in remote communities.
- Video recordings can be replayed instantaneously so that participants can see

themselves straight away. Reports take a long time to write, photographs and slides need to be sent away to be developed and printed.

- With the development of new technology, it is now possible to store video pictures on compact disks and combine it with text, diagrams and other images which can be processed on computers.

As a means of presentation

- The views of people affected by the work can be brought directly to the attention of outsiders, including senior decision-makers involved in the work.
- Video can convey a lot of information about the context of the work, the environment, living conditions, etc.
- People may find it easier to understand, criticise or disagree with a video, than with a written report.
- People are usually interested to see themselves and people they know on video. It can be a good way of taking lessons from one community to provoke discussion in another.
- Video may be a good way of presenting PLA material (maps and group discussions) to people who were not involved in the fieldwork.
- It is easy to convey technical information (for example, about the way smokeless stoves work).
- Video is often more accessible than other audio visual media, as it records sound and movement and is therefore more realistic than diagrams, slides and photos in communicating complex information.
- Video tapes of a project can be viewed repeatedly without an expert being present, whereas slides, for example, require someone to explain what you are seeing.
- If people see something on video with their own eyes they are more likely to believe it than if they are simply told.

Weaknesses of video

As a process

- If the facilitator is not good at handing the control over to participants, the camera may create a distance between the people filming and the people being filmed.
- When less powerful people are encouraged to express their views on video, this may result in considerable conflict. For example, in some situations women have been punished by their husbands for expressing their views on video.
- Enthusiasm for the technology may overshadow the issues being discussed.
- The technology is expensive, can break down and needs power.

- Editing facilities are expensive and often only available in urban centres (although new digital equipment should make it possible to edit more quickly, in the field).
- Repeated use of video tapes causes them to degrade with time, so important material may be lost unless adequate cataloguing and copying of tapes is done systematically.
- Cataloguing and listing video material is time-consuming and ideally should be done by someone present at the time of recording so that background information is noted. NGO staff are often happy to do the filming but reluctant to spend time cataloguing the resulting material.

As a means of presentation

- Video can be used to promote messages. It may be completely controlled by the person using the camera. The bias of the message can be subtly altered by the methods of filming and editing. For example, if you film someone from a low angle they look big and important. The video may be edited to show a project in a favourable or critical light depending on the editor's bias.
- It may be difficult for staff to find the time, space and equipment to view videos.

Prerequisites for success

- Proper understanding of how film works, how to construct a story and how to use moving pictures and dialogue.
- A facilitator who is as skilled in using a participatory approach as in using video.
- At least one person with sufficient technical skills to be able to use the camera without too much effort and who can be flexible. The technology should be less important than the information it conveys.
- Robust machinery, including camera and external microphone. Tripod and mobile editing equipment would also be useful.
- Appropriate video format compatible with equipment used elsewhere, so that it can be viewed on locally available equipment.
- Archives and catalogues of raw material.

Theatre for Development

Theatre is a well established means for communicating the feelings and viewpoints of different people and how these interact with each other. Theatre for Development (TfD) is an approach that emphasises both the process of making and performing plays, and the products (the performances, plays or the event which come out of that process). TfD has been used successfully with young people to enable them to explore issues that are important to them, and then present the issues to other young people and to adults in a way that stimulates real discussion.

What it is

There are two main parts to the TfD process:
1. The creation of the performance by the children, which comes from what they see as important to themselves. They are helped in this by trained facilitators who guide them through various exercises which enable them to study others and reduce self-consciousness. They decide the problems they wish to portray in their performance through group debate and discussion, which in turn develops bonding between them. The performance itself is not rigid but instead open to continual development and improvisation.
2. Discussion groups with the audience concerning what the performance meant to them, and asking other relevant questions to probe their attitudes and to bring their concerns to the surface. This part of the process is as equally important as the first.

How it is done

TfD is usually carried out through a well planned and facilitated training workshop, in which children and adults work together to improvise plays about selected issues. The workshop usually consists broadly of the following steps:
1. Exercises in improvisation
2. Thinking collectively about problems or issues that have been identified, and how these affect different participants
3. More improvisation based on expressing feelings
4. Story making: making up a story and turning it into a play by improvisation; making sure the story is interesting
5. Discussing issues raised in the plays
6. More improvisation
7. Discussing what makes a good story, introducing irony and contradiction
8. Songs, music and dances: using musical skills in the group and extending them
9. Preparation for performances and discussion
10. Performing improvisations: criticism and changes
11. More work on all the above
12. Performing to an audience
13. Group discussions with audience about issues raised.

The above steps are usually carried out over five or six days with plenty of games and exercises to develop confidence and spontaneity.

How it can be used

TfD for situation analysis
TfD can be used to find out about issues that concern children.

TfD for rights-based development and advocacy
TfD can be used to explore problems that affect children in a community, the causes of the problems, how they affect different people, and how they fit into the wider picture. The plays can be performed to adult decision-makers in order to present the children's perspective. In the right context and with proper support, TfD can help give children the confidence and skills to address rights violations with the duty-bearers.

> **For example:** Children in Ladakh used TfD to explore issues concerning school and education. They created plays around their own experiences in school and performed them to different audiences to provoke discussion about how the problems could be addressed locally and at a national level.

TfD for evaluation

> **For example:** TfD was used in an evaluation of a health promotion project for adolescents on HIV/AIDS prevention. The health promotion is carried out by training staff in HIV/AIDS prevention and by training child activists to provide correct information to their peers at school and their families at home. The evaluation was carried out by a team of adults and children. The children used TfD to develop plays which they then performed at the schools in which the health promotion activities had taken place. The plays were developed around issues of sexual health and drug use, how children could obtain help and advice, and how they could deal with inaccurate information given to them by adults. The group discussions after the plays showed what issues were most important for adolescent girls and boys, and the extent to which the health promotion project had helped address these issues. The TfD approach helped people to open up and discuss sensitive and private matters, which may not have been possible using other approaches. The skills and learning developed by activists and project staff who took part in the TfD could also be used in other contexts.

Strengths of Theatre for Development

- Can provide insight into the concerns and perspectives of children and communicate these powerfully to different audiences.
- Helps participants look into and communicate their own understanding and feelings.
- Performers and audience come to a better understanding of their problems than is possible through more conventional methods.
- By improvising plays people act spontaneously, as they would in real life. They then reflect on what they did spontaneously and why they did it. This can give great insight into why people behave in certain ways, power relations, and so on.
- The process develops important skills in participants:
  - working together
  - improvising
  - making plays, and being able to change them spontaneously
  - working out collectively the root causes of different problems, and how these might be tackled
  - developing confidence in communicating with others, including adults, teachers, those in authority
  - ability to talk about physical and emotional matters
  - ability to facilitate the responses of others.

Weaknesses of Theatre for Development

- Time-consuming and expensive. In particular it can be difficult to find time to do it with children at school.
- Where the issues raised are of a sensitive nature, this may cause problems for the participants, especially if there is no on-going support.

Prerequisites for success

- Use it for the right purpose.
- Skilled facilitators
- Proper supportive context, especially where the TfD addresses issues that are sensitive. For example, in the evaluation of the health promotion project described above, good consultation with principals and teachers was essential to make sure they felt comfortable with the way issues around sexual health were to be tackled. A bad reaction from teachers or parents could have jeopardised the project itself.
- Contingency plans for dealing with strong reactions from members of the audience.

Tool 11
Training and development in planning, monitoring, review, evaluation and impact assessment

(This Tool has been written in collaboration with Belinda Duff, Human Resource Adviser in Save the Children, with contributions from Emily Moore, Consultant.)

There is a constant demand for training in planning, monitoring, review, evaluation and impact assessment, both from programme staff and partners. Most organisations do not have enough resources to meet all these demands, and in any case training in monitoring and evaluation on its own is usually not particularly effective in developing better performance. Training and development needs to be part of a **long-term strategy** to develop skills and techniques that is integrated into the normal processes for programme management.

This Tool presents the issues that need to be addressed by a strategy to develop planning, monitoring, review and evaluation. It then considers some different approaches that can be used to develop a strategy to improve planning, monitoring and evaluation (PME) capacity. The final two sections discuss the pros and cons of possible training providers and the prerequisites for success in a PME strategy.

Which issues need to be addressed?

Recognising the value of PME, and its role in an effective programme

- For a PME system to be effective, the strategic *impact* of programmes and projects must be given primary importance. This means an emphasis on what outcomes the work is trying to achieve in both the short and the long term, and looking critically at the *effect* of a programme and who benefits from it as well as describing activities and their immediate outputs.
- It is essential that senior managers fully support the process of developing planning, monitoring, review and evaluation systems. Ensuring clarity about the importance and role of planning, monitoring and evaluation is an integral part of programme management and accountability.

Perceptions and relationships

- People can feel threatened by monitoring and evaluation because it involves a judgement about the work and will have an effect on future programmes. Managers and operational staff need to be involved to ensure they understand and are committed to PME processes.
- Monitoring, evaluation, and impact assessment need to be developed within an organisational culture that is genuinely trying to understand what aspects of the work are successful, and which are not – a culture of self-criticism. It is essential to acknowledge problems and analyse the reasons behind them. This can be difficult, especially when admitting mistakes may affect funding decisions.
- Developing relationships between programme offices, partners and with donors that encourage openness, learning and accountability is critical.
- It is important to understand cultural and linguistic differences that affect communication, how far self-criticism is an accepted form of behaviour, and how receptive to external perceptions people may be.

Skills development

- Managers, staff, partners and communities need to develop techniques and approaches to planning, monitoring and evaluation. Skills required include: managing information, data collection, data analysis, selection of pertinent indicators, prioritising, producing clear and succinct reports and analytical skills, such as how to interpret statistical and qualitative information, how to make sense of contradictory or complex results and how to draw conclusions and apply these.
- Planning skills: analysing needs, and using the analysis to set objectives and decide how best to achieve them. This is key to the whole process.
- When setting out to improve people's performance, it is helpful to distinguish between behaviours that people should demonstrate and the underpinning knowledge they should possess. This distinction can help to clarify what will be developed and which approaches are likely to be most effective.

It may be useful to distinguish between improving *system performance* – routines, practices and the way planning, monitoring and evaluation is organised – from *people performance* – the way people carry out tasks and the skills and knowledge needed to perform such tasks well.

Resources

- Human and financial resources will be required to develop an effective PME system.

Different programme offices and partners will have different needs and priorities in relation to these issues. What needs to be addressed in developing planning, monitoring and evaluation will depend on:

- the internal environment: aims, values and culture of the organisation, as evidenced by the management style and habitual ways of organising work
- the external environment: political, social and economic factors as well as stages of development of partners and community organisations.

For example:

- For some organisations, the main issue may be to develop a more strategic approach which focuses on impact rather than activities, or to provide a more systematic and analytical approach.
- Networks need to accommodate a range of different organisations, objectives and styles. The main issue to address may be how to identify common objectives and to coordinate monitoring and evaluation.
- For small community-based organisations, the priority may be to develop a simple and cheap system for monitoring and evaluation, building on existing skills, systems and resources.

Developing a strategy to improve PME capacity

What follows is a guide to the different stages of a strategy to develop performance in planning, monitoring, review and evaluation. Some stages may have been carried out as part of other processes, such as strategic planning or annual reviews, and may not need to be carried out strictly in the order below. However, they are all essential ingredients for developing PME.

1. Needs assessment

Assess existing systems and experience

The first stage is to assess existing processes for planning, monitoring, review and evaluation. Most organisations already have a variety of formal and informal mechanisms for monitoring and reviewing their own work in order to make decisions. These may include project visits, staff meetings or writing annual reports, for example.

These can be assessed by looking at relevant documents and carrying out interviews. These are likely to draw out not only information about what happens but also to reveal the degree of satisfaction or dissatisfaction with current practices.

This could be done by staff or with an outsider asking the following questions:

- What planning and monitoring activities are already carried out? Who does it and how? What is good and bad about it?

- Are there clear objectives for the projects and programme?
- How are decisions made?
- How is learning identified and what actions result from learning?
- How are organisational principles and values (eg, child rights) incorporated into planning, monitoring, review and evaluation?
- What are the problems in relation to planning, monitoring, review and evaluation?

See how other people do it

It may be worthwhile examining how other programme offices or organisations working in similar sectors use different approaches to planning, monitoring review and evaluation. It is useful to see how such approaches work in practice, and how they help to improve the quality of the work and its impact.

Analyse needs

The assessment of existing systems can then be fed into a needs analysis to work out which areas of PME need to be improved or developed. A range of methods can be used, for example, by identifying Strengths, Weaknesses, Opportunities and Constraints (SWOC analysis tool – see Tool 5), building a Problem Tree (see Tool 6) or a similar exercise. It is important to try to find a tool that can be adapted to the specific circumstances and needs of the group of people who will be using it.

Training and development is more likely to achieve intended results if people participate in setting their own learning goals and objectives. For this reason, it is helpful to involve people in discussion about the following topics:

- their own strengths and weaknesses in planning, monitoring, review and evaluation
- what institutional opportunities and constraints exist
- how changes in PME systems and practice would improve the effectiveness of the programme and be useful for them in their day-to-day work.

For example: A consultant was employed by Save the Children to help improve planning, monitoring review and evaluation practice in East and Central Africa Region (ECARO). The focus was to investigate the gap between the stated policy of giving greater attention to monitoring and evaluation, and how well the policy was being implemented. The consultant took the following steps:
  a) visited the programmes, talking to people and looking at documents to assess the situation
  b) analysed what was found
  c) recommended a course of action.

As a result, a problem tree was drawn up, and then reversed to form an overall aim and a series of objectives that would lead to accomplishing the aim.

The **aim** was: **Improved programming and better results in the region.**

The **objectives** were defined as:
- Attitude development: related to reducing fear; increasing willingness to carry out monitoring and evaluation activities
- Skills improvement in data collection, data analysis, selection of pertinent indicators, prioritising work, drawing valid conclusions based on evidence, how to apply lessons to future work, transferring skills to partners, following-up
- Reducing confusion producing simpler, clearer objectives and indicators; fewer indicators; distinguishing academic rigorous research from information collection.

A range of strategies were then drawn up to address these objectives.

Define people performance needs in terms of behaviour and knowledge

A working definition of these terms is set out below:

Behaviour – is what people do, is observable, and can be measured. It can also therefore be developed.

Knowledge – is inside people's heads, can increase or decrease, is unseen but can be manifested in behaviour. It is useful to identify knowledge that is consciously applied through actions (and so forms part of an individual's competence in day-to-day performance) from actions that are not grounded in a clear understanding of why they are being used and what their effect may be.

The distinction becomes increasingly important when making decisions about what the priorities for investment in skills development are, for example, or when choosing the best methods to improve performance. Some methods (eg, group work) are better suited to developing interactive and interpersonal skills; others (eg, individual study and reflection) can help to improve analytical skills.

2. Develop the necessary tools and processes needed

A combination of methods will be needed to address the needs identified by assessment and analysis of current systems and practices. These may include the following:
- **Workshops/training:** Focus on planning, monitoring and evaluation

approaches that are relevant for the work of a specific organisation or programme. Training should be highly relevant to the context of the work, as well as the context of the programme and its relationships with head office and partners. It should build on existing systems and skills, and distinguish between system improvements and improvements in how people perform PME tasks. Training workshops in monitoring and evaluation will be effective only if done as part of wider performance management processes such as supervision and coaching, and in the context of supportive relationships. It is important to select carefully both the facilitator and the participants for the workshop.

- **Mini-workshops** (which could be incorporated into existing meetings): Exercises to develop essential skills for planning, monitoring, review and evaluation can be carried out in staff meetings. This was one of the strategies suggested as a result of the needs analysis in the Save the Children East and Central Africa Regional Office. Exercises included short sessions on analysis, setting objectives, using mistakes as learning opportunities, building a logic model, setting goals, objectives, strategies, activities, resources and indicators.
- **Long-term planning, monitoring and evaluation accompaniment:** By a person with the relevant skills to develop the skills and tools needed. 'Companheiro critico' is an approach adopted by Save the Children in Brazil. Save the Children's partner organisations are each assigned a 'critical friend' with appropriate skills and experience, often someone from a local university or institute. The person develops an ongoing relationship with the organisation, and helps to develop the skills and systems to analyse, monitor and evaluate their work.
- **Linking monitoring and evaluation to other processes:** It is important to make sure that the development of planning, monitoring and evaluation continues to be co-ordinated with any changes in strategic planning processes and other global initiatives.
- **Newsletter:** Share lessons learned in written form with others involved in similar work or within the agency.

Who provides the training and support?

On-going training and support are required for developing planning, monitoring, review, evaluation and impact assessment skills, practices and systems. Table 11.1 (on page 300) lists some of the possible providers of training and support, and highlights some advantages and disadvantages of each.

Table 11.1. Who provides training and support?

Who does it	Advantages	Disadvantages
Central resource unit:	• Knows the organisation and programmes (including on-going developments from Head Office) • Access to experience from different parts of world – can promote sharing and learning • Develops institutional learning – pool of experience • Long-term relationship available through e-mail and occasional visits	• Cannot cover the whole world • Not familiar with local culture or languages • Not easily available for follow-up • Reinforces the view that monitoring and evaluation is the responsibility of one or two people in the organisation, whereas it should be integrated into programme management
In-house regional expert	• As above • Less widely stretched and more familiar with the region	• As above
International consultant	• Experience of wide range of different organisations, countries • Expertise	• Long-term relationship harder/more expensive to maintain • Not easy to transpose what works well in one place to another; impact is dependent on factors such as culture, language, politics and history and is not automatically transferable
Accompaniment: local adviser	• Knows language and culture • Familiar with other local organisations • Available for on-going support • Not identified with line management	• Not so familiar with organisational culture, values, etc • May not have global overview
Internal network of people with planning, monitoring, evaluation and impact assessment expertise and responsibility	• The advisers are already involved in programmes through their other areas of expertise, not just monitoring and evaluation • Stresses that monitoring and evaluation is part of everyone's job • Members of the network can learn from and support each other and pass this on to programmes through support	• Network members have other responsibilities and may not see monitoring and evaluation as priority

Prerequisites for success

A successful PME strategy will need to do the following:

- Address needs and issues identified by the field office or partner organisation.
- Build on what already exists in terms of planning, monitoring, review and evaluation systems, experience and skills.
- Be participatory in approach and ensure people understand and are committed to better planning, monitoring, review and evaluation practice.
- Provide clarity about the different roles and responsibilities that people are asked to carry out and show how PME links to their work so that PME tasks are seen to be relevant to their interests.
- Involve managers and operational staff to ensure support for planning, monitoring, review and evaluation from the top, as well as the skills required to collect, analyse and use the information.
- Ensure follow-up, both in terms of support from the outside and commitment to keep working on it from the inside;
- 'Demystify' monitoring and evaluation – particularly by reducing confusion about the terminology used. Define what monitoring and evaluation means, and the difference between the two, as well as the associated vocabulary of aims, objectives, outcomes, outputs, process and impact indicators, etc. Developing an effective PME system is a practical, not an academic exercise.

Ensure the planning, monitoring, review and evaluation system is assessed in terms of its functionality. How accessible is it for people who use it? How adaptable and how sensitive is it as an instrument for measuring impact and factors that contribute to valued outcomes? Regular reviews will help to keep the system up to date and provide a useful check of what people have to do to make the system work effectively. This will make the assessment and analysis of people performance requirements a simpler process.

Tool 12
Stakeholder analysis

Description

A stakeholder analysis is a process for identifying stakeholders, understanding how they relate to an activity, their interests and needs, in order to identify opportunities and potential threats.

There is no 'one way' of doing a stakeholder analysis. The key element is deciding what kind of analysis is relevant for what purposes.

Purposes of stakeholder analysis:

- To identify people and groups with an interest in a project
- To better understand their interests, needs, capabilities in relation to planning, monitoring, review and evaluation
- To understand needs and interests of those not directly affected by an activity
- To assess which groups can be directly involved at different stages of an activity
- To identify potential synergies and obstacles with different groups and individuals
- To inform development of future strategies.

Who are the stakeholders?

Stakeholders are people affected positively or negatively by the work, directly or indirectly. For example:
- people affected by the impact of an activity
- people who can influence the impact of an activity
- individuals, groups or institutions with interests in a project/programme (primary and secondary stakeholders)
- someone who is affected by a decision or who can affect that decision.

So stakeholders can be:
- users, groups and beneficiaries directly affected by an activity (ie, children, young people and other groups in the community)
- interest groups (ie, people and institutions with an interest in an activity, intermediaries, including those who are not involved in the activity)
- audiences for an advocacy strategy or objective (local, national and international institutions, community groups, civil society organisations, businesses, etc)

- people implementing projects
- external service providers
- financial sponsors
- unborn generations and downstream populations who will be affected by the activities
- wider public.

Carrying out a stakeholder analysis

There are different ways to approach stakeholder analysis, depending on its particular purpose and the type of analysis required. Two examples are given below: one for deciding who should be involved in planning, monitoring review and evaluation; and one for analysing the audience for advocacy.

1. Stakeholder analysis to decide who should be involved in the project cycle

The following is adapted from Neil Thin, *Training Materials on Logical Framework*, Christian Aid, 1997.

The roles played by various stakeholders and the relations between them must be clarified and negotiated at the start of a project and should be on-going as the project develops. This part of the analysis can be used to prioritise the involvement of different groups in the project cycle.

This analysis involves the following steps:

1. Identify all individuals, groups and organisations affected by the issues that the project seeks to address. (This can be done by brainstorming in a group.)
2. Categorise according to *interest groups*, gender, individual status, ethnic affiliation, organisational affiliation, authority, power, etc.
3. Discuss whose interests are to be prioritised in relation to specific problems.
4. Identify the potentials (strengths, weaknesses, opportunities and threats) which each group has for coping with the issues addressed by the project.

Stakeholders	Problems	Potentials	Linkages

5. Identify the linkages between stakeholders (conflicts of interest, cooperative relations, dependencies, and opportunities for better co-operation in project activities).

Who participates, how, and when?

(See Chapter 2.)

People's capacity for and willingness to participate cannot be taken for granted, and the nature of participation and relations will change during the lifetime of project.

A participation matrix is a convenient way to represent schematically different forms of participation at different stages of a project.

The different stakeholders can be inserted into the matrix to see who should participate and in what ways at different stages of the project cycle.

Participation matrix

	Information	Consultation	Partnership	Control
Analysis situations				
Planning				
Bearing costs				
Implementation				
Monitoring				
Evaluation				

2. Stakeholder analysis for planning advocacy

This is taken from a process developed by Ian Chandler.

In this context, a stakeholder is someone who is affected by a decision, or who can affect that decision. By doing a stakeholder analysis around an issue, it is possible to identify allies and opponents, and those channels of influence that can make the most impact on a decision.

Go through the following process:

1. Brainstorm all the stakeholders for the issue. The aim here is to be creative and get a long list, which you should write in the table below.

2. Next, you are going to apply three filter questions to the list of stakeholders:
    •   To what extent does the stakeholder agree or disagree with your position?
    •   How importantly, relative to the others, does the stakeholder view the issue?

• How influential, relative to the others, is the stakeholder over the decision?

Hopefully, you and your colleagues will be able to make informed judgements to answer these questions. It may be that you need to subdivide the category of stakeholder into groups that can be said to share a common position.

The issue			
Your position			

Stakeholder	Attitude of the stakeholder to your position	Importance of the issue to the stakeholder	Influence of the stakeholder over the issue
	AA A N P PP	L M H	L M H
	AA A N P PP	L M H	L M H
	AA A N P PP	L M H	L M H
	AA A N P PP	L M H	L M H

AA = Very Anti   L = low
A = Anti   M = medium
N = Neutral   H = high
P = Pro
PP = Very Pro

3. Having answered the questions, transfer the information to the audience prioritisation matrix and the allies and opponents matrix by writing the stakeholders' names into the appropriate boxes. The information is easier to interpret on the matrices than it is directly from the table.

Audience prioritisation matrix

Importance of the issue to the audience		Low	Medium	High
	High	Secondary Audience	Priority Audience	Priority Audience
	Medium	Ignore	Secondary Audience	Priority Audience
	Low	Ignore	Ignore	Secondary Audience

Low   Medium   High
Influence of audience on the issue

Allies and opponents matrix

	Very Pro				Main allies
	Pro				
Attitude of the audience to your position	Neutral				Key battleground
	Anti				
	Very Anti				Main opponents
		Low	**Medium**	**High**	
		Influence of the audience on the issue			

To interpret the results

From the audience prioritisation matrix you can immediately identify whether the stakeholder is an important audience who cannot be ignored – due to the combination of their influence and how much importance they give the issue.

From the allies and opponents matrix, you can identify which of the following five influencing strategies would be most appropriate:

- Build alliances (with allies).
- Persuade the stakeholder that the issue is important (mainly for allies with high influence but low interest).
- Persuade the stakeholder that your position is right (mainly for influential neutrals and soft opponents).

Audience targeting table

Audience Audience definition	Knowledge What does the audience know about the issue?	Attitudes/Beliefs What does the audience believe about the issue?	Interests What does the audience care most about? (even if unrelated to the issue?

- Help to increase the influence of the stakeholder (mainly for allies with low influence).
- Reduce the influence of the stakeholder (mainly for opponents with high influence).
- Overall you need to identify how many stakeholder groups you can realistically target as audiences, given your level of resources. Having identified which stakeholders you will be targeting, you can apply further analysis using the audience targeting table on page 307.

Tool 13
Frameworks to help analyse the advocacy process

This Tool contains three sections. The first looks at frameworks that have been developed to help monitor and evaluate policy change and implementation. The second looks at processes and frameworks developed to monitor and evaluate capacity for advocacy. The final section looks at ways of monitoring and evaluating advocacy networks and movements. This Tool should be read in conjunction with Chapter 11.

1. Monitoring and evaluating policy change and implementation

Pathways of influence

The pathways of influence approach[1] helps teams develop conceptual clarity about **whom** they are trying to influence, **how** they will go about this (given the activities and strengths of partners and other agents) and **what** they should monitor to assess progress. The flow diagram below illustrates a hypothetical example of pathways of influence for pressurising decision-makers. This can help to monitor the advocacy **process.**

Indicators

Breaking down the advocacy process and achieving clarity of objectives in different areas of work makes it possible to select qualitative and quantitative indicators to monitor progress in key areas. If selected indicators show no change, this can be because the advocacy strategy is not working, or because the model of change needs to be modified.

Indicators are needed for **intermediate changes** and final expected change at the targeted institution. See figure 13.1, figure 13.2 and table 13.1 (pages 310–313), for example.

---

[1] Proposed by Action Aid; see Ros David, 1998

Figure 13.1. Pathways of influence

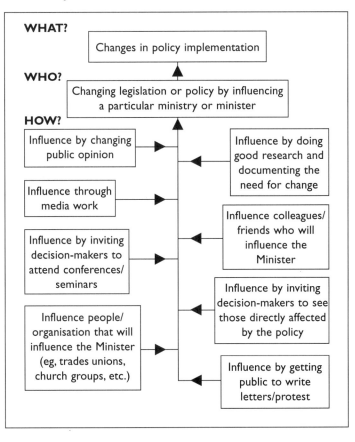

Figure 13.2. An alternative approach: target analysis
(Suggested by David Norman, Save the Children)

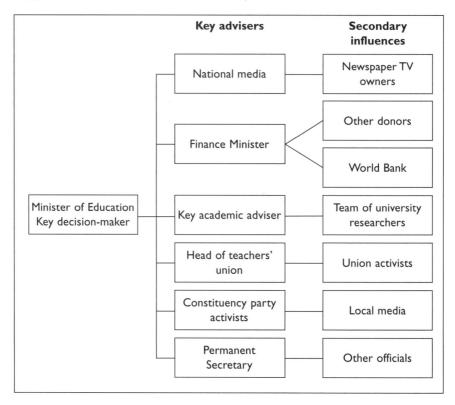

Table 13.1. Identifying advocacy indicators

What to monitor	Possible indicators
Your relationships	• Changes in the frequency and content of conversations with external sources and target audiences. Are you discussing new ideas? Are you becoming a confidant or a source of information or advice? • Face to face. Wide range of characteristics of meetings in particular contexts signal significant achievements or changes. Generalisations are difficult and possibly inappropriate. Certain events signify the establishment of trust between parties, but not necessarily the movement of the relationship towards advocacy objectives.
The media	• Quantitative: volume and range of publicity. Qualitative: analysis of contents and media response. For example: Column inches on your issue and the balance of pro and anti comment. The number of mentions for your organisation. Analyse whether media is adopting your language.
Your reputation	• Record the sources and numbers of inquiries that you receive as a result of your work. Are you getting to the people you wanted to get to? How and where have they heard of your work? How accurate are their preconceptions about you and your work? • Perceived legitimacy of the NGO as advocate can be an indicator.
Public opinion	Analyse the popular climate through telephone polling, or through commissioning surveys. (Can be very expensive.)
The target	• Changes in knowledge and attitudes of immediate recipients of the advocacy communications. What types of changes would they expect if advocacy messages were having an effect? • Indicators showing changes in areas have been identified as strategically key from past campaigns.
The stages	These stages can be: • **Changes in rhetoric:** Record and observe changes in the rhetoric of your target audience. Keep a file of

their statements over time. What are they saying about you and your campaign? Are they moving closer to your position, adapting to or adopting any of your language or philosophy? (but beware of co-option.)

- **Changes in policy or legislative outputs:** It is possible to differentiate between generic types of policy change and their relative importance. For example, through looking at the authorities involved, and the explicit and public nature of policy statements.
- **Budgets:** Are important policy statements, signalling a real commitment to specific priorities. Can monitor budget allocations and expenditure in stages. For example:
- whether the budget is allocated
- whether the budget leaves the Ministry of Finance and is received by the relevant Ministry which will be involved in implementation.
- whether the resources are received by the relevant local government agencies
- whether this translates into resources available to service users and citizens.
- **Changes in behaviour: Policy implementation.** To what extent has new legislation or policy been translated into administrative procedures or institutional practice? (This is often not monitored well, but is crucially important.)
- Where policy change is local it may be possible for local groups to monitor its implementation.
- Include within the policy change the commitment to report on progress.
- Seek agreement for allowing independent monitoring, often in addition to internal monitoring.
- Who bears costs for monitoring? Implementers bearing costs may signal greater commitment.

As in any monitoring system, the number of indicators should be kept to a minimum. Different ones will be useful at different stages of the advocacy process.

Budget monitoring

As shown in Chapter 11, budget monitoring is a tool for analysing public expenditure. It allows us to build on the policy-practice steps elaborated in Chapter 11 and above and investigate the detailed steps in the implementation process.

For more information on the techniques and tools to use for budget monitoring, see Lindelow M, *Holding Governments to Account: Public expenditure analysis for advocacy*, Save the Children, 2002.

2. Monitoring and evaluating the capacity for advocacy

This section looks at frameworks developed to help understand the changes in the ability of people, organisations and society to become involved in advocacy work. These might be termed empowerment, civil society capacity and social capital.

Building the capacity of groups to undertake advocacy work

This can also be applied to an organisation's programme offices and to partner organisations.

- To what extent have organisations accumulated the necessary skills, infrastructure, policy information, contacts, allies and resources to carry out successful advocacy?
- To what extent are these translated into realistic policy objectives, careful planning, sensible divisions of labour?
- Are they making appropriately timed interventions in decision-making processes, without compromising their own values?

Some approaches assess a group's capacity by looking at its interaction with the outside environment; others focus on their interaction with partners or donors. Some approaches help groups assess their own capacity in undertaking advocacy work.

One example from Chris Roche identifies stages in group cohesion and effectiveness[2]:

1. Group formation
2. Group carries out activities
3. Group sets up or joins a federation beyond village level
4. Movement is launched which takes on groups with vested interests
5. Groups of poor are involved in framing legislation and have control over resources.

---

[2] See Roche, C, *Impact Assessment for Development Agencies*, Oxfam/Novib publications, 1999

Self-assessment of group capacity for advocacy

Organisations are often best placed to assess their own capacity for advocacy work, perhaps with the aid of an outside facilitator.

One approach is for an organisation to select the competencies that it feels are important for effective advocacy. The organisation can then assess where it stands in relation to the different aspects it has identified for areas of capacity-building. It can judge its initial capacity, changes in capacity and reasons for them against a scale of 0–3:

0 = undesirable level calling for a large amount of improvement
1 = poor level having much room for improvement
2 = good situation with some room for improvement
3 = ideal situation with little room for improvement.

The spider diagram below is one way of representing this assessment diagrammatically. Each aspect of organisational change should be vigorously discussed during participatory monitoring meetings.

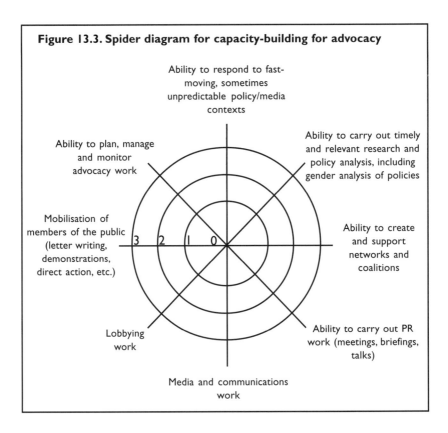

Figure 13.3. Spider diagram for capacity-building for advocacy

Ability to respond to fast-moving, sometimes unpredictable policy/media contexts

Ability to carry out timely and relevant research and policy analysis, including gender analysis of policies

Ability to plan, manage and monitor advocacy work

Mobilisation of members of the public (letter writing, demonstrations, direct action, etc.)

Ability to create and support networks and coalitions

Lobbying work

Ability to carry out PR work (meetings, briefings, talks)

Media and communications work

Save the Children UK has developed a tool for self assessment of advocacy capacity for internal use. For more information contact the Human Resources Department.

Ladder exercise

A similar way of assessing organisational change is by using a ladder exercise (see below). Once again the organisation sets its own targets and (after a reasonable period) assesses its own performance. The organisation ranks the degree to which it has increased its capacity to carry out its advocacy work on a ladder of changes. It can then assess to what extent the changes (be they positive or negative) are attributable to a particular organisation's support or to other agencies or external factors. An explanation for these changes can be written alongside the diagram. This gives the support NGO more feedback on what elements of its support are considered most effective and useful.

Table 13.2. Hypothetical ladder exercise for partners of Action Aid[3]					
	BEFORE	AFTER	AA SUPPORT	OTHER FACTORS	REASONS
Research and Policy Analysis			+++	– – – –	Progress despite a key researcher leaving the team
Media and Communica-tion			++	++++++	Developed mainly through involvement in a particular campaign without AA support
Network and Coalition Building			+++++	++++	Progress due to AA capacity-building work and involvement with other CSOs
PR work (meetings, briefings etc)			++	++	Helped slightly by AA due to secondment of staff

KEY	Range	+ positive support	– negative factors

Empowerment

How do we know that a previously powerless group has been empowered?

There is still no consensus on how to do it, but different approaches have been tried.

---

[3] Adapted by Ros David (1998) from original work by Gosling and Edwards (1995)

For example: ActionAid in Nepal supported "Organising for Rights", a movement working to liberate bonded labourers (Kamaiya) whose families have been in debt to landlords for generations. As part of the activities of the movement, training sessions were organised to provide hands-on skills for advocacy through organising communities for rights. Workshops were held at district and village level to discuss Nepal's constitution as well as other relevant legislation and civic rights against slavery and bondage. Bonded labourers from Organising for Rights have described the impact that being part of the movement had on them. The table below shows the changes in their awareness and perception levels. These have been conceptualised as a shift from traditional perception to naïve understanding, and finally to more critical awareness of their situation, strengths and capacities. This illustrates the importance of attitudinal changes related to political awareness and personal self-worth, and how to identify and track these changes.

Bonded Labourers' changes in awareness and perception levels

Traditional	Naïve	Critical
"We are *Kamaiya* by age-old tradition"	"We can't repay the *Sauki.* (debt) How can we be liberated?"	"We can survive freely. We do not want to be bonded like a bull"
"We are *Kamaiya* by birth and it is our *Karma*" (believe in fatalism)	"We are exploited and sold by landlords time and again. What option do we have to be liberated?"	"Slavery is illegal. It must be punished by the law in practice."
"We will not die of hunger in landlord house being *Kamaiya*"	"How to secure our daily wages?"	"Our labour must be valued and be calculated"
"Without having a piece of land, how to cope with survival?"	"We are not interested to be bonded, but we are landless."	"Government should guarantee our food and shelter"

3. Networks and movements

There has not been much experience in monitoring and evaluating networks and movements except in terms of their specific activities. Any attempt to do so needs to take into account political nature and 'invisible' effects, like putting people in touch with each other, stimulating and facilitating action and trust that enables concerted action.

The Open University has developed a framework for collaboration methods among environmental NGOs, based on the strength of the links between them.[4] (See figure 13.4) This framework is useful in that it stresses different degrees of collaboration and gives precise definitions for words that tend to be used very loosely. It can usefully be extended to apply to collaboration between NGOs working on development issues. What it lacks is an analysis of where the power is centred.

Figure 13.4. Global collaboration methods among environmental NGOs

Degree	Style	Methods/Characteristics	
Increasing degree of global contact and organisation	NETWORKING	Decentralised/**unpredictable** use of information from elsewhere. Publications, IT 'nets' used **passively**/occasionally. Open access opportunities to information flows.	*Increasing co-ordination, time, people resources*
	NETWORKS	More **active** exchange of info. With co-ordinating secretariat. **Fewer specific** tasks, more long-term support-boosting morale. More **regular personal** contacts especially with trusted buddies. Emphasis mostly on info-sharing **rather than** joint campaigning.	
	COALITIONS	Single event joint campaigns often among fairly diverse NGOs. Attempted division of labour into most appropriate tasks. Limited life recognised and accepted, given diverse missions.	
	ALLIANCES	Long-term allegiance to common ideals among very trusted partners. Northern partners committed to empowering southern NGOs. Very regular consultation by fax, IT and personal meetings. Time investment justified by 'certainty of shared values'.	

[4] See Eccleston, B (1996) 'Does North-South collaboration enhance NGO influence on deforestation policies in Malaysia and Indonesia' in Potter, D (ed), *NGOS and Environmental Policies: Asia and Africa*, London: Frank Cass.

The dynamics of networks and power relations within them can also be monitored and evaluated. Several frameworks for analysing these different structures of collaboration have been suggested. For example:

Research by the New Economic Foundation differentiates between three different structures of network:

- the **pyramid**, where information flows up and down to a co-ordinating secretariat
- the **wheel**, with one or more focal points, but also with considerable flow of information directly between member organisations
- the **web**, where information flows in all directions in roughly equal quantities.

Each of these has different strengths and weaknesses, and may be good for different roles in advocacy.

The challenge for networks is often to avoid internal bureaucracy and setting up secretariats that consume huge resources and deplete the effectiveness of the campaign. It is now becoming more common to see 'light-footed' alliances, where organisations come together for a few public profile events and divide up functions (such as research and publicity) between themselves. This is made possible due to the growth of internet and e-mail technologies, and the growing experience amongst pressure groups. A recent report for the Development Planning Unit at the University College London looks at this in more detail. See Church et al (2003) *Participation, Relationships and Dynamic change: New thinking on evaluating the work of international networks*, DPU working paper 121.

Tool 14

Frameworks for developing monitoring and evaluation questions in emergency situations

This Tool should be read in conjunction with Chapter 10.

SPHERE Minimum Standards

The SPHERE handbook (see reference on page 330) gives minimum standards and indicators for several key sectors covered by most disaster responses. These can be used to assess how effectively a programme is addressing problems in these sectors.

The following is a summary of the minimum standards. A list of indicators and guidance notes for each standard are given in the SPHERE handbook.

Minimum standards applicable to all sectors:

Analysis standards	• Initial assessment: decisions based on clear analysis of needs relating to the sectors • Monitoring and evaluation: performance of programme and effectiveness in responding to problems, as well as changes in the context • Participation: the disaster-affected population has the opportunity to participate in the design and implementation of the assistance programme.
Human resource capacity and training	• Competence: programmes implemented by staff with appropriate qualifications and experience, and adequately managed and supported • Support: members of affected population receive support to enable them to adjust to new environment and make optimal use of assistance provided • Local capacity and skills used and enhanced by programmes where relevant.

Water and sanitation

Water supply	• Access and water quantity • Water quality • Water use facilities: so people can collect, store and use water.
Excreta disposal	• Access to and numbers of toilets • Design and construction of toilets.
Vector	• Individual and family protection from insects and lice where this is a health risk • Good practice in use of chemical vector control methods.
Solid waste management	• Solid waste collection and disposal • Solid waste containers/pits available to population.
Drainage	• Drainage works: people have an environment free from risk of water erosion and from standing water • Installations and tools: means to dispose of domestic wastewater.
Hygiene	• Hygiene behaviour and use of facilities: population aware of priority hygiene practices • Programme implementation: facilities reflect vulnerabilities, needs and preferences of all sections of the affected population. Users involved in the management of facilities where appropriate.

Nutrition

General nutritional support to the population	• Nutrient supply • Food quality and safety • Food acceptability • Food handling and safety.
Nutritional support to those suffering malnutrition	• Moderate malnutrition: public health risks associated with moderate malnutrition reduced • Severe malnutrition: mortality, morbidity and suffering associated with severe malnutrition reduced • Micronutrient deficiences corrected.

Food aid

Requirements	• Food basket and rations designed to bridge gap between the affected population's requirements and own food sources.
Targeting	• Recipients of food aid selected on basis on food need and/or vulnerability to food insecurity.
Resource management	• Food aid commodities and funds managed, tracked and accounted for using transparent and auditable system.
Logistics	• Agencies have necessary capacity to manage procurement, receipt, transport, storage and distribution of food commodities safely, efficiently and effectively.

Distribution	• Method of food distribution is equitable and appropriate to local conditions. Recipients are informed of ration entitlement and its rationale.

Shelter and site planning

Housing (shelter)	• Living quarters: sufficient covered space to provide protection from climate, warmth, fresh air, security and privacy.
Clothing	• Sufficient blankets and clothing to provide protection from the climate, dignity, safety and well-being.
Household items	• Items for households and livelihood support: utensils, soap and tools • Environmental concerns: fuel-economic cooking implements and stoves available, and use promoted.
Site selection and planning	• Site selection: site suitable for number of people • Site planning: sufficient space for household areas, supports security and well-being, provides for effective and efficient provision of services and access • Security: ensures personal liberty and security for entire population • Environmental concerns: minimises damage to environment.

Health services

Measles control	• Vaccination • Vaccination of newcomers • Outbreak control • Case management.
Control of communicable diseases	• Monitoring: occurrence of communicable diseases monitored • Investigation and control: diseases of epidemic potential investigated and controlled according to international standards.
Health care	• Appropriate medical care: based on initial assessment and ongoing health information system • Reduction of morbidity and mortality: follows primary health care principles and targets health problems that cause excess mobidity.

Education

A 'Basic Education Framework' has been developed by Save the Children which emphasises the need for a holistic view in educating the child. The package is based on the UN Convention on the Rights of the Child with its call for universal basic education, and emphasises the participation of children. This outlines the areas of curriculum that should be covered in education in emergencies, and can be used to develop objectives and indicators for both process and impact of emergency education programmes.

Education for children in emergencies should be relevant and teach them to:
Live where they live, to participate safely and productively in communities;
Be, to develop resilience and competence and a sense of belonging;
Learn, to continue developing basic academic skills of literacy and numeracy.

Life Skills: Learning to live where you live

Curriculum Area	Purpose
❏ *Safety measures*	To understand the dangers in the immediate environment and be capable of implementing survival strategies.
❏ *Vocational skills*	To acquire practical vocational skills that enable the reconstruction of homes and livelihoods.
❏ *Health promotion*	To understand basic health and survival issues, develop practical skills and implement strategies to reduce health risks. ➡ *Community Health* To promote and improve individual, family and community health and well being. ➡ *Reproductive Health* To facilitate informed choices based on HIV/AIDs and other risks. ➡ *Environmental Hygiene:* To be able to address pro-actively personal and environmental hygiene issues that include appropriate water, sanitation and waste disposal resources and practices.
❏ *Contextual analysis and understanding*	For children to understand the effects of conflict, what is going on around them and how this impacts on their lives, their families and their communities.
❏ *Understand unity in diversity*	To recognise the similarities and respect the diversity of people from different cultures, religious, ethnic and political groups.
❏ *Education in environment*	That children recognise and understand the effects of conflict and the impact of human activities on their environment.
❏ *Parenting and care-giving*	To enable and encourage care-givers (children, youth, adults in the family and community) to take an interactive role in the children's care and emotional, intellectual, physical and social development.

Developmental Skills: Learning to Be

Curriculum Area	Purpose
❏ *Social development*	To be able to confidently participate, interact and take responsibility at individual, family and societal level in all aspects of everyday life.
❏ *Communication*	To be able to communicate effectively in a variety of ways and situations in a manner that respects, understands and recognises others.

❏ *Social harmony, peace and tolerance*	To understand, respect and be open to differences in opinion, religion, ethnicity and background with a commitment to overcoming discrimination and building a tolerant community inclusive of and responsive to all members.
❏ *Conflict resolution*	To develop capacities and use peaceful means to resolve day-to-day conflict.
❏ *Moral education*	To observe and respect the moral and ethical codes of one's own society and of the host community, drawing on positive aspects of his/her culture.
❏ *Civic responsibility and ability to effect change*	To demonstrate the initiative and confidence to represent and promote the best interests of individuals, family and the community.
❏ *Awareness of rights, responsibilities and obligations*	To understand and respect that all individuals have basic human rights and to take practical measures to advance them in their daily life.
❏ *Psychological development*	To strengthen self-esteem, ability to cope and to be resilient within the changing circumstances of the day-to-day context in which they live and more towards becoming an independent, capable and responsible person.
❏ *Emotional well-being and development in conflict*	To provide support and encouragement to children so they are better equipped to maintain an emotional balance within the changing circumstances created by the conflict.
❏ *Recreation and creativity*	To allow the time and space for leisure, with the opportunity to participate in and express themselves through a variety of recreational activities.
❏ *Coping with effects of conflict*	To cope with fear and stress and develop capacity to recognise the impact of conflict on themselves and their families and to develop practical coping mechanisms to deal with these.
❏ *Spiritual development*	To allow for individuals' spiritual development (thought, conscience, religion) within the socio-cultural context.
❏ *Physical development*	To develop a variety of physical skills to improve physical health and mental well-being, (includes strength, agility, stamina).
❏ *Cultural identity and heritage*	To develop skills which know and appreciate one's own culture in order to develop a sense of belonging, while enabling functional integration and appreciation of the host community.
❏ *Language (mother-tongue)*	To learn one's own mother tongue in order to function within one's own culture and community in addition to other languages as appropriate.

Learning Skills: Learning to Learn

Curriculum Area	Purpose
❏ *Functional literacy*	To be able to use reading, writing and oral skills effectively for enjoyment, to acquire information and to interact with others.
❏ *Functional numeracy*	To be able to apply basic mathematical skills in order to undertake financial transactions, use basic measurements and to think analytically in daily life.
❏ *World learning*	To understand and appreciate one's relationship with one's physical and social environment and the wider world.
❏ *Science*	To develop an investigative approach to learning about the world and the way things work.
❏ *History*	To develop a sense of history and change.
❏ *Geography*	To give children a sense of themselves, their family and community, in relation to their environment, and the wider world.

Child protection

The following framework, developed by Sarah Uppard at Save the Children, highlights key questions and areas of focus related to child protection that can be used to help to develop indicators for monitoring and evaluation:

Key questions	Where to focus
Services: What particular issues are faced by girls, boys and disabled children in using camp services?	Registration Security Shelter, and distribution of non-food items Food distribution and feeding programs Health problems Educational services and opportunities Water and sanitation Recreation Community support and networks.
Vulnerable groups: What is the awareness of these groups in the general population, and camp facilities? What issues do they face? How are these addressed?	Separated children Disappearances Female-headed households Children-headed households Children with special needs Youth.
Exploitation and abuse: What evidence? Who is involved? What action is taken?	Recruitment for employment, prostitution, Child soldiers Child labour Sexual abuse Violence.

| Resources and coping | What coping actions are taken to resolve issues identified?
Role of community in addressing issues
Role of camp authorities and service providers
Skills and resources amongst refugee population. |

References and further reading

Evaluation and impact assessment: core reading

Cracknell, B.E.,**Evaluating Development Aid**. 2000. Sage Publications. ISBN 0 7619 9404 1.
This book provides a comprehensive guide to the subject of evaluating development aid. The first half reviews the basic issues of evaluating aid – objectives, methodology, the difference between monitoring and evaluation, and feedback. The second part focuses on the role of the recipient of development aid. Topics discussed in this section include the importance of evaluating impact and sustainability, stakeholder analysis, problems particular to various sectors including research and development, poverty alleviation and structural adjustment, international cooperation, the participatory approach, and the "Fourth Generation Evaluation".

Estrella, M (eds.) **Learning From Change: Issues and experiences in participatory monitoring and evaluation**, 2000, IT DG Publishing, ISBN: 1853394696
This book brings together a broad range of case studies and discussions between practitioners, academics, donors and policy makers about PME from around the world.

Feuerstein, Marie-Therese, **Partners in Evaluation: Evaluating development and community programmes with participants**, 1986, Macmillan, TALC, ISBN 0–333–422619.
A practical field handbook designed for field workers with little or no formal training in evaluation methodology. It advocates the participation of people at community level in various parts of the evaluation process. It is geared towards technologies which are centred on people working as a team, in partnership with project teachers and managers. It contains practical advice on how to plan an evaluation, organise resources, use existing knowledge and records, collect and analyse information, report the results of evaluation, and use evaluation results.

Roche, C., **Impact Assessment for Development Agencies: Learning to value change**, 1999, Oxfam/NOVIB publications ISBN 0 85598 418 X
A book produced by Oxfam considering the process of impact assessment, showing how and why it needs to be integrated into all stages of development programmes from planning to evaluation. There is a significant section that covers participatory methodologies, which, though not focused on children, offers a useful outline to

approaches taken. It offers a useful balance between theoretical approaches and practical examples.

Rubin, Frances, **A Basic Guide to Evaluation for Development**, 1995, Oxfam publications, ISBN: 0855982756
This book addresses questions often asked about evaluation in the context of the work of a Northern NGO working with Southern partners and international donors. It aims to help the reader understand the underlying principles of evaluation and to be clearer about its uses and limitations. It recognises issues of power and control, and the political nature of evaluation.

Wilkinson, J., **Children and Participation: Research, monitoring and evaluation with children and young people** 2000, Save the Children, London.
This is a fairly brief overview on where to go for information on including children and young people in research projects and in monitoring and evaluating on-going work. The main sections cover good practice, ethics and tools and methods.

Webb, D. and Elliot L, **Learning to Live: Monitoring and evaluating HIV/ AIDS programmes for young people**, 2000, Save the Children, London ISBN: 1841870358
A Save the Children UK handbook that provides an introduction to the concepts that underline project monitoring and evaluation and how they are applied in projects addressing HIV/AIDS. The handbook also offers an overview of existing good practice along with examples and methods from HIV/AIDS projects.

Goyder, H., Davies, R., and Williamson, W., **Participatory Impact Assessment.** 1998, ActionAid.
This paper reviews the background, methodology and key findings of an applied three year research project into finding more reliable participatory impact assessment approaches in four countries where ActionAid works: Bangladesh, Ghana, India and Ghana.

Participatory Monitoring and Evaluation: Learning from change, 1998, Institute of Development Studies (IDS), , IDS Policy Briefing 12.
A good place to start for a brief introduction to PME.
Contact: http://www.ids.ac.uk/ids/bookshop/briefs/brief12.html

Estrella, M. And Gaventa, J, **Who Counts Reality? Participatory Monitoring and Evaluation: A literature review**, IDS Working Paper 70, IDS Sussex.
This is an extensive literary review of experiences in PME from around the world. It introduces key principles, its applications and a number of tools and methods used,

including participatory and more conventional methods. Finally it also raises key challenges emerging from the literature.
Contact: Http://Www.Ids.Ac.Uk/Ids/Publicat/Wp/Wp70.Pdf

Methods of information collection and analysis

Ennew, Judith, **Street and Working Children: A guide to planning**, 1994, Development Manual 4, Save the Children, ISBN 1–870322–82–7.
This manual draws on different experiences of work with street and working children in various settings and with different resources. It assumes the reader knows little about the topic, and gives a basic guide on planning a project. It covers the following areas: using secondary data; investigating the local situation; types of project and how to set them up; organising human resources; and how to avoid some of the most common problems encountered in working with street children. The emphasis is on working with children, rather than for them. The section on research goes into detail on the research process, who should do it, and different research methods including participatory methods and surveys.

Nichols, Paul, **Social Survey Methods: A fieldguide for development workers**, Development Guidelines No 6, Oxfam 1991, ISBN 0–85598–126–1.
Formal and non-formal survey methods are dealt with in detail, and there is helpful advice on statistical analysis of results, design of survey forms, and interview methods. Based on the author's extensive field experience of conducting social research, this book is intended to be of use to those without a formal training in statistics.

Pratt, Brian and Loizos, Peter, **Choosing Research Methods: Data collection for development workers**, 1992, Development Guidelines No. 7, Oxfam, ISBN 0–85598–177–6,115 pages.
This book discusses the various ways in which research can be carried out, and how to select the most appropriate method for particular circumstances. The advantages and disadvantages of a wide range of research methods are assessed, and guidance is given on how to decide exactly what information is necessary and how to obtain it, given the resources available.

Pretty, J, Guijt, I, Thompson, J, Scoones, I, **Participatory Learning and Action: A trainer's guide**, 1995, IIED Participatory Methodology Series, ISBN: 1 899 825 00 2
This useful and practical guide is designed for both experienced and new trainers who have an interest in training others in the use of participatory methods, whether they are researchers, practitioners, policy makers, villagers or trainers.

Protz, Maria, **Seeing and Showing Ourselves: A guide to using small format**

videotape as a participatory tool for development Vdeazimuth, 3680 rue Jeanne Mance, bureau 430, Montreal, Quebec, Canada H2X 2K5.
An excellent guide to using video in development. There are two sections: one covers technical issues; the other considers issues of participation and development.

Johnson, V, Ivan-Smith, E, Gordon, G, Pridmore P, and Scott, P. Eds., **Stepping Forward: Children and young people's participation in the development process**, 1998, IT Publications, ISBN 1 85339 448 3
This book presents the key issues and challenges facing those facilitating children's and young peoples participation. The book has evolved from an international workshop on children participation held by the institute of development studies, the Institute of Education and Save the Children UK in September 1997.

Advocacy

Chapman, J. & Wameyo, A. (2000), **Monitoring and Evaluating Advocacy: A scoping study**, ActionAid
A very useful overview of tools for monitoring and evaluating advocacy work that focuses on changing policy, increasing the capacity for people-centred advocacy, and enlarging political space. Different frameworks, indicators and methodologies are explained. The report can be downloaded from: www.actionaid.org/resources/impactassessment/impact.shtml

Chapman, J. & Fisher, T. (1999), **The Thoughtful Activist: A toolkit for enhancing NGO campaigning and advocacy**, New Economics Foundation (draft available on their website www.neweconomics.org)
This document is a guide to help think through campaigning. It sets out frameworks and tools developed by NEF for use in understanding NGO campaigning and advocacy work. They are not meant to be fixed tools but guides to help innovative thinking towards better understanding of how campaigns work and how they can be made more effective.

Church, Madeline et al (2002) **Participation, Relationships And Dynamic Change: New thinking on evaluating the work of interneational networks**, Development Planning Unit. 9 Endsleigh Gardens London WC1H 0ED Tel. +44 (0)20 7388 7581. www.ucl.ac.uk/dpu/
A very useful report that looks at ways of evaluating the work of networks, suggesting models, frameworks and indicators.

Coates, B. & David, R. "**Learning for Change: The art of assessing the impact of advocacy work**", in *Development and Practice*, Vol. 12, Nos. 3 & 4, August 2002

This paper starts by exploring the complex and changing nature of advocacy work, arguing that standardised forms of monitoring and evaluation/impact assessment are likely to be inappropriate. It suggests that NGOs should identify essential elements of their advocacy work and ensure they monitor and evaluate the most important areas, guided by an analysis of power and power structures. To be successful, monitoring and evaluation needs to be flexible enough to adapt to external events, and to reshape an advocacy campaign. New tools are needed for this.

Cohen, David, de la Vega, Rosa and Watson, Gabrielly, (2001) **Advocacy for Social Justice: A global action and reflection guide**, Oxfam/Advocacy Intitute, Kumarian Press, ISBN 1-56549-131-9
A comprehensive guide to advocacy, that explores the elements of advocacy and includes a toolkit for taking action, detailed case studies, and extensive resource listings.

Davies, R. (2001), **Evaluating the Effectiveness of DFID's Influence with Multilaterals Part A: A review of NGO approaches to the evaluation of advocacy work**, DFID
This is a wide-ranging and constructively critical review of the information available about different approaches to monitoring and evaluating advocacy work. The author looks at different NGOs' approaches to evaluating their advocacy activities and identifies next steps that could be taken in developing tools and techniques. This can be downloaded from: www.mande.co.uk/docs/EEDIMreport.doc

Save the Children (2003) **Closing the Circle: From measuring policy change to assessing policies in practice. An overview of advocacy impact.**
This paper presents an overview of the current literature regarding the impact assesment of advocacy. This review is carried out on the basis that advocacy is not limited to policy change, but rather is seen as an integral part of rights-based programming, concerned with the long term transformation of children's lives.

Emergencies

Seaman, J, Clarke, P, Boudreau, T, and Holt, J, **The Household Economy Approach: A resource manual for practitioners**, 2000, Development Manual 6, Save the Children, ISBN 1-84187-029-3
This manual describes the Household Economy Approach, a method of analysing the impact of crop failure and other shocks on household income and access to food. This approach enables rural and development workers to: build up a picture of the economy of a defined population using rapid field methods, and analyse the relationship between a shock (for example a crop failure) and the ability of households to obtain food and other essential items.

The Sphere Project: Humanitarian Charter and Minimum Standards in Disaster Response. The Sphere Project, 2000. Oxfam Publishing ISBN 0-85598-445-7; Sphere Project ISBN 92-9139-059-3.
This book is the result of more than two years of inter-agency collaboration to frame a Humanitarian Charter, and to identify minimum standards to advance the rights set out in the Charter. These standards cover disaster assistance in water supply and sanitation, food aid, shelter and site planning, and health services.
www.sphereproject.org

Humanitarian Action: Improving performance through improved learning, ALNAP Annual Review 2002. London: ALNAP/ODI.
ALNAP c/o ODI
111 Westminster Bridge Rd
London SE1 7JD.
Can be downloaded from www.alnap.org

Humanitarian Action: Learning from evaluation, ALNAP Annual Review 2001. London: ALNAP/ODI. Can be downloaded from www.alnap.org

Mitchell, John and Slim, Hugo, **Registration in emergencies**, 1990, Oxfam Practical Health Guide No. 6, Oxfam, ISBN 0–85598–128–8.
This book shows how registration can be used to collect information valuable for assessment, monitoring and evaluation. The manual gives a step by step guide to assessing the need for and setting up a registration system. Sometimes a community managed registration is more appropriate and the manual assesses the advantages and disadvantages of both systems. The layout of the registration site, selection and training of staff, organisation of the registration process, design of ration cards and the recording of information are all covered in detail. The need for careful planning, involving the full participation of community leaders and consultation with local authorities is stressed, as is the need to explain the process at all stages to the people being registered.

Richman, Naomi, **Communicating with Children: Helping children in distress,** 1993, Development Manual 2, Save the Children, ISBN 1–870322–49–5.
This book aims to help those working in conflict situations and emergencies to develop their listening and communication skills, in order to identify and help children with special needs. It deals with the importance of understanding different cultural ways of communicating and coping with stress, overcoming blocks in communication, giving comfort, talking to families, preventing 'burn-out', and more.

Community Emergency Preparedness: A manual for managers and policy makers. 1999, World Health Organization,. Also available in French.
This manual is primarily aimed at local managers and decision-makers. It provides

an overall view of all aspects of disaster management, including policy development, vulnerability assessment, identification, description and ranking of potential hazards, analysis of available resourcces, definition of the roles and responsibilities of different groups and individuals, training, and public education.

Assessment of Nutritional Status of Adolescents in Emergency-Affected Populations. Refugee Network Information Systems, UN Food & Nutrition Dept. 1999. Can be downloaded from http://acc.unsystem.org/scn (click on Publications, then select RNIS). Note that there is also a publication dealing with adult malnutrition on this website.
This publication looks at the use of BMI (Body Mass Index) of individuals compared to a reference population and concludes that additional solutions may be required to achieve accurate assessments of the nutritional status of individuals.

Reducing Risk: Participatory learning activities for disaster mitigation in Southern Africa. 1996, International Federation of Red Cross and Red Crescent Societies. ISBN 0 85598 347 7
This book is a collection of participatory learning activities for people who work with at-risk communities, either in development or relief. It is intended to increase the understanding about community risk and vulnerability as well as strengthen the training capacities of those involved in community-based disaster management

Evaluation Humanitarian Assistance Programmes in Complex Emergencies. Good Practice Review 7. Humanitarian Practice Network. 1998. Also available in French.
This paper is the written output of an OECD/DAC project initiated to identify and disseminate best practice in the evaluation of humanitarian assistance programmes.

Guidance for Evaluating Humanitarian Assistance in Complex Emergencies. Development Assistance Committee, OECD, 1999. Available in French. Can be downloaded from http://www.reliefweb.int/library/documents/human_en.pdf **Free.**
This guidance is aimed at those involved in the commissioning, design and management of evaluations of humanitarian assistance programmes principally with donor organisations but is also likely to be of use to UN agencies, NGOs and other organisations involved in the provision of humanitarian assistance.

Evaluation

A small selection of key texts on evaluation for those who wish to read more.

Marsden, David and Oakley, Peter, Eds., **Evaluating Social Development Projects.** 1990, Development guidelines No. 5, OXFAM, , ISBN 0–85598–147–4.
A book which brings together the main papers and workshop discussions from an international conference held in Swansea in 1989. The four major themes covered are: qualitative indicators to be used in evaluation; methodologies for social development evaluation; partnership in evaluation and the changing nature of relationships between funders/donors and recipients; and the role and position of the evaluator. It gives useful background to the ideas, principles and discussions concerning the evaluation of social development projects.

Marsden, David, Oakley, Peter and Pratt, Brian, **Measuring the Process: Guidelines for evaluating social development.** 1994, INTRAC, ISBN: 189774806X
A unique attempt to set out guidelines for evaluating social development processes. Intended as a practical guide for undertaking the evaluation of social development projects, this book combines a theoretical overview of the concepts involved, and insights into evaluation planning and implementation. Three substantial case studies from Colombia, India and Zimbabwe are provided.

Oakley, Peter, Pratt Brian and Clayton, Andrew, **Outcomes and Impact: Evaluating change in social development.** 1998, INTRAC, ISBN: 1897748213
Building on the experiences of many different agencies, this book provides a comprehensive discussion of the difficulties, dilemmas and opportunities of understanding the outcomes of social development programmes and projects: How can development agencies evaluate the long-term impact of their social development programmes? What types of methods do they need to employ? How effective are formal planning, monitoring and evaluation systems at understanding social change? The book shows that while there are no easy solutions to evaluating impact, a range of methods and approaches can be employed in order to provide an adequate understanding of social change.

Omidian, P, **Impact Of Save The Children's Child-Focused Health Education Project: Effects on children's self-esteem and status in the family**, 2000, Save the Children UK, Afghanistan Office, Peshawar, Pakistan.
An impact assessment of the changes in the self-esteem and status of children in the family as a result of Save the Children's child-focused health education project in refugee camps in Pakistan. Uses an innovative write and draw technique with the children.

Disability and evaluation

Man, K, **Community-based Rehabilitation: Global review and seminar report,** 2000, Save the Children, London.
A review of Save the Children's experience of Community-Based Rehabilitation, pooling experiences and insights, to develop a greater understanding of what has happened in the past, to look at what is occurring now and begin to think through where to go in the future.

Stubbs, Sue, **Engaging with Difference: Soul-searching for a methodology in disability and development research**, 1996, Save the Children, London.
Personal reflections on evaluation work at a Community-Based Rehabilitation project in Lesotho.

Monitoring and evaluation sources of information on the Internet

This is a small selection of sites for more information on monitoring and evaluation.

M and E News
http:// www.mande.co.uk/news/htm
An Internet based news service oriented towards NGOs. Focusing on developments in monitoring and evaluation methods relevant to development projects with social development objectives.

The Participation Group
www.ids.susx.ac.uk/ids/particip/
The Participation Group is a group of people at the **Institute of Development Studies** in Sussex, UK, working in support of participatory approaches to development. The website gives details of how to make contact with participation people and networks in over 50 countries.

Resource Centre for Participatory Learning and Action
http://www.iied.org/resource/
For those seeking practical information and support on all aspects of research on participatory methodologies with a particular focus on their application and integration into institutional structures.
Resource Centre for Participatory Learning and Action.
International Institute for Environment and Development.

The World Bank Group's Poverty Net website
http://www.worldbank.org/poverty/impact/index.htm
The site includes an Impact Evaluation Web Site which aims to disseminate information and provide resources for people and organizations working to assess and improve the effectiveness of projects and programs aimed at reducing poverty. There is also a section specifically on the Monitoring and Evaluation of Poverty Reduction Strategies.

Monitoring and Evaluation Capacity Development
http://www.worldbank.org/evaluation/me/
This World Bank web site page provides an annotated list of a range of documents on building M and E capacity. The full text of each document is available via the links provided.

The World Bank OED website
http://www.worldbank.org/oed/
This is the website of the Operation Evaluation Department of the World Bank. It provides useful information on the department's activities, including country and thematic evaluation reports and evaluation guidelines.

ELDIS
http://www.eldis.org/
Eldis is a gateway to on-line information on development in countries of the South. Coverage includes social, economic, political and environmental issues. ELDIS makes a qualitative selection of materials and structures it for easy access.

Glossary

(Definitions of the words in italics are found elsewhere in the glossary.)

aims: the broad, long-term goals set for a piece of work. For example, to improve the health of children under five in district X.

Aims relate to the agency's mandate, principles and values, which are the fundamental standards against which the success of the work can be measured. They should also relate to the long-term goals of partners, to national goals, and to the aims identified in broader strategies.

It is often difficult to demonstrate that aims can be achieved through any one particular programme. For example, the improvement of health of children under five in district X will be affected by a large number of factors, including social, economic, and political changes completely out of the control of the programme. While it should be possible to demonstrate that a programme will contribute to the achievement of a long-term aim, it may not be possible to measure its precise contribution.

appraise: to examine a project or programme objectively and in detail. This may be in order to determine, for example, the appropriateness of the activities in relation to the experience and priorities of an organisation, or whether the costs of the project are reasonable for the expected outcomes.

baseline study: a collection of data about the characteristics of a population before a programme or project is set up. This data can then be compared with a study of the same characteristics carried out later in order to see what has changed.

brainstorming: asking a group to contribute ideas and suggestions as quickly as possible. Ideas could be recorded on a flipchart or board. They should not be discussed or clarified further until all the ideas have been recorded.

capacity: the resources (people, money, assets), skills, knowledge and organisation required to carry out a particular task.

children's rights: the specific rights of children are set out in the UN Convention on the Rights of the Child (and in other international, regional and national legally binding instruments).

In defining the specific rights of children, the UNCRC addresses the particular vulnerabilities and needs of childhood and ensures that these rights receive special attention from governments and others. Children's rights are for all people under 18. They include the full spectrum of human rights (civil, political, economic, social and cultural), and all of them need to be treated with equal respect. They are universal and allow no discrimination of any kind (for example, against girls or disabled or rural children).

diagram: a model that presents information in an easily understandable form. Different types of diagrams include maps, transects, seasonal calendars, time trends, time lines, historical profiles, daily routine diagrams, livelihood analysis diagrams, flow diagrams, causality diagrams, Venn diagrams.

disaggregate: analyse data according to different groupings to show differences between certain groups (by gender, age, ethnic group, etc) and therefore to reflect the true variations within the sample.

duty-bearers: Duty-bearers are all those who have a responsibility to respect and protect and fulfil the rights of others. In rights-based programming the duty-bearers responsible for delivering on specific rights must be identified, and made accountable and responsive. In terms of child rights, governments have a duty to ensure that those rights are secured. Duty-bearers also include individuals with direct responsibility for protecting and fulfilling the rights of children, for example the immediate family, carers, teachers, doctors, and so on. It also includes institutions responsible for protecting and fulfilling rights such as schools, education ministries, ministries of justice, and all development organisations which have any impact on any rights of the children. It further includes all those with an impact nationally or globally on child rights, for example international bodies including UN, and national and international businesses.

facilitator: a person who will coordinate, rather than lead, an exercise, encouraging participation by others.

feedback: the process of presenting the findings of an assessment, monitoring, review or evaluation exercise to any of the people involved in the work, so that the findings are incorporated into discussions, plans and policy relating to the work.

focus group discussions: A particular form of interviews and group discussions involving people with knowledge and interest in a particular topic, normally with a facilitator.

framework: a framework is a way of organising information so that it can be more easily understood and interpreted. For example, a child rights framework for a situation analysis may mean that information about a situation is collected and interpreted according to violations of selected child rights. Examples of frameworks are given in Tools 13 and 14.

household economy analysis (HEA): this is the analysis of the household economy, where the household is defined as the smallest coherent economic unit, defined as a group of people who contribute to a common economy and share the food and other income from this. The size and nature of households may vary widely from "nuclear family" (a man, a woman and their dependent children) to units of a hundred or more people. A household is most often, but not necessarily, a family. Household economy means the sum of the ways in which the household gets its income, its savings and assets holding, and its consumption of food and non-food items.

impact chain: this is a way of representing how one change will lead to another. It is a useful tool for modelling the assumptions that are made about the expected impact of a programme. It shows the expected links between the immediate impact of a programme, and longer-term or wider impacts.

indicators: objective ways of measuring (indicating) that progress is being achieved. These must relate to the aims and objectives of the project. For example, the height of a child would be an indicator of growth; the ability of a health worker to perform a task learnt on a training course would be an indicator of the effectiveness of the training course. Indicators provide an indication that something has happened, or that an objective has been achieved; they are not proof.

Impact indicators: are needed to assess what progress is being made towards reaching the objectives and what impact the work has had on different groups of people. Process indicators show whether the activities that were planned are being carried out, and how they are being carried out. Quantitative indicators can be measured using figures. Qualitative indicators can be measured using qualitative questions – for example, the level of satisfaction with a particular service. Proxy indicators measure things that represent (or approximate) changes in areas that cannot be measured directly.

inputs: the organisation and provision of resources to implement activities.

interviews: face-to-face or long distance (eg, by phone) consultations between two or more people, with the aim of collecting data and the opinions of those involved.

maps: diagrams showing specific kinds of information about an area.

model (of change): a model is a simplified representation of reality. It is a way of showing how different factors are connected, and how different causes and effects may interact with each other. A model of change shows how you would expect a change in some factors to affect others. You can then look at a real situation and see whether the changes you expect are taking place. This can help understand what changes your programme is helping to bring about and what processes lead to those changes. If the expected changes don't take place, the assumptions are wrong, can the model be altered and the activities re-oriented?

objectives: are specific, time-bound and measurable goals for projects or programmes, which contribute to achieving the longer-term aims, for example, to achieve 80 per cent immunisation coverage in the next five years in district X. (See also SMART below.)

Programme or project objectives should indicate what changes the project is hoping to achieve – for example, an increase in the effective use of family planning methods.

observation: direct observation means observing objects, events, processes, relationships or people's behaviour systematically and recording these observations; it is a useful qualitative research method.

participatory approaches: when staff, partners, people affected by a piece of work, managers and others involved with the work participate directly in planning and carrying out (for example) an assessment, monitoring, review or evaluation exercise.

participatory learning and action (PLA): a form of qualitative research used to gain an indepth understanding of a community or a situation. (See Tool 1 for full description and methods.)

plan of action: draws together activities that address an objective and specifies how they will be carried out, what resources are required, etc.

process monitoring: gathering information about the use of resources (or inputs) in a programme, the progress of activities and the way these are carried out.

programme: a collection of projects supported by an agency within the same sector, theme or geographical area, to which a coordinated approach is adopted.

project: a discrete series of activities in a particular location aiming to achieve common objectives (see 'programme' above).

qualitative analysis: methods of analysing and interpreting data provided by qualitative research (see 'qualitative research' below) and to answer questions like what, how and why something happened. Methods include meetings, diagrams, maps, interviews and observations (see 'quantitative analysis' below).

qualitative research: a flexible and open-ended method of building up an in-depth picture of a situation, community, etc; methods used include observation, discussion, interviews and mapping (see 'quantitative research' below).

quantitative analysis: methods of analysing and interpreting data provided by quantitative research (see below) to answer questions like what, how much, how many, or how often; methods include numerical or statistical analysis, graphs and charts (see 'qualitative analysis' above).

quantitative research: is used to collect data which can be analysed in a numerical form; things are therefore either measured or counted, or questions are asked according to a defined questionnaire so that the answers can be coded and analysed numerically (see 'qualitative research' above).

questionnaire: a series of questions listed in a specific order, used to gather information from a range of people.

ranking: placing something in order; it can be used to help identify the main preferences of people and to compare their priorities.

rights-based programming: rights-based approaches to programming are ways of programming which aim to make a reality of people's human rights. Such approaches build on the belief that all human beings have certain rights which cannot be taken away from them and which enable them to make claims on others when their rights are being denied or violated. These rights are set out in international law, where they are presented as standards and norms that all societies should aim to achieve.

rights-holders: everyone has human rights as set out in the UN Convention of Human Rights. Everyone is therefore a rights-holder in relation to those human rights. All rights holders have entitlement to their rights, and can legitimately claim them. The United Nations Convention of the Rights of the Child confirms that children are active and legitimate holders of children's rights which they can exercise in accordance with their maturity and experience.

situation analysis: this involves collecting and analysing information about a particular issue in its broader context in order to make a sensible assessment of what needs to be done. This usually includes: what are the causes of the particular problem, what are its effects on different groups, how do different people perceive it, what environmental factors affect it or are affected by it; what is the political context; what different groups and institutions are stakeholders; what are the links between different organisations, what policies are concerned, and how are they implemented? A situation analysis for rights-based programming looks at the situation in terms of rights which have been violated. Who are the rights holders, what are the causes of rights violations, and who are the duty bearers responsible for protecting those rights?

SMART: stands for Specific, Measurable, Achievable, Relevant, Time-bound. These should be essential characteristics of any objective.

SPHERE Project: this is a programme of the Steering Committee for Humanitarian Response (SCHR) and InterAction with VOICE, ICRC and IVA. The project was launched in 1997 to develop a set of universal minimum standards in core areas of humanitarian assistance, published in 2000 as The Humanitarian Charter and Minimum Standards in Disaster Response.

stakeholders: stakeholders are all those who have an interest in a project or will be affected by it. This includes all individuals, groups, and organisations affected by the problems which the project seeks to address, and those who are affected positively or negatively by the project; people implementing the project; external service providers; financial sponsors; the wider public, and so on. (See Tool 12, Stakeholder Analysis). Stakeholders differs from the term *participants* in that some stakeholders, such as unborn generations and downstream populations won't take part in a project but will be affected.

survey: used to gather a broad range of information about a population.

terms of reference: a plan of action for an exercise; they clarify aims, objectives, methods, organisation, tasks, etc.

variable: any characteristic that can vary: for example, the height of a child, the number of years a mother spent in school.